Caught by Don Hutson!

ALSO BY LEW FREEDMAN
AND FROM MCFARLAND

*Johnny Mize: A Biography
of Baseball's "Big Cat"* (2022)

*Lightning Strikes Twice: Johnny Vander Meer
and the Cincinnati Reds* (2021)

*Buffalo Bill Cody: The Man Who Shaped
the Wild West Legend* (2020)

Cy Young: The Baseball Life and Career (2020)

Ernie Banks: The Life and Career of "Mr. Cub" (2019)

*Connie Mack's First Dynasty:
The Philadelphia Athletics, 1910–1914* (2017)

*Baseball's Funnymen: Twenty-Four Jokers, Screwballs,
Pranksters and Storytellers* (2017)

The Boyer Brothers of Baseball (2015)

Joe Louis: The Life of a Heavyweight (2013)

DiMaggio's Yankees: A History of the 1936–1944 Dynasty (2011)

*The Day All the Stars Came Out: Major League
Baseball's First All-Star Game, 1933* (2010)

Hard-Luck Harvey Haddix and the Greatest Game Ever Lost (2009)

Early Wynn, the Go-Go White Sox and the 1959 World Series (2009)

BY GEORGE ALTMAN WITH LEW FREEDMAN

*George Altman: My Baseball Journey from the Negro Leagues
to the Majors and Beyond* (2013)

Caught by Don Hutson!
A Biography of Pro Football's First Modern Receiver

Lew Freedman

McFarland & Company, Inc., Publishers
Jefferson, North Carolina

ISBN (print) 978-1-4766-8782-7
ISBN (ebook) 978-1-4766-4633-6

LIBRARY OF CONGRESS AND BRITISH LIBRARY
CATALOGUING DATA ARE AVAILABLE

Library of Congress Control Number 2022046397

© 2022 Lew Freedman. All rights reserved

*No part of this book may be reproduced or transmitted in any form
or by any means, electronic or mechanical, including photocopying
or recording, or by any information storage and retrieval system,
without permission in writing from the publisher.*

Front cover: Green Bay Packers
wide receiver Don Hutson (B.E. Callahan)

Printed in the United States of America

*McFarland & Company, Inc., Publishers
Box 611, Jefferson, North Carolina 28640
www.mcfarlandpub.com*

Table of Contents

Preface   1

Introduction   5

1. Growing Up in Arkansas   9
2. High School Play   17
3. The Passing World Gets Ready for Don Hutson   24
4. Alabama   31
5. Alabama Reigns   37
6. Last Days at Alabama   44
7. The Rose Bowl   52
8. Off to Green Bay   59
9. Starting with the Packers   66
10. Making a Mark   73
11. Baseball Still Beckons—For a While   85
12. First Championship   92
13. Aiming for Another Title   103
14. Close to Winning It All Again   111
15. 1939—Another Crown   119
16. The Biggest Little Town   128
17. Trying to Repeat   134
18. 1941   142
19. War-Time Football   155
20. Making the Most of It   161

Table of Contents

21. New Looks for 1943	169
22. One More Crown	176
23. The Last Go-Around	184
24. Legacy	192
Epilogue	201
Chapter Notes	209
Bibliography	217
Index	219

Preface

Don Hutson was grace and speed personified on the football field. He possessed a dancer's moves that enabled him to run away from defensive coverage and a track sprinter's burst with his churning legs.

When he came into the National Football League in 1935 from the University of Alabama, where he was a teammate and roommate of the soon-to-be iconic college coach Paul "Bear" Bryant, the professional football passing game was in its infancy, rough around the edges, lacking in sophistication, and even distrusted as a worthy weapon by many coaches.

Hutson, who had been making waves with his ability when given the chance in the college game, was viewed as a savior by legendary Green Bay Packers coach Earle "Curly" Lambeau. Lambeau was a true believer in the passing game as the explosive offense of the future, and in Hutson he saw a talented and exciting player who could add a fresh dimension to the Packers' style and effectiveness. Hutson's nickname with the Crimson Tide was the "Alabama Antelope." Never mind that antelope were much more common in the western United States, it was more about the alliteration.

Lambeau would do just about anything he had to do to add Hutson to his roster and bring more championships to Green Bay. It was the year before the NFL player draft was instituted, so it was every man for himself in seeking to sign players. By then, Hutson had come to realize his own value, and he also had the foresight to recognize that passing the football would revolutionize the sport as it moved away from the dark ages of simply running the ball. The era of "three yards and a cloud of dust," the cliché about football's offensive play, was soon (although only gradually) to be de-emphasized.

In 1935, pro teams did not operate an intricate network of scouts. Nor was there easy access to tape to help judge players' abilities.

Preface

Word-of-mouth was a heavily used tactic to find out about players and whether they might fit in with your club. Coaches had to rely on the analysis of talent observers. In this case, however, Lambeau did see Hutson play live and instantly recognized how much he could help the Packers.

Stanford was favored in the Rose Bowl of 1935, but Alabama, with Hutson putting on a show, upset the California host, 29–13. Hutson's freewheeling maneuvers shredded Stanford's secondary. Lambeau had no doubt that Hutson's ability would be a huge asset for Green Bay. "I'd always dreamed of an end who could do the things Hutson did," Lambeau said. "And out for [sic] the Rose Bowl in Pasadena that day, there he was."[1]

By the time he graduated from Alabama, Hutson weighed somewhere slightly north of 168 pounds, distributed over 6 feet, 1 inch of height. Some wondered if the young man who looked so slender could take the pounding that would be dished out in the very rough pro game. That was despite doing everything asked of him in college, including the first-rate performance in the Rose Bowl game.

Doubters need not have worried about his size. When Hutson began matriculating at Alabama, coming out of his home in Pine Bluff, Arkansas, four years earlier, he weighed just 145 pounds. He must have eaten better in Tuscaloosa. Hutson's skill translated to the next level, and he promptly began setting records while running pass patterns for the Packers. Some of those marks lasted for decades. He also successfully added around 15 pounds.

Lambeau was not the only NFL coach who could spot talent, though he seemed the one most committed to the passing game. The Chicago Bears, under the leadership of George Halas, made a bid for Hutson, but Halas was notoriously stingy with player salaries, and he could not compete in the dollar range. The old Brooklyn Dodgers, who took their name from the baseball team, were the other serious suitor. A character called "Shipwreck" Kelly was the point man in the frenzied pursuit of Hutson.

Hutson ended up in Green Bay and never played for anyone else again. He established his reputation in northern Wisconsin, where he is still revered even though he passed away in 1997. The current-day Packers work out in a large practice facility named after Hutson. His old-style No. 14 football jersey is for sale in the team's gift shop, which workers claim is the world's largest such sports souvenir store.

Preface

Hutson was so dazzling that his name had spread long before the technology was developed to bring interstate fame to high school athletes during the latter part of the 20th century. Bear Bryant said that once Hutson's exploits were so well-known as a high schooler, he hitchhiked to Pine Bluff from elsewhere in Arkansas to watch Hutson play.

Don Hutson only caught one football at a time during his NFL career, but he could juggle many if he had to (courtesy Neville Public Museum of Brown County).

Preface

When the Professional Football Hall of Fame was founded in Canton, Ohio, in 1963, Don Hutson was a member of the inaugural class. As recently as 2019 (with updating from 2016), an Alabama online sports site referred to Hutson as the greatest football player who competed for the Crimson Tide. The headline in part referred to Hutson as "the Babe Ruth of wide receivers."[2] That was in addition to the claim that he remained Alabama's finest football player some seven decades after he last took the field for the school.

Though Hutson was never as flamboyant as Babe Ruth or many other sports stars, those in the know still recognize and praise him for his greatness as a Green Bay Packer, where he helped the team win three NFL titles. He earned eight trips to the Pro Bowl as a first-teamer and won two league Most Valuable Player Awards.

A member of the Green Bay Packers Hall of Fame, the College Football Hall of Fame, and the Pro Football Hall of Fame, Don Hutson lives on in the sport's memory through his enshrinement in those prestigious institutions.

Introduction

The forward pass was non-existent when the sport of football began, in a sense like the slam dunk in basketball. Although some colleges had begun playing games, professional football's origin story dates play-for-pay development to 1892.

That year, the Allegheny Athletic Association signed William "Pudge" Heffelfinger for a big game on November 12, 1892, against the Pittsburgh Athletic Club and paid him $500 to show up and slip into the good guys' uniform. While this type of activity in various sports came to be called bringing in "a ringer," there was nothing illegal about the Association's move. However, it was pricey in the context of the times, given that $500 was worth the equivalent of $16,275 in 2022 money.

Later in 1892 and again in 1893, the Allegheny group had no qualms about shelling out for a bonus player to bolster its chances. The second time around, one week after Heffelfinger's debut, Allegheny paid out just $250 for the services of Ben "Sport" Donnelly. The Association also hired some individuals for $50 a game for a whole season.

Don Hutson, light-footed and athletic, would not have recognized much about the earliest days of football, going back to the college version, which was birthed November 6, 1869, when Princeton and Rutgers faced one another, or even the early-20th century professional version. Football then was all about brute force and power, about gimmicks like the flying wedge and hammering the other guy, not so much eluding him.

And there was no passing game. Zero. Zilch. Throwing the ball was not included in the early rules. With football's roots in rugby and soccer, there was not much reliance on using the hands to advance the ball downfield. It was not until 1906 that passing was legalized. A highly controversial, "illegal" forward pass was completed in an 1876 game between Yale and Princeton. Football pioneer Walter Camp was about

Introduction

to be tackled when, in a quick-thinking gesture, he tossed the ball to teammate Oliver Thompson. Without even the benefit of instant replay provoking doubt, Princeton instantly protested. Apparently, Camp bamboozled the officials sufficiently. They tossed a coin, and it came down in favor of Yale, so the play was okayed.

Passing is so ingrained in the minds of fans today that they have to wonder what all of the kerfuffle was about. It took outright violence on the field, at least 19 deaths, and many more serious injuries during the 1905 college season for a rules change to be implemented. Academicians howled for the game to be banned, but President Theodore Roosevelt, who liked physical outdoor activity very much himself, convened a gathering of school representatives. Roosevelt's effort, presiding over these meetings, is credited with saving the sport. The idea of passing was approved, a move that would open up the offensive game and diminish some of the hand-to-hand combat that had become so dangerous. It was not as if hard-throwing, deep-throwing, frequent-throwing quarterbacks appeared overnight, however. Coaches seemed wary of the pass and reluctant to try it, never mind hurriedly blending it into regular formations.

Finally, almost with an attitude of "OK, we'll give it a shot," a couple of famous attempts were made that introduced the forward pass to college football. The first legal, authorized pass was hurled by St. Louis University under the direction of Billikens coach Eddie Cochems. St. Louis quarterback Bradbury Robinson threw incomplete to receiver Jack Schneider in a September 5, 1906, game against Carroll College in Wisconsin.

That was the milestone inaugural throw in a college football game, but while notable, it pretty much led nowhere. Other teams and coaches did not incorporate passing into their offenses much. It took until the 1913 season, when the passing-catching combination of Charley "Gus" Dorais and Knute Rockne, later one of the most esteemed coaches of all time, put the style on the map for Notre Dame.

This was not spontaneous but premeditated. Dorais and Rockne practiced pitching and catching over the summer, and on November 1, 1913, in a major confrontation, they whipped out the weapon to beat favored Army, 35–13, dizzying the Cadets with their passing. "Perfection of the forward pass came to us only through daily, tedious practice," said Rockne.[1]

Football was catching on in popularity during the second decade

Introduction

of the 20th century. The college game was pre-eminent and would remain so for many years, but there was a continuing interest in playing the sport by some who had exhausted their eligibility. They did not look upon football as a genuine career choice in the way Major League Baseball was, but some sought to keep going, competing week-by-week for a small remittance. Also, companies began sponsoring their own in-house teams, stocking the roster with employees.

There was also an attempt in 1902 and 1903 by Pennsylvania cities to jump-start a first National Football League. The Philadelphia Athletics and Philadelphia Phillies baseball clubs were involved in this creation. Still, the focal point of non-college football swiftly shifted to the Midwest, especially Ohio. The Massillon Tigers and the Canton AC, later the Bulldogs, featuring the fabulous Jim Thorpe, emerged as key clubs.

In 1919, the Green Bay Packers were formed by Curly Lambeau and George Calhoun. The team was sponsored by the Indian Packing Company. The firm provided $500 to pay for start-up equipment and allowed the use of a field it owned for practice. Green Bay finished its first season with a 10–1 record. More important for the Packers was their timing.

One season later, a group of enthusiastic backers who believed professional football had a good chance to succeed gathered at an overcrowded automobile dealership in Canton, Ohio. August 20, 1920, was the kickoff of the National Football League as we know it, although for one season the organization was known as the American Professional Football Association. Just about every club that had ever kicked a football wanted in, though after a second organizational meeting, reality collided with dreams and representatives realized they could not make an effort to go pro full-time.

The first group of teams included the Canton Bulldogs, Dayton Triangles, Muncie Flyers, Rock Island Independents, Decatur Staleys, Racine Cardinals, Akron Pros, Buffalo All-Americans, Rochester Jeffersons, Detroit Heralds, Columbus Panhandles, Hammond Pros, Cleveland Tigers, and Chicago Tigers. Racine became the Chicago Cardinals, and the Staleys became the Chicago Bears.

It should be noted the Green Bay Packers spent 1919 and 1920 playing a schedule built around opponents in Wisconsin and Michigan.

Teams played uneven schedules, and soon there was a grand shaking out of surviving teams still playing in 1921, when the league changed its name to the National Football League, and then throughout

Introduction

the 1920s when clubs located in small cities could not keep up and folded.

The Packers, who moved into the league with the 1921 season, could easily have become one of those casualties. In 1923, losing money, the club began selling stock in the team to members of the public and became a non-profit outfit. Nearly a century later, Green Bay is the smallest city represented by a North American sports franchise in football, baseball, basketball, or hockey. Much of the early success was owed to the acumen of Curly Lambeau, whose team now plays its autumn games in a stadium named after him.

Lambeau's hand could be seen in keeping the team afloat, coaching his roster to championships, becoming an early acolyte of the passing game, and making astute personnel moves. That included signing Don Hutson, though not quite yet. In 1921, Hutson was turning eight years old.

1

Growing Up in Arkansas

As a youth growing up in Pine Bluff, Arkansas, a community whose name makes it sound more rural than it is, at least in the 21st century, Donald Montgomery Hutson joined the Boy Scouts.

As evidence that he possessed sufficient boldness of spirit and a willingness to try just about anything once, when sportswriters inquired about his early days on the planet, he informed them that he played with snakes. Somehow this was couched under the cover of saying he was a Boy Scout, as if there was a merit badge awarded for avoiding the fangs of a rattler.

Hutson told people he developed his athletic agility in this manner. It is not known if any other accomplished football players gave credit to fooling with swift-moving reptiles for their own ability to dodge tackles or otherwise employ the sleight of hand that could have helped with the job of dealing cards in Las Vegas. Nonetheless, it was Hutson's story and he stuck to it. Hutson did reach the rank of Eagle Scout, though it was not clear if he gained bonus points for dazzling the snakes the way he would someday confuse football pass defenders.

Hutson was born on January 31, 1913, in Pine Bluff, which is located on the Arkansas River. In 2020, Pine Bluff was the 10th-largest city in Arkansas, with a population on the decline over the previous decade to 42,323. However, it is only 45 miles south-southwest of the capital and largest city of Little Rock. In the years shortly before Hutson's birth, Pine Bluff was a much smaller place of about 15,000 residents.

The riverbank area was populated with pine trees, and the community had a long history of settlement that included Native-Americans and future generations of European trappers. At the time of the Civil War, Pine Bluff was mostly known as a shipping site for exported cotton, and it had a large slave population. Union troops occupied the city

Caught by Don Hutson!

for a few years during the latter portion of the war, and in one instance, freed slaves joined with the blue coats at the Battle of Pine Bluff in 1863 to repel the Confederate Army's attempt to reclaim it.

A half-century later, the same year Hutson was born, optimistic businessmen got behind the establishment and construction of a luxury hotel called the Hotel Pines at the corner of Main Street and West 5th. Viewed as a destination property, the hotel was a local landmark but eventually fell on hard times, ceasing its star-turn role for accommodations in 1970.

The Hotel Pines was added to the National Register of Historic Places in 1979, and eventually, a $35 million restoration was begun in 2018 to revive it. That had not concluded by the summer of 2022, however. That may dovetail with the overall historical review of Pine Bluff, including some good times tinged by optimism, some tough times resulting from war, and some links to America's greatest shame in history with its involvement in slavery.

Don Hutson made his way through an upbringing in such a town to emerge as one of its most famous citizens and arguably its greatest athletic son. Among other prominent figures from Pine Bluff the world outside may have heard of are future governor of Arkansas Mike Huckabee, five-time Major League Baseball All-Star Torii Hunter, Willie Roaf, another Hall of Fame National Football League star, pro basketball player Lafayette Lever, Olympic gold medal sprint champion Charlie Greene, Olympic shot putter Dallas Long, novelist Chester Himes, and numerous singers, actors, and actresses, including Broncho Billy Anderson, an honorary Academy Award winner.

The future football star Hutson was ahead of most of them. His father was Roy B. Hutson, who earned the family's finances as a conductor on the long-defunct Cotton Belt Railroad. Don's mother, Mabel, was a stay-at-home housekeeper. In that sense, Hutson and his two brothers did not have a privileged upbringing. He made his own breaks and opportunities, and mostly developed his own talents.

There was little doubt that at a young age, Don Hutson was a gifted all-around athlete. While he made his enduring mark in football, the gridiron was neither his favorite environment for sporting competition nor where he most distinctly excelled as a teenager. These days, there are three public high schools in the Pine Bluff School District, but the original was founded in 1868, and when Hutson attended secondary school in the early 1930s, it was the only one. Pine Bluff High's sports

1. Growing Up in Arkansas

teams' nickname is the Zebras. The school has a proud sports heritage and one of long standing, dating to Hutson's days.

Pine Bluff has won 24 state high school football championships, and in 1925 the school finished 16–0 and was regarded as the national titlist. In 1930, Hutson, truly ahead of his time, caught five touchdown passes in a game, still the state record, although it has been tied twice. Even in high school, when the forward pass was still very much a fledgling weapon, Hutson could take advantage of his skills to score.

However, in his local environment, Hutson the athlete was much better recognized for his achievements in other sports. The high school did not have a baseball team when Hutson attended, but there was what was commonly known as a "town team." Communities routinely fielded baseball clubs during the summer and competed fiercely against other nearby cities and towns on weekends.

Hutson invested more time in interscholastic basketball than football when attending Pine Bluff High. When asked later, he said the round ball sport was his favorite, not football. During the high school year, Hutson focused more on basketball and was chosen all-state. He was a track and field competitor, too. In terms of a career, though, he gave more thought to baseball than the others.

In the 1920s, Major League Baseball was *the* professional sport in the United States. Pro football was just nudging its way into the consciousness of the sports fan after its founding in an organized league in 1920. The football that counted in the South was college ball. The National Hockey League was around, but mostly a Canadian sport, with only a few big cities of the Northeast and Midwest concerned with the game. And while Hutson loved basketball, there was no true professional basketball league until after World War II.

"I'm like most athletes," Hutson said in a newspaper interview in 1989.

> I'd rather see football, but I'd rather play basketball. In those days [the early 1930s], there was no future in either football or basketball. When Bear [his friend and teammate Paul "Bear" Bryant] and I were at Alabama, the daily papers never printed a word on pro football. They gave you the NFL scores on Monday and that was all. So from the start, I concentrated on baseball. My goal was the big leagues—until I found that there was more money in the NFL.[1]

That may have been for Hutson, by the time he got there, but not for very many others. George Halas, founder of the Chicago Bears, was

Caught by Don Hutson!

legendary for being a tightwad with players. That reputation began in the early days of the league and continued for decades. It was one of Chicago's greatest stars and heroes, Mike Ditka, as both a player first and then a coach, who uttered the most legendary comment on Halas' tendency towards being cheap. In a fit of anger following salary negotiations in 1966, Ditka spouted that Halas "throws nickels around like manhole covers."[2] By the autumn of 1967, Ditka, a future Hall of Famer, was playing tight end for the Philadelphia Eagles, not the Bears.

When the pro game began and throughout the 1920s, when Don Hutson was forming his impression about the relative attractiveness of pro football as a paying career, most players were paid by the game, between $100 and $300.[3] In the 1930s, some of the best and most popular players began making some dough, especially by the standard of the Great Depression, when things were grim economically everywhere.

When Hutson was in junior high and high school (and thinking ahead about making a career in the business world), those game-by-game payments were not encouraging to college men who spent four years earning degrees. Decades later, based on his production, Hutson would have become a millionaire just from his exploits on the field. In 2020, 77 players each made at least $15 million for their season of play in the NFL.[4] Astoundingly (it certainly would have been to Hutson), Kansas City Chiefs quarterback Patrick Mahomes was at the top of the earnings list with a payout of $45 million a year. The Arizona Cardinals' DeAndre Hopkins was the highest paid receiver, making $27.3 million for the year, but another 39 receivers (Hutson's position) made at least $5 million.

Before he was universally known by his nickname of "Bear" to all but his closest relations, Paul Bryant knew about Hutson's football prowess, even if it had not been on display as often as his basketball talent or his track sprinter's speed.

Bryant was born in what was always called Moro Bottom, Arkansas, on September 11, 1913, in Cleveland County. That was seven-and-a-half months later than Hutson and 25 miles south of Pine Bluff. Moro Bottom was an unincorporated tract of land with seven families, and the Bryant clan filled up its share of the local population, since Bryant was the 11th of 12 children belonging to Wilson and Ida.

The Bryants were also close kin to poverty, and even later, as a young coach, before Bryant became famous, he ate on the cheap three

1. Growing Up in Arkansas

meals a day at the Krystal fast food chain. That was the story the coach told in the late 1970s, when he became a celebrity endorser for the hamburger outfit (founded in 1932) which throughout the region is appreciated essentially as the McDonald's of the South.

Bryant took up football in junior high school, when he was already 6-foot-1, on his way to 6–4. His tiny home area did not have its own high school, so he matriculated at Fordyce High. By then, Bryant already had connected with his lifelong nickname. It glommed on to him early, when he was 13. Bryant wrestled a bear in a carnival-like setting, not a pastime available nearly a century later, but no less impressive sounding, even if the animal was described as captive. Maybe Bryant felt that if he could tackle a bear, he could tackle any human being on the football field.

"Football has never been just a game to me," Bryant once said. "Never. I knew it from the time it got me out of Moro Bottom, Arkansas—and that's one of the things that motivated me, that fear of going back to plowing and driving those mules and chopping cotton for fifty cents a day."[5]

In his autobiography, Bryant wrote that three of his siblings died in infancy, and as he was the 11th child, most of the others had grown up before him. He also wrote that his father was a semi-invalid by the time the boy was coming of age, weakened by illnesses such as high blood pressure and shortness of breath. The family raised crops like black-eyed peas, watermelons, and turnip greens, his mother transporting them by mule-pulled wagon to different neighborhoods. Paul had to be ready to go by 4 a.m. The family worked 260 acres of land, later reverted to timber, he said, with his childhood home vanished.

Bryant was the last boy left at home, and he took his sisters to school daily before helping his mother on the wagon sell the produce. "I hated every minute of it, making those rounds," Bryant said.[6]

Later, after both Bryant and Hutson were famous in the football world, Bryant said Hutson's pass-catching reputation was well-known, though they were at different high schools. "He was something to see, even then," Bryant said. "We'd hitch-hike to Pine Bluff just to watch him play. I saw him catch five touchdown passes in one game in high school."[7] That had to be a reference to Hutson's record-setting performance that still stands.

Anyone who could tell the bear story which Bryant recorded deserved the nickname. Bryant was hanging out at a touring carnival

Caught by Don Hutson!

with some other football players, ones he later teamed with at Fordyce High and who made the more common choice during that era to compete for the home-area University of Arkansas after high school. They came upon a poster advertising a wrestling bear and a challenge paying $1 a minute to anyone who could stay up with the beast. "I was chopping cotton for fifty cents a day at the time," Bryant said, "and I felt I'd wrestle King Kong for a dollar a minute."[8]

Bryant said the master of ceremonies introduced the bear to the crowd as a ferocious creature, but it seemed scrawny and skinny to him. He initiated a takedown move and held the bear down for as long as he could, counting pennies in his head with the passing of seconds. The MC interrupted and got Bryant to move. He tackled the bear again and hung on as time passed. The third time, Bryant said, the bear no longer wore a muzzle. After the bear bit him on the ear, drawing blood, Bryant leapt from the stage.

After the show, when he went to collect his money for riding time, the man was nowhere to be found. Bryant got cheated out of his hard-earned fee. That was a disappointing denouement to the incident, but there was a postscript. Years later, Bryant and pal Hutson were bird hunting in another Arkansas town and came upon the same act, with the same bear, and the same guy in the carnival.

"By then I was an assistant coach at Alabama and had achieved a certain amount of dignity, so I was able to stifle the desire to go choke my money out of the man," Bryant said. "He probably needed it more than I did, anyway."[9] Then, perhaps, but not years before when it was earned. It would have likely caused quite the scene if two well-known football figures confronted the man who scammed Bryant. There was a decent chance the duo could have beaten up the guy and claimed Bryant's few dollars.

One summer, Bryant went to Cleveland to stay with a sister and worked in a factory. He jumped the job hurriedly after knocking down another employee in a fight and rode the rails illegally back to Arkansas. That worked until he reached Pine Bluff, where he was nabbed. But the crew chief's son had played with Don Hutson, recognized Bryant as a player, and let him go the rest of the way home.

Bryant's father did not want his youngest boy to play football. He wanted him to keep farming the land. Bryant said his dad threatened to whip him if he played, but his mother seemed to quietly lobby for him, and Bryant ended up on the Fordyce team.

1. Growing Up in Arkansas

Bryant was full-grown in high school, and that helped his football. Fordyce fielded some good teams, and during his junior year, Bryant's bunch defeated Pine Bluff's group—Hutson's team—7–0. The next year, it wasn't that close. Fordyce demolished Pine Bluff, 50–12. Pine Bluff also had a tough tackle named Charlie Marr, who joined Bryant and Hutson at the University of Alabama and was an All-Southeastern Conference star for the Crimson Tide. In 1934, Marr, Hutson, and Bryant together were SEC selections.

Bryant's Fordyce team crushed Hutson's Pine Bluff team in that high school encounter, but Bryant made clear that he knew who the better athlete was. Hutson, he said, scored both touchdowns for the losers. "He was already a great all-around athlete," Bryant said, "a baseball player, and a basketball and a track star, as well, and we became friends even though we were rivals."[10]

Players like Hutson and Bryant would have been welcome at the University of Arkansas, and there were other football-playing colleges in the state that could have been options, if they wanted to stay closer to home. But they were lured to Alabama for different reasons. Alabama was already renowned throughout the South as a good football school. As Bryant put it in comparing Alabama to any of the Arkansas programs, "But we read and heard more about Alabama and that's where I wanted to go. If you were any kind of football fan, you knew about the Crimson Tide and Wallace Wade, who had been head coach there since 1923 and took them to three Rose Bowl games."[11]

It was a different era in college football. Unlike a century later, when there are so many bowl games after the regular season that teams barely have to record winning records to gain an invitation somewhere, there were hardly any. The Rose Bowl, "The Grand-daddy of Them All," dates to 1922. This was decades prior to the Big Ten and Pac-10 (now Pac-12) making a contractual arrangement to send regular-season champions to the game in Pasadena, California, and long before anyone contemplated a series of bowl games to determine a national champion. That is why Alabama appearing in the Rose Bowl three times over a short time would have made an impact on Bryant.

Not so for Hutson. Some may chuckle to learn that Hutson was not attracted to Alabama because of its football charms. By the end of high school, Hutson was still more fixated on the likelihood that if there was any opportunity to play professional sports, it would be by making it big

Caught by Don Hutson!

in Major League Baseball. So Don Hutson, pioneering wide receiver for the football team, chose to attend the University of Alabama in Tuscaloosa on a partial baseball scholarship. Initially, he did not intend to play college football at all and said the coaches in the game didn't view him as much of a prospect.

2

High School Play

It was a quiet afternoon in the neighborhood. The sun was strong and the temperature mild in March. There were no children playing on the grass of simple Don Hutson Park in Pine Bluff. A couple of months later on the calendar, the temperature might well hit a stifling 100 degrees and the humidity reach breath-stealing proportions.

This small patch of ground is perhaps the most public way the city of Hutson's youth celebrates his memory, even if no one was really paying attention on this given day. It was surrounded primarily by residential homes, and it would not be described as a palatial neighborhood, some houses even bordering on dilapidated.

A pavilion stood in one area of the East 6th Street location, with its concrete benches and tables going unused, as were the basketball courts, swings, and slide for smaller children. School had not let out for the day yet. A clerk at a local hotel and a librarian at the public library were asked if they had any knowledge of Don Hutson, probably the greatest athlete produced by the community. But they said they had never heard of him.

It is likely that Don Hutson is appropriately remembered best in Pine Bluff through the record and newspaper reports of his high school football exploits, especially his senior year, when he truly shined. The fall of 1930 began Hutson's last year of high school, and he graduated in the class of 1931 the following spring. The yearbook was called "The Zebra," consistent with the sports teams' nickname. The typical yearbook head shot of the students showed Hutson with a thick head of hair, slightly curly, wearing a sport coat and tie and smiling slightly, if not broadly. The word space devoted to individuals was tight, with not even full sentences allotted to their time invested in the school. The complete entry for Hutson reads this way: "Lettermen's Club. Basketball. Football. Hi-Y. President of Senior Class. Best

Caught by Don Hutson!

Boy Athlete." Then in its own paragraph was this: "Not only good in athletics."[1]

From this one source, you could glean that Hutson was popular enough to win election as class president, and there was more to his personality and character teased by the final line that went beyond his stellar sports performances. Hutson himself confirmed with sportswriters that by this stage of his life, he already knew he wanted to be a successful businessman of some kind. In between, he became a renowned college and professional athlete. However, readers of the hometown newspapers might well have guessed that sport was in his future. The *Pine Bluff Daily Graphic* and the *Pine Bluff Commercial*, competing newspapers, chronicled Hutson's important senior season as a football player.

The Zebras wore striped uniform jerseys to match their team nickname, and those shirts could be gaudy with stripes not only across the shoulders, but up and down the arms as well. They would probably be referred to as retro cool today. This was not one of the seasons when the Zebras, who were rebuilding and had just five returning lettermen, walked away with an Arkansas state football championship, though the writers in the yearbook did not seem too put out by the results, in part penning in a laconic manner:

> The football season is finished. The last punt is kicked; the last plunge is made. Pine Bluff again has failed to win the state championship. But are we discouraged? No. What if we didn't win the championship? What if we didn't beat all of our ancient rivals? One thing will always stand out. Pine Bluff put her usual gentleman-like team on the field. Whether it be track, basketball, or on the gridiron, Pine Bluff is always represented by nothing but sportsmen of the first calibre.[2]

Although the yearbook also mentioned a paucity of fans in the stands, pre-season, at least, the community showed off the kind of small-town local support that is common. Businesses demonstrated they were all in by purchasing team-related advertisements in the newspapers to kick things off. Ballard's Drug Store shouted that it was "ALWAYS ZEBRA BOOSTERS," and "We Know Drugs Like the Zebras Know Football." Also, the Cotton Belt Route, providing rail service and road service by bus proclaimed, "Let's Go Zebras—And Go Via Cotton Belt Route."[3]

The season did not open until mid–September, but the papers paid perfunctory attention to early practices involving the 47 players out for the team. "The Pine Bluff Zebras went through another stiff workout

2. High School Play

today—and oh what a workout it was," The *Commercial* reported the demands of returning punts and of suffering through the extreme heat.[4] A few days later it was noted that "Old Sol," as in the scorching sunshine, had knocked out four players, and the team was "praying for rain" to make workout conditions more tolerable.[5]

Meanwhile, The Daily Graphic, reporting in much more detail, explained how the young football players were coping with the draconian heat as they worked their way into condition at a pre-season camp. "Just like a great, big family of hungry boys—that is the impression made by the gridders who are getting into shape ... as they dove into the 15 ice cold watermelons brought to them by Sam Cook and A.H. Miller of the Ice Service Co. yesterday."[6]

The newspaper said the players were "slaving like madmen to form a machine that will represent Pine Bluff High School on the gridiron this fall." It also noted that after just four practices, "It is still pretty hard to predict just what kind of team Pine Bluff will have this year." Players were listed in no obvious order, not alphabetically, by size, or position. It can be assumed that the newcomer "Donald Huston" was Don Hutson, whose name would become better known.[7]

The *Graphic* was so into the upcoming season that after a week of workouts, it published a story about a day of non-practice, of what was termed a Sunday day of welcome rest. However, it mentioned the team holding a kangaroo court, which is an in-team operation where justice is meted out for minor infractions. Some 90 years later, such an activity would likely be viewed with suspicion and defined as hazing.

Even then, before Pine Bluff began amassing many Arkansas championships, the state title seemed to be on their minds. The *Graphic* teased matters with a sub-head that read, "Pine Bluff to Make Desperate Bid for State Championship This Year."[8] It was not clear if that meant everyone believed it was the Zebras' turn in 1930, or the squad was just desperate since it was so young and had few returning starters.

The town's businesses had reached into pocketbooks to support the kickoff with their ads. Sears, Roebuck and Co. broadcast "May Victory Be Yours Zebras." The Ice Service Co. that had delivered the watermelons announced, "You Can Do It Zebras." The J.C. Penney Co. stated, "Zebras ... let's go for the 1930 championship."[9] And more.

A day later, Pine Bluff opened Don Hutson's senior year with a 20–0 victory over Benton before a crowd of merely several hundred. The defense did the job in what had to be a confidence-boosting start for a

Caught by Don Hutson!

team with only a handful of holdovers. It was intriguing to note that in these simpler times, head coach Allen Dunaway had just one assistant coach. These days in high school programs, never mind at the college and professional levels, coaches number in double figures along the sidelines.

It was noted in game reports that the weather was brutally hot and humid and seemed to be as big an obstacle as the opponent. The *Commercial* reporter called the "weather conditions much too warm for football, good or bad. Aside from the first few moments of excitement that always accompany the opening game of the football season in Pine Bluff, the game was generally slow and listless. The terrific heat caused that." The Zebras had practiced for just two weeks, and the group's lack of experience seemed to show.[10]

What also showed in the eyes of the reporter was a fledgling passing connection between quarterback Harold Davis and Don Hutson. There was a sense that the duo might make beautiful music together. "The passing combination of Davis to Hutson might be developed into something worthwhile," the story observed. "Hutson is a rangy, sure-fingered receiver and Davis appears to have the knack of heaving the ball with all of the uncanny accuracy of the well-known Ebbie Alexander of 1925 fame."[11] Perhaps only of local fame.

The Zebras seemed to mature fast. In the second week, Pine Bluff trounced Texarkana, 48–0. Much excitement stemmed from adding Guy Reeves to the lineup as a starting halfback, while moving Red Davis, brother of the quarterback, back to the offensive line. Reeves made two dazzling touchdown runs, and the Harold Davis-Hutson tandem teamed up for two touchdown passes. Heck, Pine Bluff High might have had as worthy a passing game as any college in America. The duo added two two-point conversions through the air.

Pine Bluff kept rolling in its third game of the season. The Zebras moved to 3–0 by romping over the Dermott Rams, 51–0, the huge plurality following a 0–0 first quarter. Hutson was not the main man this time, but he did turn in a long touchdown run with a pass near the end of the first half and employed a notable straight-arm to fend off a tackler. That culminated a 75-yard pass play. Hutson also blocked a punt. As a side job, Hutson also kept busy returning kickoffs when needed.

A week later, Pine Bluff pushed to 4–0—one of four unbeaten teams remaining across Arkansas. This time the passing game was paramount

2. High School Play

as the Zebras handled North Little Rock, 44–20. Praise was heaped on Hutson as he scored 32 points for his team, but the *Daily Graphic* had an unfortunate typographical error in a sub-headline, giving credit to "Hudson."

North Little Rock geared its defense to stopping the ground game and was successful with that objective. But the Zebras adjusted and overpowered the visitors with their air attack. "Donald Hutson [the story spelling his name correctly], lanky Zebra wingman, picking forward passes out of the ozone like so many ripe apples from an overburdened tree, earned the victory for the locals with his five touchdowns and two extra points," the *Daily Graphic* gushed.[12]

Hutson made one of his touchdown grabs in highlight fashion. Two Wildcats defenders got hands on one throw, deflecting it into the air near the goal-line, only for Hutson to reach in and gain possession for the score. That gave the appearance of the Zebras enjoying a charmed season, but things turned a week later.

This was a lengthy road trip. Pine Bluff traveled to Marshall, Texas, some 225 miles away at the nexus of Arkansas, Texas, and Louisiana. It took a tremendous rally for the Zebras to come from behind to tie Marshall, 20–20, in the last minute. Pine Bluff was down at the half and was three touchdowns behind starting the fourth quarter. There was a notable history behind this finish. In 1929, the teams also tied, 6–6, and in 1927, the Zebras defeated the Mavericks by one point in the last minute. This time Pine Bluff scored all of its points in the fourth period to stay unbeaten at 4–0–1.

That tie pretty much felt like a win, given how bleak the situation looked. But it was a hint that the Zebras might be vulnerable. Definitely for Hutson, who incurred a lacerated hand requiring stitches, an injury serious enough that in the lead-up to the next week's big rivalry game against Fordyce, the coach announced that he would not be able to play. "Unable to handle a forward pass," the *Daily Graphic* said, "the young man will in all probability be forced to assume the uncomfortable post of bench-warmer."[13] Much ado was made about the game, which was played in Monticello, and a special train was put on to accommodate traveling fans.

Fordyce was Paul Bryant's school, but with Hutson sidelined, the two future teammates did not go head-to-head. Fordyce had the upper hand just about the whole way, winning 50–12 after scoring 32 points early. The Zebras made big miscues, fumbling in inopportune places.

Caught by Don Hutson!

Fordyce benefited from Pine Bluff kickoff man J.W. Cutrell breaking his leg. It was not a good day to be a Zebra.

Pine Bluff coaches inserted two new faces into the starting backfield the next week, and Hutson returned to the lineup from his injury. The expected resurgence on offense, however, did not take place, and the Zebras dropped their second straight game, 12–7, to Camden. This was the first loss ever to the Camden team, though there had been a 1929 scoreless tie.

Pine Bluff was shut out again until the fourth quarter. Hutson made the big play on defense, recovering a fumble at the Camden 25-yard line. The Zebras followed up with a touchdown pass. Interestingly, in an era when stat-keeping was more haphazard, the reporters disagreed on who caught the touchdown toss for Pine Bluff. The *Commercial* credited the catch to one player, and the *Daily Graphic* wrote that Hutson made the score. The *Graphic*'s description was indeed graphic, calling the TD play this way: "A Camden back was covering the lanky [Hutson was regularly characterized as lanky by the local press] Zebra end. Both battled for the ball frantically, the pigskin bouncing into the air and then the madly clawing Hutson snared it with one arm to make good the touchdown."[14]

That was certainly a highlight play, but the longer the season went, the fewer highlights the Zebras produced. As October turned to November, the team had five remaining games, and workouts were eased up. It was not a strategy that paid off. The Zebras were crushed, 68–8, by the El Dorado Wildcats. No amount of rest would have changed the outcome. Hutson was in the middle of a second-half double lateral play that gained 35 yards.

After this dismal stretch, dropping the record to 4–3–1, the Zebras regrouped and ground out another victory, topping Jonesboro, 19–7. Although active in catching passes, Hutson seemed to make more of a mark on defense, in the secondary, in this one.

The turnaround didn't last. Pine Bluff was blown out, 32–7, by Little Rock, and as an indication of how much that hurt, the Zebras brought a six-game winning streak against this rival into the contest. It was just 14–7 at halftime and sure enough, Hutson had the only touchdown for Pine Bluff. Hutson made a fingertip catch just out of the reach of a defender as he stepped into the end zone for the Zebras' only score.

The season wound up with Pine Bluff's first Homecoming event that featured a parade, the naming of a queen, whose identity was kept secret until the game, and a contest against Malvern. It was a better day

2. High School Play

for the royal Sterling Virginia Ussery than it was for the football-playing students, who dropped the game to the Leopards, 19–7.

That was basically it for Don Hutson and Pine Bluff Zebras football. He excelled beyond the overall level of his team but was hamstrung by its shortcomings, as well. The Zebras began the season with a shortage of seasoned talent and played well in spurts, but could not rise to the level of the best teams on its schedule. Soon enough, the high school basketball season began and Hutson recorded an All-State season.

He may have opened eyes and made friends with his often flashy and stellar showings on the football field, but chances are his contemporaries remembered him athletically more for his basketball prowess than his gridiron skills. Or his baseball talents. Like so many high school multi-sport stars, Hutson seemed as if he could do it all. He was nimble, quick, and athletic in ways that would be recalled, but few among those students who shared space in the yearbook would have staked rich bets on Hutson becoming one of the all-time greats of professional football.

Truly, in the fall of 1930, he was just getting started in the game, and no one even knew he would even distinguish himself as a football player for Alabama. As far as the Pine Bluff folks knew, Hutson was going off to play baseball and probably baseball only.

3

The Passing World Gets Ready for Don Hutson

It is remarkable that a high school record Don Hutson set roughly 90 years ago with five touchdown passes caught in a single game still stands in Arkansas. But even more remarkable, given the times and era, is that the ball was thrown his way often enough to provide those scoring opportunities.

Unlike the modern era, when NFL quarterbacks throw the ball 600 times a season, the pass was very slow to catch on following that debut with the St. Louis Billikens and the follow-up efforts of Notre Dame pre–1920. College teams sporadically incorporated the passing game into their game plans, high schools hardly at all. Similarly, the first decade of the National Football League's existence was much more closely linked to variations within the running game, with not much reliance on a quarterback cocking his arm and flinging.

A coach at a high school had to be considered very forward-thinking indeed to throw the ball with any regularity. Of course, not many high schools had a Don Hutson on the roster, capable of out-running defensive coverage with his speed and catching them off-balance with his moves. This was merely a taste, a hint, of what was to come from Hutson later. Unless a coach was sophisticated, keeping up with the latest trends and developments, he didn't dare try those high-risk plays.

It should be remembered that in the 1920s and early 1930s, the shape of a football used by the NFL had about the same amount in common with a basketball as it does with the aerodynamic ball in use today. It was more round than oblong until it was recognized that the ball could be heaved better if shaped more to the liking of the human grip.

3. The Passing World Gets Ready for Don Hutson

George Halas, one of the NFL's co-founders and player-coach-owner of the Chicago Bears, once said of the old ball that a tape measure showed it was "a plump 23 inches around the middle."[1]

The most famous football player of the 1920s was Red Grange. He burst into public consciousness as a running back for the University of Illinois, leading the Illini to a national championship in 1923. He scored six touchdowns in a game against Michigan in 1924, was on the cover of *Time* magazine in 1925, became a three-time All-American, and through the machinations of agent C.C. Pyle, nicknamed "Cash and Carry," toured the nation playing exhibition games with the Chicago Bears. Pyle's ingenuity and chutzpah then led to the formation of an entire league to showcase Grange and compete with the NFL.

Most media attention regarding football centered on Grange as the NFL sought to build something enduring. Except for Green Bay, the clubs in small towns and small markets were gradually weaned out. Yet almost none of the hoopla, as it is these days, revolved around players filling the skies with passes.

One quarterback who rose to the top was Michigan's Benny Friedman. In one 1926 game, Friedman threw for five touchdowns and by passing, running, and kicking accounted for 44 points against Indiana University. Friedman, who stood 5-foot-10 and weighed 183 pounds, was a shrimp by modern quarterback standards. Sometimes on the cranky side, Friedman wanted to be allowed to pass more often than legendary coach Fielding Yost endorsed. Still, Friedman was a two-time All-American and a College Football Hall of Famer.

Representing his original hometown Cleveland Bulldogs, then the Detroit Wolverines, New York Giants and Brooklyn Dodgers over eight seasons, Friedman led the National Football League in passing four times. Nearly a decade into fighting for the spectator dollar among sports fans, the NFL was dragged into a more open era of offense by young men like Friedman. Left to his own devices, Friedman would have thrown more pitches than a baseball starting pitcher. In 1929, when he completed 20 passes for touchdowns, he set a single-season mark that stood until 1942.

Friedman was a herald of the future but an outlier in the present. During seasons when he tossed 10 TD passes, the second-highest total was five. He demonstrated that passing could be a very useful tool, but there was still considerable hesitancy among coaches. They believed in employing running plays on first and second downs, and only on third

Caught by Don Hutson!

down, when still more than a few yards shy of a first down, took the risk of putting the ball in the air. There was little clamor of public opinion demanding that coaches open their style of play and trust field generals to throw more regularly.

Partially due to the fame and exploits of Red Grange, who sported the magnificent nickname of "The Galloping Ghost," there was an incorrectly perpetuated notion that college football players, who might attract 60,000 or 80,000 fans to a game, played a higher quality brand of football than pros. This pervading thought drove the Bears' Halas wild. Pro football was not yet a coveted profession for a college graduate, nor appreciated for its level of performance, but he knew from the first moment the ball was hiked in the new league in 1920 that the pros were better than the amateurs.

Halas, despite being conservative in his tendencies, was almost jealous of Friedman's talents. In the long run—the very long run—Halas understood that Friedman's arm had done the NFL a service with his commitment to passing. Friedman, probably because his statistics were far less gaudy than those belonging to later quarterbacks, was not elected to the Pro Football Hall of Fame until 23 years after he died. He had long felt overlooked and obsessed over a lack of acknowledgment of his important role in those early days of establishing what a throwing quarterback could accomplish.

"Benny revolutionized football," Halas said.[2] That kind of praise was more widespread than many realize for a player somewhat forgotten by time. Friedman had his fans among heavy-duty contemporaries besides Halas.

"There are some who say Friedman is the greatest passer of all time," said Notre Dame's Knute Rockne, who died young before the passing game truly took hold. "They are not far wrong. He could hit a dime at 40 yards."[3]

Grange lived a much longer life, staying around football as a broadcaster for decades. He remained a Friedman supporter. "He was the best quarterback I ever played against," Grange said. "There was no one his equal in throwing a football in those days. Anybody can throw today's football. You go back to Benny Friedman playing with the New York Giants ... he threw that old balloon. Now, who's to tell what Benny Friedman might do with this modern football? He'd probably be the greatest passer that ever lived."[4]

Many statistics routinely taken for granted in the current football

3. The Passing World Gets Ready for Don Hutson

world were not closely tracked in the 1920s, but in 1929, when Friedman threw his 20 touchdown passes, end Ray Flaherty was credited with receiving eight of them, and Hap Moran caught five. On Pro Football Reference.com's season summary, five other players are given at least one touchdown reception, but the total apportioned is 19, not the 20 Friedman was said to throw for the lasting single-season record.

Moran played pro ball between 1926 and 1933, with the Frankford Yellow Jackets as well as the Giants. In a 1933 game against the Philadelphia Eagles, he set the league record for most yards receiving in a game with 114, a record broken many times over, but evidence of how little it took to establish passing and pass-catching records at the time.

As for Flaherty, inducted into the Pro Football Hall of Fame as a coach, the individual record of his season, according to the same source, takes note of those eight TD catches, but has no figure available for total catches. It seems the early days of record-keeping of the NFL were a little sketchy.

The Giants of 1929 were a darned fine outfit, outscoring opponents 312–86 while compiling a 13–1–1 record, even if they did not win the title. The champs were the undefeated Green Bay Packers. It was the start of a three-year run of dominance in 1929, 1930 and 1931, with the Packers putting up a combined record of 34–5–2 under Curly Lambeau. Those were the first three championships earned in the Packers' illustrious history.

Lambeau observed intently as the Giants and Friedman performed superbly. The Packers did not have a quarterback on the 1929 team as the position is currently played. The snap, or hike, went to the player called the tailback, not the quarterback, to initiate the offense. There is little doubt the 12–0–1 Packers fielded all-around talent, with such players as Johnny "Blood" McNally, Verne Lewellen, and Lavvie Dilweg.

That three-season Packers run was timely in more than one way. As one by one the small communities that dreamed of becoming big-league in football fell by the wayside, Green Bay was the one that persevered. As the Packers beat up on the Bears, Giants, and representatives of big cities, they became a symbol to the little man as the ultimate underdogs. Lambeau was the constant and the front man for the team as the sport gradually gained legitimacy and attention.

The Packers played in City Stadium, and slightly more than a decade into their existence, the seating expanded to 10,000. That was big-time for a small operation. There was something special about the

Caught by Don Hutson!

atmosphere. Even Johnny Blood, a big-city playboy and partier at heart, said there was a uniqueness about the team founded by a meat packing company and the way people treated the players. "Green Bay was definitely the place for me," said Blood, who competed for the Packers every season but one between 1929 and 1936 in his Hall of Fame career. "My destiny, maybe. I loved the place, and I have to say, the place, the people, loved me. If you play for the Packers the people know you better than they know their own brothers."[5]

As those who live in small towns are aware, everyone seems to know everything about everyone. In Blood's case, he couldn't keep his wild drinking nights quiet. It even became a subject of contract negotiation with Lambeau. Before the 1929 season, Lambeau offered Blood $110 per game if he refrained from drinking alcohol from Wednesday until after the weekend's game. Blood made a counter-offer, saying, "Make it $100 a game and let me drink on Wednesday." Lambeau said he appreciated Blood's honesty and would still pay him $110 a game and allow for the Wednesday imbibing.[6]

It was not as if Lambeau was a teetotaler himself, but his separation of church and state was the separation between football and bars. Another indicator of how different things were on the field with offenses in the late 1920s and 1930s is that Blood called the plays on the field, without the title of quarterback. "I got along pretty well with Curly, for a while anyway. I was one of the only ones who did. Most didn't like him at all. But for the first three or four years he put up with my antics."[7]

Lambeau signed local Arnie Herber for the 1930 season, and he was slowly molded into the quarterback of the Packers' future. He was not a major offensive factor in 1931 and 1932, but starting in 1933 he emerged as a long passer of sufficient renown to be ultimately chosen for the Pro Football Hall of Fame. Those first two seasons, Herber did not play much, but in 1932 he was the top passer in the NFL, and he was again in 1934. His statistics were forgettable by later standards, just 101 attempts and 639 yards gained the first year and throwing for only 799 yards in 11 games two years later.

Herber totaled 8,041 yards passing and 81 touchdown passes across his entire career, but he played for four championship teams. He also teased Lambeau with glimpses of what might be if he had all the tools at his disposal in the lineup needed for an all-around passing game.

Lambeau himself had been a passer for the Packers. In 1920, Lambeau demonstrated his very first serious flirtation with the football

3. The Passing World Gets Ready for Don Hutson

traveling through the air. This was pre–Benny Friedman, but the statistical confirmation of a story Lambeau told was elusive, as were many football statistics at the time.

Lambeau said he attempted 45 passes in one game, completing 37, which had the ring of exaggeration, a habit Lambeau was critiqued for later. George Calhoun, who was the sports editor of the Green Bay newspaper and Lambeau's business partner running the team, said Lambeau threw 17 times in that game, a bit of a discrepancy. However, the NFL average was six pass attempts a game, so it was still notably high.

"Forward passing had been permitted for 14 years," Lambeau said in 1920, "and most of the original restrictions had been removed. But the passer still had to throw from at least five yards behind the line of scrimmage, which greatly reduced the possibility of deception."[8]

Herber signed for $75 a game and became the beneficiary of a coach who was enthusiastic about passing, but also of a timely change of rules that benefited NFL passers. After the 1932 season, the league held a meeting under a new Rules Committee to consider changes to open up play and alter rules previously patterned after the college game. Foremost for quarterbacks, throwing a forward pass became legal from anywhere behind the line of scrimmage.

Lambeau and Bears rival Halas were among supporters of this change, and coaches began creating more creative plays for their quarterbacks. Herber pre-dated Hutson in Green Bay but became one of his great partners in Packers success. When young, Herber sold Packers programs at City Stadium. A star athlete at Green Bay West High, he tried college at the University of Wisconsin and Regis College in Denver, but within a couple of years was living in Green Bay again.

Herber was working as a handyman for the Packers when Lambeau gave him a tryout prior to the 1930 season, and to most observers' surprise, he made the cut. Nobody would have imagined a future Hall of Famer was already on the premises toting a hammer and a screwdriver.

Lambeau had a nose for talent. Herber might well have been handicapped by having small hands, but he developed his own style of throwing and possessed a very strong arm. One day, Packers veterans Johnny Blood and Mike Michalske issued a betting challenge to test that arm power. Essentially, the three-way conversation on the practice field went like this: "Rookie," Michalske said to Herber, "I'll bet you can't throw a football a hundred yards." The low-key Herber responded, "You're right, Mike, I guess about 80 yards is my limit." Blood interjected that

Caught by Don Hutson!

Michalske really meant 100 yards including any post-landing roll. Herber was surprised to hear he would be given the benefit of the bounce, but Michalske confirmed that he and Blood would each ante up $25, contending Herber could not heave the ball from one goal-line to another. That would be a heck of a throw. Herber said, "You're on."[9]

Herber took a running start, powered a long toss through the air, and watched the ball hit the ground about 85 yards away. However, when the ball struck the ground, rather than rolling, it bounced backwards. The reason why Michalske and Blood were so confident the bet would turn in their favor was that they knew the professional football hitting the ground nose-first would retreat. Herber got a lesson out of the incident from a lighter wallet. Somewhat lost in the telling was just how strong Herber's arm really was. It would not be necessary to throw the football the length of the field in games.

While all of this was going on, Don Hutson was making a name for himself in Alabama, where he was learning his trade and developing the tools that would make him Arnie Herber's best pal on a football field.

4

Alabama

The fact that Don Hutson's nickname was the "Alabama Antelope" right there announces where he first became prominent beyond Arkansas. He could have been the "Arkansas Antelope" if he stayed within the state to play college ball for the University of Arkansas Razorbacks. But as Bear Bryant said, Alabama was the crème de la crème of the region at the time.

And, it must be recalled, Hutson may have been marginally wooed by Alabama's bigger name on the gridiron at the time, but his intent was to focus on college baseball.

Although Arkansas, notably under the late Frank Broyles, who coached where the "woo pig sooie" cheer predominates as one of the most colorful in the sport for nearly two decades, and then served as athletic director for 30 additional years, has had its moments in the sun, it has played mostly in Alabama's shadow.

When it comes to football, the University of Alabama Crimson Tide has had a nearly unbroken record of success for a century, if only barely interrupted by a lower level of success than regularly pursuing national championships. Hutson was an on-field competitor as part of that history, but his friend Bryant played a larger role as a dominating coach, leading up to the present status of Alabama greatness under Nick Saban.

The first flirtation with football at the university was in 1892, introduced by a law student named William Little, who had picked up the game at Andover Academy in Massachusetts. The school's first game was played November 11 of that year, but in Birmingham. The school's first All-American was Bully Van de Graaff, a lineman who also punted and place-kicked, after the 1915 season. Coach Xen Scott built the school into a fledgling power, but resigned after becoming afflicted with cancer and died soon after. The new coach was Wallace Wade, who

Caught by Don Hutson!

had been an assistant at Vanderbilt when the Tennessee school went unbeaten with two ties over two seasons.

In 1925, Alabama gained its first critical Rose Bowl invitation, won the contest, and for the first time won the national championship. By besting the University of Washington Huskies, 20–19, and winning the crown, Alabama played a role in elevating the importance of college football in the region—and Southern pride. The phrase "The football game that changed the South" was attached to the performance.

This was 60 years after the conclusion of the Civil War, but the South was still often portrayed as a backward geographic area of the United States by Northern observers. Poverty was more common and extreme than in many other sections of the country, and development lagged behind following the devastation of the War and Reconstruction. An inferiority complex was part of the big picture. While wildly popular in Southern states, college football's power base was the North and Midwest, where schools in the Ivy League, the Big Ten, Army, and Notre Dame reigned. The caliber of Southern ball was denigrated, compared to larger schools in the West.

In 1925, however, Alabama overran the Southern Conference, as well as non-league foes, going 9–0 while allowing just one touchdown throughout the regular season. Among the shutout casualties were Georgia, Florida, Kentucky, and Georgia Tech. Alabama accepted an invitation to test itself on New Year's Day, 1926, in the Rose Bowl, and spent four days on a train traveling to California. The consensus was that Washington would handily defeat Alabama.

Alabama's star that season, and in the game itself, was back Johnny Mack Brown, called "the Dothan Antelope," antelopes apparently being popular creatures for nicknames in that state. He scored two touchdowns in the Rose Bowl and was selected Most Valuable Player. Brown later became a film star, playing mostly in Westerns.

Perhaps the most striking aspect of the Alabama victory was the return trip to Tuscaloosa. Going by slow train was not such a burden in this direction because at every stop through the South, the Crimson Tide were met by bands playing welcoming music and hailing their victory. If ever one game meant more than the singular score on the board, this was it.

Much later, a documentary film was made about the game and the times, and historians analyzed the meaning of the sporting event. "You can look at the 1926 Rose Bowl as the most significant event in Southern

4. Alabama

football history," commented Andrew Doyle, a Winthrop University professor. "What had come before was almost like a buildup, a preparation for this grand coming-out party. And it was a sublime tonic for Southerners who were buffeted by a legacy of defeat, military defeat, a legacy of poverty, and a legacy of isolation from the American political and cultural mainstream."[1]

This big-time win was something the university administration felt could be exploited to spread the university's name and image nationwide. Victory by the football team in the Rose Bowl became a recruiting tool for the student body, with the school's top officials placing advertising in major metropolitan newspapers. Seizing the moment and leaping onto the map all at once, students from elsewhere, athletes and otherwise, began flooding Tuscaloosa.

An overall 10–0 mark sounded pretty sweet to potential football candidates, and one season later Alabama finished 9–0–1, with the tie coming in a second-time-around visit to the Rose Bowl and a deadlock with Stanford. That pace could not be maintained, however, and after the Crimson Tide rolled to five-win and six-win seasons, Wade's luster dimmed somewhat. He resurrected his genius label in 1930, when Alabama won the Rose Bowl, 24–0, over Washington State and registered its third national title. Then Wallace split for Duke University, where except for World War II he spent the next 20 years. When he retired, Wade's college coaching record was a resounding 171–49–10. Duke's football stadium was named after him in 1967.

It was not as if Alabama fell apart after Wade departed. Frank Thomas had been a winner at the University of Chattanooga, and he remained a winner—an even bigger winner—at Alabama. Thomas stepped in as Wade's successor and coached the Crimson Tide from 1931 through 1946. His career record was 141–33–9, and at Alabama Thomas won four league titles and recorded two 10–0 seasons. Thomas's first Tuscaloosa season was in 1931, when Don Hutson and Paul Bryant were freshmen.

Bryant pretty much always had football on the brain, but initially it seemed certain he would stay in-state and compete for Arkansas. But Bryant wasn't exaggerating when he said Alabama was always in the news and everyone knew the heights the Crimson Tide reached in the Rose Bowl. Bryant and Hutson graduated from high school in 1931, and Arkansas coach Fred Thomsen was hungry to get Bryant for the Razorbacks.

Caught by Don Hutson!

Apparently, before so many rules were put in place governing recruiting by the NCAA, what coaches could do to convince a recruit to come to town was more wide-open. Bryant said Thomsen took him to an all-star game in Dallas, perhaps to impress him with good seats. The game did not do much for Bryant, especially not in swaying him to move to Fayetteville.

> At the half I slipped off and rode a street car back to town to listen to Alabama beat Washington State, 24–0, in the 1931 Rose Bowl, Wade's last Alabama team. So when they came over to ask the Jordan twins [brothers who had helped Fordyce whomp Hutson's Pine Bluff team] about coming to Alabama, they didn't have to recruit me. I was ready.[2]

Hutson was ready, too, attracted by the partial baseball scholarship. Baseball was foremost in his athletic thoughts. Still, by the time autumn came around on the calendar, the notion of playing for a powerhouse football team lured him into trying out. So the great Don Hutson, member of the inaugural class at the Pro Football Hall of Fame, was a walk-on as a college freshman.

Hutson may have possessed terrific raw talent and was easily able to take advantage of high school defenses in his single season as a player in Pine Bluff, but he was short on experience for the college game. He was 6–1, and that was helpful, but weighed around 160 pounds and needed some beefing up. Hutson's raw speed, though, impressed Frank Thomas. Hutson could run the 100-yard dash in 9.7 seconds. These were the days when the century sprint was measured in yards, long before the focus changed to meters.

The 100 yards was a glamor event at track meets. The then-record for 100 yards of 9.4 seconds was set by Frank Wyckoff on June 7, 1930, without the use of starting blocks. In 1933, Jesse Owens equaled that mark while still in high school, and no one ran so much as one-tenth of a second faster for 15 years. Hutson was track fast, as well as football fast. That earned him a place on the Alabama football roster, but he saw very little playing time as a freshman or sophomore. He grew from there, adding bulk, and became a better player during his stay in Tuscaloosa.

During their years as teammates with the Crimson Tide, Bryant and Hutson both played the end position on opposite sides of the field. By their senior year together, after Hutson gained more fame as a player, there were references to Bryant being "the other end" in Alabama's

4. Alabama

offense, and later, Bryant made the same self-deprecating joke. But they were both driven players. "We were both farm boys from Arkansas," Hutson said, "and Paul must have said it a million times that he didn't want to go back to plowing, and I guess I didn't either."[3]

Nope. Hutson was definitely not interested in a farming career back in Arkansas or anywhere else. He was determined to make a mark in the business world. In what segment of the business world, he did not know, but he was no man of the soil. At one point a couple of years after they finished schooling at Alabama, and just as the Great Depression was ending, Hutson and Bryant went into business together. They started Captain Kidd's Cleaners in Tuscaloosa. The business folded after two years, though.

Bryant said not everyone back home at Fordyce High thought he was going to make it as a college man, or as a college player, at big-time Alabama. Plus, this was the worst of the Depression, and the families of these young men were hurting financially. Bryant almost gave up college because he felt obligated to help out his family.

> Daddy had died eating watermelon, got poisoned or something, and Mama was having a tough time. Daddy shouldn't have died, actually. But neither one of them believed in doctors. No dancing, no movies, no sports and no doctors. Anyway, with Daddy gone and most of my brothers and sisters living elsewhere, in Cleveland or Texas, or someplace, if I was looking for an excuse to go home, I had one.[4]

Bryant wrote a letter to a cousin and told him he was going to quit school and move to Texas to get a job in the oil fields. That cousin zipped him back a telegram back so quickly, Bryant barely had time to reflect on what he had originally written. Cuz's telegram read: "GO AHEAD AND QUIT, JUST LIKE EVERYONE PREDICTED YOU WOULD." That stung. "I wasn't about to quit after that," Bryant said.[5]

Imagine how different Alabama football history would have been if Paul W. Bryant, "Bear," had been erased from its pages. By that point, a couple of years into their Tuscaloosa sojourn, practically no one in the state of Alabama had heard of Bryant or Hutson. They were just names on a roster sheet, numbers dashing onto the field periodically in front of spectators. They were not the locus of newspaper writeups or fans' attention as Frank Thomas established his reputation with some good teams, if not always good enough for a soon-to-be spoiled and greedy fan base. In 1931, the Crimson Tide went 9–1. In 1932, the Crimson Tide finished 8–2. In 1933, Alabama ended up 7–1–1. Those were talented

Caught by Don Hutson!

teams. Hutson was at least a regular by then, even if the passing game was barely involved in the offense. By 1934, though, Hutson and that other end were starters and cemented their stature in school lore.

Hutson, the gifted receiver, was not on the receiving end of much most of his time at Alabama, but he burst through with startling numbers—by the era's standards—as a senior. In 1932, Hutson caught three passes all season and did not score a touchdown. In 1933, he caught four passes, and none went for touchdowns.

In 1934, a milestone highlight in early Alabama football history, things were different. Hutson and passing partner Dixie Howell lit up the atmospheric conditions. Although the numbers seem insignificant through the lens of time, Hutson's 19 passes caught, averaging 17.2 yards per grab, and three touchdowns made big news and garnered national attention. This was still the Deadball era of the passing game, so anyone making a splash regularly by weaponizing the air game was lionized.

For Alabama, that 10–0 season can be looked at as a bridge to the second round of school football greatness, which continues today, or a continuum perhaps. While Hutson was the bigger star on the field, the fact that Paul "Bear" Bryant did not drop out of school and returned to Tuscaloosa to become one of the most famous coaches in college football history meant more to the university in the long run. Friends and teammates, Hutson and Bryant were legends in the making, right alongside the program itself in 1934.

The Rose Bowl, a post-season bowl that in the 2020s is almost never on the radar of Alabama football teams, played a pivotal role in the team's and Hutson's reputations. Nearly a decade had passed since Alabama won that first Rose Bowl to lift the entire South. But the 1934 season showed that the Crimson Tide was not going away, and Hutson's demonstration showed just how a creative-thinking coach could utilize the forward pass. It was a little late for Frank Thomas to come to awareness, but the display paved the way for Hutson's future.

5

Alabama Reigns

For someone who became so famous in the sport, for someone who became so renowned that he was inducted into the Pro Football Hall of Fame's first class in 1963, Don Hutson was the ultimate late bloomer. Football was neither his first nor second sport of choice, or skill, or maybe not even his third. He had shown more talent in basketball, baseball, and track, and football seemed an afterthought until senior year in high school.

Making that leap from high school play to college ball, especially at a school like Alabama, which was one of the most prominent in the country, was not as smooth a transition as just taking up the game in high school was, either. "Don didn't make all that much of an impression when he made the varsity as a sophomore," said teammate Buck Hughes, a fullback who later coached the high school game in Alabama. That was a viewpoint made some 60 years later. "As I recall, he played just enough to earn a letter in '31, '32, and '33. Now 1934, that's another story."[1]

Teammates remembered him as being behind the curve, far from an impact player during his first seasons in Tuscaloosa, a guy not valuable enough to gain much playing time, and, as his statistics showed, a receiver the team seldom threw to. He was not a factor in game plans because he hardly received playing time, never mind the ball.

Jim Dildy, a tackle on those Alabama teams, basically said Hutson was a lousy football player at the time. "He was so inept in football that the Arkansas group [Crimson Tide teammates from Arkansas, including Bear Bryant] called a special meeting to set him straight. They told him, 'Look, you'd better get your butt in gear. You're not going to embarrass the guys from Arkansas.'"[2] Was it really that bad?

Apparently, appearances counted against Hutson early on, too. "He had short legs and he didn't pick 'em up real high, so it looked like he

Caught by Don Hutson!

was just shuffling along," said Young Boozer, a halfback in that group who was from in-state. "People didn't realize he was flying."[3]

Sometimes athletes are late bloomers, but Hutson was a great athlete earlier. It just took him longer to make a major impact in this particular sport. His reputation gained steam on a weekly basis during his senior season, that 1934 year which the Crimson Tide turned into a special place in the school scrapbook. It was a season to remember, bordering on perfection when no perfection can ever be achieved. The Crimson Tide won every game and nearly prevented every opponent from even scoring. It is always notable to score a shutout, but to record shutouts week after week is virtually unheard-of in the annals of the sport. Alabama's defense notched five shutouts, gave up one score in a game three times, and never allowed more than 14 points in a game.

The starting ends on the 1934 Alabama team were Don Hutson, a future pro Hall of Famer, and Paul "Bear" Bryant, who became the winningest coach in college football history. But the biggest star, day-in and day-out, coming into the season was quarterback Millard Howell. He was a known quantity, the team leader, and better known by the nickname "Dixie." As time went on, he became overshadowed by the others, and most likely is best remembered (even in Alabama) as the man who threw the ball to Hutson that season.

Coach Frank Thomas' teams had been very good over the preceding couple of years, but there were no off-hand predictions of greatness issued in anticipation of the 1934 season. One newspaper story a week before play began suggested that Alabama was taking Howard "more seriously than any initial contest in years. The reason is that the Howard Bulldogs are doped to be in great shape for the Tide battle."[4]

Alabama's season opened September 29 with a 24–0 victory over Howard College, with the Crimson Tide nearly scoring a touchdown in each quarter. This school is not to be confused with Howard University, the traditionally Black school located in Washington, D.C. This Howard is in Alabama and later changed its name to Samford. Howell, who was on his way to first-team All-American honors, scored one of the touchdowns on a day when Alabama converted none of its extra-point tries.

Sewanee, The University of the South, was the next opponent. Sewanee and Alabama had been playing football regularly since 1893, and this was the 29th meeting. The Tigers, based in Tennessee, were once a football power, but now compete athletically in NCAA Division III, including on the gridiron. Alabama won that game, 35–6, a contest

5. Alabama Reigns

that was played in Montgomery, a somewhat neutral site. This was supposed to be a night game, played on a Friday, but heavy rain disrupted the surface at the Cramton Bowl and caused a postponement until the next afternoon. It would have been Alabama's first-ever night game, but that evolution in the sport did not happen for the Crimson Tide for another six years due to this delay.

In mid–October, Alabama crushed Mississippi State, 41–0. Bryant beat Hutson to the scoreboard with a touchdown catch in the second quarter of a game completely dominated by the Crimson Tide.

By the fourth week of the season, when Alabama out-struggled Tennessee, 13–6, Howell finally made Hutson's acquaintance. This may be the moment when Hutson first gained some notice as a college football player. It was a big stage, a big game between regional rivals. A 33-yard pass from Howell to Hutson set up Alabama's first touchdown.

A fight broke out and Bryant took the blame, ejected from the game even though he was not near the confrontation. Twice in the second half, Hutson's number was called for a trick end-around play. On the same drive, he picked up good yardage on the ground, caught a pass for nine yards, and scored a touchdown on a slick run that eluded potential tacklers and culminated with him diving into the end zone. Dixie Howell gained more kudos than anyone for the way he handled the ball, prompting Tennessee coach Robert Neyland to call him the best back in the South.

> This boy Howell is the best back we've ever played against. Howell is a backfield in himself. He runs like a deer, passes with utmost accuracy, and is among the best punters in the nation. Howell has what might be termed "a change of pace" in baseball language. He runs fast, lopes, quickens and sidesteps his way, and his style has made him one of the most elusive backs in the country. Frank Thomas has everything it takes to make a good football team there at Alabama.[5]

A week later, Howell sought to live up to that review. He scored two touchdowns as Alabama pushed around Georgia, 26–6. He ran for 152 yards without even playing in the second half. Alabama chose not to run up the score. That carried the team through October, and it was obvious this was a special squad, thank you very much, Mr. Neyland.

The Southeastern Conference was new in those days, formed in 1932. Alabama was a charter member, along with neighboring Auburn within the state, the two Mississippi schools, Mississippi State and the University of Mississippi, Georgia, Louisiana State, Vanderbilt, Florida,

Caught by Don Hutson!

Kentucky, Tulane, Georgia Tech, and Sewanee. The latter three are long gone from the group. Tennessee came in one year later, in 1933. Arkansas (1991), South Carolina (1991), Missouri (2012) and Texas A&M (2012) came along much later. In the 2000s, the SEC has morphed into the strongest college football conference in the country, and Alabama's presence is a big part of that.

In 1934, the next opponent was traditional foe Kentucky, and November 3 was Homecoming for the Wildcats in Lexington. Alabama showed little respect, crunching the hosts, 34–14. This was the Crimson Tide's first game of the year played outside the state. Howell and backfield mate Joe Riley must have seen openings they liked in the Kentucky secondary. It was a big deal that combined, they threw the ball nine times. An early completion of 22 yards went to Hutson, but he scored the first touchdown on a run, a 10-yarder on another end-around. Although the game was not close, the margin could have been wider. Alabama lost out on another six-pointer by stalling on downs on the one-yard line.

Talk had begun in newspapers about which team from the East should be chosen to face a top power from the West in the Rose Bowl. Syndicated columnist Damon Runyan (who wrote the stories that were the basis for the Broadway hit *Guys and Dolls*) nominated Alabama as his choice in early November, and that news was spread around by the Tuscaloosa newspaper. In a piece that traveled nationwide, Runyan highlighted Alabama's track record in the Rose Bowl, noting that the Crimson Tide had won twice and tied once in previous swings.

> Runyan's opinion was so widely valued the Tuscaloosa newspaper printed his column. It read in part, The Tide, in the writer's opinion, can beat any team on the Coast this year. The Alabamans think this year's team is the best in Alabama's football history, though this seems to be taking in a great deal of territory. But that is what the Alabamans think, according to old grads. [Southern football teams] accept the Rose Bowl game as a most solemn assignment, as something that involves the honor and dignity of all southern sport, and generally put up a great battle.[6]

Howell left Clemson dizzy in a November 10 game. Current Alabama fans would chuckle at the news that a Homecoming game drew just 8,000 fans. The result would leave them pleased, however. Collecting 23 first downs and 413 yards of offense, Alabama blasted Clemson, 40–0. It was Howell-to-Hutson for a touchdown in the first period through the air, but several Alabama players made big plays. On a third-quarter

5. Alabama Reigns

drive, Hutson hauled in passes of 21 yards and 26 yards, too. The Crimson Tide even turned in a 75-yard punt return, but the play was called back on a holding penalty.

Once essentially a non-entity on the roster, Hutson was now a visible presence on more than the practice field. Following the destruction of Clemson, Hutson's name even made it into a sub-head in the *Tuscaloosa News* which read, "Don Hutson, Millard Howell Lead Mates in Season's Seventh Victory." The praise expanded from there in the game story with a definite elevation of his status, almost as if the school's sports information director had chosen the words:

> Don Hutson, Alabama, end who bids fair to grab an All-American berth, definitely established himself as one of the greatest Alabama ends of all-time Saturday afternoon. This alert speedster was all over the field, doing everything that could be wished for. Hutson caught six passes for a total gain of 83 yards. Two of them were good for touchdowns, while each of the others went for nice gains. He also played a brilliant defensive game, out-smarting the most alert Clemson backs.[7]

As the season progressed, the Alabama defense stifled everyone, and the diversified offense ran up points. There seemed to be more faith from Frank Thomas in his passing game and more confidence shown by Howell in his own arm and in Hutson's hands. Opponents sought to dig up fresh plans to stop Alabama but couldn't come up with the correct answers. Meeting in Atlanta, Georgia Tech fell by the same 40–0 score, and a Howell-to-Hutson toss set up the first TD. In the second quarter, Hutson cradled the ball through the air and scored himself. Passing might still not have been the first option, but Alabama proved it knew how to utilize the method for advancing the ball by mixing in runs and catching foes off-balance with timely throws. The hometown Tuscaloosa newspaper observed, "Hutson Again Turns in Brilliant Game at End."[8] The senior was gaining last-minute fans.

Before Alabama met Vanderbilt on Thanksgiving, it was noted just how powerful the Crimson Tide had been throughout the season. The win over Georgia Tech was by the largest plurality—by either team—in the rivalry that dated to 1902. Also, all other Alabama victories were by the largest point spreads incurred by every opponent.

A few days before Alabama's last regular-season game, the announcement of the Newspaper Enterprise Association All-American team came. Howell was a first-team choice, and Hutson was a third-team selection. The day before the game, United Press International

Caught by Don Hutson!

announced its All-American squad, and it included Howell and Hutson. Also, Bryant, guard Charlie Marr, and tackle Bill Lee, the captain of the Crimson Tide, were chosen honorable mention All-American.

The Crimson Tide had generated considerable excitement on both sides of the ball and in the win column. Dixie Howell was still the big name on the team, and he left his fans in awe in his final regular-season game November 29. Alabama took on Vanderbilt at Legion Field in Birmingham, and 24,000 spectators watched the 34–0, one-sided match, a sellout.

This was truly Howell's day to savor. Between running, passing, and returning punts, he amassed 318 yards, and he also averaged 40 yards on his own punts. His longest punt return was 42 yards, his rushing totaled 162 yards, and on one 76-yard drive in the fourth quarter, Howell ripped off 48 yards in three attempts, the last for a 15-yard touchdown. The showing provided Alabama with a 9–0 regular-season record, and in those days such outstanding play could mean only one thing—another shot at the Rose Bowl. Indeed, the school's marching band broke into a rendition of "California, Here I Come," as the time ticked down.

The win over Vanderbilt gave Alabama its second straight Southeastern Conference title. As soon as the final gun sounded, Alabama was presented with an invitation from the hosts in Pasadena to come celebrate New Year's with them again. There was not much debate about whether Alabama would accept. The school officially did so immediately, making the fourth time the Crimson Tide's presence was requested at the Rose Bowl. The opponent was scheduled to be Stanford, in a rematch of the 1927 game that concluded in a 7–7 tie. Stanford, at that time known as the Indians, not the Cardinal, as the school's sports teams are now, was also undefeated, though with one tie, and the champion of what was then called the Pacific Coast Conference. From Stanford, Alfred Masters announced in a press conference the Rose Bowl selection of Alabama to come West, saying, "Well, boys, it is my pleasure to tell you that Alabama has been invited. I am informed they have one of the greatest football teams in the history of the South. We could make no other choice."[9]

Soon after, advertising by the Southern Pacific Lines assured Tide fans they could reach the Alabama-Stanford game by taking a special train. For $109.30, the passenger would receive a round-trip ticket by rail from Tuscaloosa to California that also included a ticket to the Rose

5. Alabama Reigns

Bowl, a hotel room in Los Angeles, a tour stopover in El Paso, and sightseeing in "Old Mexico." The Pullman car would be attached to a lounge car, a dining car, and an observation car, and a barber would ride along. Presumably, the Alabama football fan would have to spring for his own champagne to toast a Crimson Tide victory.

6

Last Days at Alabama

It is difficult to overestimate the importance that the Rose Bowl of January 1, 1935, played in Don Hutson's life. Alabama's tremendous regular season, going 9–0, helped put him on the map as an outstanding player who gained All-American recognition. But Alabama's and Hutson's performances in the bowl game against Stanford elevated his stature tenfold.

Hutson was transformed from a National Football League prospect who could aid a team that was interested in developing an offense around the forward pass into someone who could be the savior of a club. In that sense, this one game was a career-maker. Hutson was presented with an empty canvas and filled it with images that rivaled Van Gogh. For those who already had it in their imaginations that the passing game represented pro football's future, he was a potential miracle gift darting across the stage. At least two teams realized instantly that Hutson was the player they coveted above all others.

Pro scouting does not work quite the same way in the 2020s as it did in the 1930s. Nowadays there is more film of a star player available for viewing than there is of Clint Eastwood. Statistics ranking a player, especially a runner, receiver, or thrower, who heavily interact with the ball, are readable with the tapping of fingertips on a computer keyboard. Coaches can parachute into a campus and attend a game in person on short notice to determine if a player passes the eyeball test. There are major combine camps where college players dreaming of pro careers are measured and timed, weighed, and have body fat and body power dissected.

Not so in 1934, when Hutson was a senior. NFL teams cast a local net in seeking to boost rosters with the best players excelling in their immediate area. Coaches who had friends in the business, trusted friends with experience and a reputation for recognizing talent, men

6. Last Days at Alabama

who were on their side, relied on their judgments to recommend young players. There was no game film to study, no television sending games via the air waves across the country.

For what it was worth in informational and scouting value, newsreels playing in movie theaters provided the public with highlights about some of the finest athletes of the day, the first ones showing in 1911 and their quality improving over the ensuing decades. While it might be nice to see your favorite sport portrayed on the screen, it probably wasn't much help as a source in finding the right player for your team.

Still, Don Hutson had gone from an unknown in the Alabama lineup to an All-American in a single year. Sportswriters spread his name amongst themselves, and their reporting spread his achievements to honors voters. Stanford knew of Hutson leading up to the Rose Bowl, and any coach in the pros who wanted to know something about a previously anonymous wide receiver could have access to his statistics and gleaned background about what type of player he was.

The scheduled match between Stanford and Alabama loomed as a special one, certainly likely to be the game of the year. Alabama, of course, was undefeated, with an explosive offense led by Dixie Howell, and a ferocious defense that somehow made the word deny rhyme with defense. Stanford was 9–0–1 and headed into its fifth Rose Bowl. Some suggested Stanford might be the finest Western team ever, and the Indians were called "a team without a weakness." As for Alabama, there were some doubters about the Crimson Tide's true strength "despite its great record compiled during the regular season."[1]

There was tremendous anticipation for the game and, consistent with bowl organizers' dreams, demand for tickets was so intense that the Rose Bowl sold out—some 85,000 seats—by December 23. Many said the demand for more tickets kept increasing even when none were left to be had.

The Tide football team journeyed from Alabama to California by train and arrived at its Pasadena destination at 9:30 a.m. on December 24, a week prior to the Rose Bowl. The travel party of some 250 members started with 35 players, but one was afflicted by unexpected illness. Back-up tackle Bill Young suffered an appendicitis attack and was taken off the train in Del Rio, Texas, for an operation. The team had paused for a practice in San Antonio, and Young seemed fine, but then became sick. Originally, he sought to keep his discomfort to himself, but it worsened,

Caught by Don Hutson!

and an onboard doctor from Birmingham took a look into the situation. The physician, H.P. Ledbetter, recommended action be taken, so Young stopped in Del Rio, population 9,000. Young's teammates waited aboard the train, anxious for news. A report that the surgery was successful allayed their worries, and everyone moved on, leaving Young behind to recuperate.

It was a festive circumstance when the Alabama train chugged out of Tuscaloosa, with many fans cheering on the Crimson Tide. At stops along the way west, other fans turned out at stations to add well wishes. In some places, football fans lined the tracks, waving and shouting when the train did not even stop. In Tucson, Arizona, a scheduled stop, the players were greeted by a Mexican orchestra playing tunes.

As is common even today at bowl-game stayovers, the team was scheduled to see the local sights in California. Alabama was invited to visit Warner Brothers movie studios. Events in Pasadena were orchestrated by the Alabama Club of Southern California. There was plenty of time for such low-key enjoyments. Alabama coach Frank Thomas said there would be light scrimmages at Occidental College's field, but not heavy practices. He was concerned about risking injury.

Stanford stayed in Northern California through Christmas, plus a day. The Indians featured their own stars, such as back Bobby Grayson, and their own defensive reputation, utilizing a four-man front that had been nicknamed "the butterfly" defense. One early-arriving Southern sportswriter representing the *Atlanta Constitution* expressed skepticism about the hullabaloo being made over Stanford's greatness in West Coast newspapers and how the Indians might be the best Coast team in the last decade. "You may put this down as strictly baloney, and sliced quite thin," wrote Ralph McGill. "The Stanfords cannot be as good as the Trojans [Southern Cal] of 1931 and 1932. They don't come that good in more than once in a very great while." McGill also thought Grayson was "not quite as good as Dixie Howell."[2]

Was that regional pride, a truly informed opinion, or a voice of reason drowned out by those residing in another region? "Boys," McGill wrote, "the ozone out here does things. It creates delusions and illusions of grandeur."[3]

The day after Christmas, the Alabama football team took its fun trip to Warner Brothers in Culver City. This was the early days of talking motion pictures. In 1927, *The Jazz Singer*, starring Al Jolson, was introduced to the public as the first "talkie." The movies had been around for

6. Last Days at Alabama

a while, but they were silent pictures, no dialogue spoken aloud by the characters on the screen. This was only seven years later, so the revolution was a young one. Jolson was one of the stars the Crimson Tide met during its tour, along with such other luminaries as Ruby Keeler, Joe E. Brown, Pat O'Brien, and Dick Powell. Brown signed autographs, and Powell wanted to meet the Arkansas players since he was from Little Rock.

Jolson sang "My Mammy." Lyrics in that tune include "My heartstrings are tangled around Alabammy." Did that mean Jolson believed the Crimson Tide would be victorious in the Rose Bowl? It seemed so, since he fell to one knee and said, "Now, I guess Alabama will win."[4] It did not seem Jolson had a song to make Stanford feel so at home.

Players egged on center Kavanaugh Francis to sing because they knew he had a good voice and they wanted to give something back. Usually, Francis called out blocks for teammates on the line, but this time he belted out the song "The Man on the Flying Trapeze." It was a performance in the clutch, though unlikely to earn him more playing time from Coach Thomas.

The scribes were the loudest proponents, taking sides between Alabama and Stanford, but Thomas would not be caught issuing bulletin board material for the newspapers that could be read by the opposition. He was careful in his analysis of the upcoming game. "Stanford doesn't know much about us," Thomas said, "and we don't know much about Stanford. I think it should be a close, interesting game. But you can never tell when two teams of apparently even strength get together. One may be hot and win by 30 points. We are glad to be out here, and I think the fans won't be sorry after they attend the game because it looks like a tough battle from any angle."[5]

Alabama had gone through changes of personnel, from the head coach to the players, since the Crimson Tide made its first trip to the Rose Bowl. However, Hank Crisp, the team's line coach as well as athletic director, had been present with each of the westward-bound teams for previous Rose Bowls. He liked Alabama's chances in the 1935 game. "This team is faster than any of the others," Crisp told local sportswriters, "and it has a more diversified attack. We are going to enjoy your good weather because we had quite a bit of rain down home before we left."[6]

The Rose Bowl was the culmination of the Don Hutson-Paul Bryant playing partnership. They were not only the twin ends in the Alabama

Caught by Don Hutson!

lineup, they had also become roommates. They had a brotherly relationship, but Bryant, coming from deeper poverty and struggling more as a college man, seemed to view Hutson as the one who could handle things in easy fashion. At one point, Hutson, Bryant, and four other guys were roommates, sleeping on bunk beds in a compartmentalized area of the school's gymnasium. Not so much privacy, but the cost was cheap.

Fancy, the digs were not. Bryant described the living quarters this way: "They had partitioned three rooms out of what was an old dressing room and there were more rooms on the second floor where they had the basketball court. Near our room number ten, they had the so-called A Club Room, for lettermen, with a pool table and some benches and a couple of chairs for hanging around. That was the entertainment portion of the deal."[7] It is unlikely that this apartment would go too far in impressing girls the players might want to take home and get to know better.

Bryant said Hutson was the first-rate student between them, and it came from his upbringing. "Hutson breezed through school," Bryant said. "His mother was a school teacher and he knew how to study, and the value of it. I wouldn't swap my mama and papa for anybody's, but neither one of them had been to school, there were never any books around the house, and I was a lousy student."[8]

At Alabama, in general Bryant and Hutson hung out together, were part of the same group of guys, some players and some not, who spent their free time together. They didn't have much money and their social lives were limited, but Bryant said they always had a good time together. Bryant quoted his wife, Mary Harmon, as saying the girls thought the football players were the best dancers, but they were the worst ones to risk getting into relationships with, though he was not more explicit. Bryant hinted that this group did a little bit of mischief-making, but was not into lawbreaking. By his account, Bryant's and Hutson's college days sounded pretty tame on a small-town campus in the 1930s.

"Ours was a simple time," Bryant said, without emphasizing that their college days occurred during the Depression, when money was tight and pressures were everywhere, "and the discipline problems were simple. A crisis consisted of a couple of guys getting caught smoking or drinking beer or something, that kind of thing. We all wanted to win so badly, we never strayed too far off the line, and those who did would hide it from other players."[9]

Bryant, Hutson, teammates like Riley Smith and Jim Dildy, and

6. *Last Days at Alabama*

other friends like Hillman Walker and Sam Friedman, called themselves a club of sorts. Friedman's family did own a place in the country, and the others pooled their money and rented cars so they could take their dates out of town for picnics on the weekend. Bryant said they would "go riding around," and that meant picking up the girls at a sorority house, buying baloney and bread, and going out of town. The football team was subject to a curfew, and the girls had deadlines for being back in the sorority houses.

"We had two flat tires," Bryant said, "and when we went to check the car in, we couldn't come up with enough cash. So we kept it and it was a week before we could raise enough to turn it in. Every day the bill got higher. And every day we drove those girls around." Might as well use the car if they were paying for it.[10]

The boys got bolder and bolder, though they weren't exactly wild men. They skirted the rules, not the law. They did some drinking and some partying with young ladies, and Hank Crisp, Thomas' chief disciplinarian, got a handle on their behavior. He decided to put his foot down with a loud stamp, Bryant said.

> We were caught one night in our rooms with a gallon of old corn likker we paid six bits for, and another night over at the Chi Omega House after hours. There were about ten of us saucering around. The girls had the music going and we were dancing and having a time. When the house mother started down the stairs to find out what was going on we tried to escape. [Teammate] Charlie Marr grabbed the door handle to pull it open and the son of a gun was so strong he pulled the knob off. We were trapped.[11]

It was not a clean getaway, and reports were filed with Crisp. "His favorite punishment was to make us run laps at 4 a.m.," Bryant noted. "But this time he took us over to the track, where they were having a meet, and all of the students were there, and he made us run a hundred laps. Run them, he said, or get going."[12] Rather than be thrown off the team, they all ran them ... and ran them. They did not finish for hours.

Once during junior year, Bryant said, Hutson was trying to be a good boy, to get in the football coaches' good graces so they would let him out of spring ball to play for the baseball team. Bryant and some of the usual gang had plans to attend a sorority dance, and one of the fellows rented a riverboat and obtained some grain alcohol to spike the punch. Hutson refused to go along. He wanted to show well at a football scrimmage and convince the coaches they should let him switch to baseball for the rest of the spring.

Caught by Don Hutson!

"Oh no, not me, I'm going to bed," Hutson said. "I'm going to be ready for that damn game so I can play baseball." Everyone else got plastered, stayed out late, and was hung over the next day. When a peppy Hutson rose feeling grand and was getting dressed, he made fun of the others. "Oh, you poor sonsabitches," he said. "I feel sorry for you."[13]

Bryant said the temperature was at the melting level, and although he struggled, staggering into the end zone on a play (courtesy of Hutson, who blocked two men out of commission with one shot), the coaches lifted him and thankfully rested him. For some reason, Coach Crisp got all over Hutson that day, denigrating his hustle, pointing to Bryant as a good example, and making Hutson play the entire game. He threatened to keep him playing football until school let out, never mind considering baseball as an excused absence. It was apparently part of a ruse because a couple of days, later Hutson was permitted to go to the diamond.

Crisp may have meted out the punishments, but Frank Thomas was not in the dark about what his players were up to. Bryant, Hutson, and the others were playing a bit too hard to suit him, and one day senior year when he passed by the Bryant-Hutson duo in his car, he stopped and had them climb in with him. "I understand you boys are pretty big with the ladies," Thomas told them. "Well, that doesn't mix too good with football. You better make up your minds whether you want to play on this football team or not."[14] Then they were let out of the automobile.

That was not the end of things, however. This was the week of the Sewanee game in Montgomery. Bryant saw the newspaper that speculated Alabama was going to start two different players at the ends for that encounter. Bryant said, "He may not start me, but I know he's going to start you." The next day at practice, Thomas named the starting lineup and did not mention Hutson or Bryant. On game day, the Montgomery paper printed the starting lineups, and those guys weren't listed there either. Hutson and Bryant did not start, though Thomas did put them into the game about halfway through the first quarter of the 35–6 win. Bryant said, "the message was clear. Coach Thomas meant business, and what he was really doing was getting us ready for Tennessee, which was only two weeks away."[15]

Bryant said Thomas was a good worker of psychology, and on the train on the way to California for the Rose Bowl, when Bryant walked in on the coach sitting with the Louisiana State athletic director and a few newspapermen. Thomas noticed and said, "This is my best football

6. Last Days at Alabama

player. This is the best player on my team. I would have gone out there and killed myself for Alabama that day."[16]

According to Bryant's upbringing and the need to scrap for money, he viewed Hutson as well-off because his father, the railroad man, brought home steady wages. When he spoke of Hutson doing on-campus jobs like waiting on tables in dining halls, Bryant made it sound as if Hutson didn't really need the money, but did the work to blend in. That was not an accurate portrayal. Hutson wasn't that well off.

When it came to dissecting Hutson's athletic ability at the time, Bryant is the most reliable witness, however. It was obvious he thought highly of Hutson's talents, but as much ink as Hutson gathered as a senior, there was little written about him at Alabama before that because he did not make a real splash. Bryant knew what Hutson accomplished in high school, but he didn't accomplish that much in college athletics, even football, until that senior season.

Bryant said Hutson got his weight up to as high as 194 pounds before it dropped down to pretty much a steady 183–185 over the following pro years. Hutson loved to eat, but it didn't seem to matter what he ingested, Bryant said, he didn't gain any fat from his snacks.

"He was, in every respect, a complete football player," Bryant said, clearing up the notion espoused by others that Hutson wasn't very good, though that could have been true early on. "A good defensive end, a fine blocker, and an intelligent player. But, oh my, could he catch passes. In all my life, I have never seen a better pass receiver. He had great hands, great timing, and deceptive speed. He'd come off the line looking like he was running wide open, and just be cruising. Then he'd *really* open up. He'd look like he was gliding and he'd reach for the ball at the exact moment it got there, like it was an apple on a tree."[17]

That was the Don Hutson receiver the sell-out crowd at the Rose Bowl and all of the sportswriters saw in action against Stanford in that big game.

7

The Rose Bowl

The official attendance at the Rose Bowl for the showdown between Alabama and Stanford was 84,474, a huge crowd, especially for the time, but nowhere near the size of the more recent turnouts since the stadium was expanded. That was nearly 50,000 more people in attendance than in 1934, the record low. The all-time record for spectators is 106,869 at the 1973 game, with No. 1 ranked University of Southern California against No. 3 ranked Ohio State. That attendance is the largest for any college football bowl game.

Numerous regular-season college football games have topped that Rose Bowl mark, including the Battle of Bristol, a matchup between Virginia Tech and Tennessee played at the Bristol Motor Speedway, a NASCAR auto racing track, on the border separating those two states. That September 10, 2016, game recorded an attendance of 156,990.

Still, given that Alabama competed in the fall of 1934 in front of crowds that were only one-tenth as large as the Rose Bowl viewership, that 84,000-plus was notable. That was a lot of people gathered together, even if it was an open-air stadium, not under one roof. So much for the in-person mob. It was predicted that about five million people would listen to the game on the radio as well. Of course, there was no televising of sporting events nationwide just yet.

These were still the days of leather helmets with no face guards, tiny shoulder pads, and limited padding in the football pants. The players really did dress differently, not much resembling knights in armor with much heavier-duty protection. The speed of the sport had not reached modern-day proportions, either, but the tandem of Alabama's Don Hutson and Dixie Howell teased the future with their air game, and it was recognized immediately on the scene.

Fans had their pre-game favorites, allegiances, and beliefs about which was the stronger of the two regional powerhouses. Despite no

7. The Rose Bowl

outright bragging noted by coaches and players, the supporters had some deeply held convictions. My Alabama is better than your Stanford. My Stanford is better than your Alabama. Upsets take place every day in sports, so regardless of what fans thought might happen, somebody was going to be surprised. Maybe the coaches, Frank Thomas for the Crimson Tide or Claude Thornhill for Stanford, really did have closely held expert opinions they did not reveal to anyone outside of their immediate families.

The manner in which the game began and the first quarter played out, it seemed everyone might be right. It was a major struggle to make big gainers by either team, and after the first 15 minutes the score was 7–0 Stanford. Star back Bobby Grayson scored on a one-yard run followed by an extra-point kick. Stanford's defense came out looking very sharp and held Alabama to just four yards in the quarter.

However, one period of feeling things out was all Alabama needed to solve puzzles presented by Stanford. The Crimson Tide exploded in the second quarter, running off 22 points for a 22–7 halftime lead. Howell, who was ultimately named Most Valuable Player, pulled off the first touchdown on a five-yard run, but 'Bama's extra-point kick missed, and the Southerners still trailed, 7–6. That didn't last much longer, though. Riley Smith, who flubbed the one-pointer, atoned with a 27-yard field goal for Alabama's first lead.

The next time around, Smith demonstrated that his toe was all limbered up. That was after Howell proved *his* legs were all limbered up with a 67-yard touchdown run that improved the margin. Smith made good on the extra-point kick this time. Before the period ended, Howell and Hutson began showing their stuff. Alabama's next big score was imprinted on minds, as well as the scoreboard, when Howell heaved a 54-yard TD to his favorite end. This was a back-breaker, raising the lead to 15 points, though it could have been more if Hutson had successfully booted the extra point. The play had fans on both sides buzzing, since longer completed passes were still quite rare. The completion likely helped demoralize Stanford as well, which was not used to surrendering such explosive touchdowns.

For the most part, the second quarter was the game, not only the turning point, but the clinching point. Pasadena, whether in the Tournament of Roses Parade, or at half-time of the Rose Bowl game, is quite good at showing off marching bands. This time when the music stopped, it was a bit like musical chairs, with Stanford having nowhere to sit.

Caught by Don Hutson!

The avalanche of points by Alabama in the second period gave the Tide ownership of the game. The rest was pretty much playing out the clock. Stanford did its best to come back, but Alabama's defense, solid throughout, mostly repelled the challenges, with one exception. Stanford did manage to inch a little bit closer in an otherwise scoreless third period. Alabama did not score, but Stanford posted a 12-yard touchdown run by "Buck" Van Dellen. Whether exhausted from so much productive expenditure of energy in the second quarter, or merely stifled for the 15 minutes by Stanford's still-in-there-trying defense, Alabama could not break through on the scoreboard in the third period.

With the score 22–13 entering the fourth period, the game was not a rout. But it was in Alabama's control. Once again, the Crimson Tide was king, deflecting all attempts to penetrate the end zone by Stanford. Finally the duo of Howell and Hutson crushed Stanford's hopes with another big-play touchdown bomb. Hutson collected a 59-yard toss from Howell for six more points, and Smith kicked the extra point, raising the spread to 29–13. Stanford never got closer, and that was it for the scoring.

Essentially, it was a valedictory performance for Howell and Hutson on their way to exiting Alabama. It almost made watchers wonder why the Tide had not passed more during the regular season. Of course, the Crimson Tide had not needed to most of the time since they put up a 10–0 season. In Pasadena, Hutson caught six passes for 165 yards, a show that left most football fans gasping.

One sportswriter who covered the game for the *Los Angeles Examiner* was observant enough to realize what he was seeing, a fresh incarnation of a new generation of forward pass wizards working together. In his game story, he referenced the famed Gus Dorais-Knute Rockne partnership at Notre Dame and the University of Michigan's Benny Friedman working with All-American end Bennie Oosterbaan. He capitalized the last names of Hutson and Howell—HOWELL TO HUTSON—and made it clear he did not do so by accident. "And let the last stand in capital letters because it should top the list of two-men combinations in football to make history and to make for the total eclipse of the West in 1934 annals, at least."[1]

Calling Stanford's loss "a stunning defeat," he ascribed the result to the passing game, saying, "What the air routes have done to land travel in the line of national transport, this pair did to prove that the pass is

7. The Rose Bowl

more potent than the carry. The arm is mightier than the torso, or the foot."[2]

The report sent to the *Tuscaloosa News* was no less glowing, reading in part, "Alabama's Crimson Tide, acclaimed by all sides as the greatest team ever to represent the South and East in the Rose Bowl, sang 'Alabama bound' today."[3] That was a reference to the team beginning its eastward trip by train the morning after the game.

That acclaim and reaction was indeed widespread. Even though Stanford was not wiped out, Alabama did its best to dominate and led by a decent margin for most of the game. Another account attributed Alabama's superb performance to "its aerial circus," a combination of "dizzy loop the loops with power drives." The 22-point, second-quarter burst was called "the most amazing fifteen minutes of streamlined, mile-a-minute football that those 85,000 spectators ever saw."[4] The big plays, Howell's run and his throws to Hutson, accounted for 256 yards in that quarter.

This was not an era in sports reporting when the writers entered the locker room to pump players for quotes about what they did. Instead, the sportswriters inked what they saw, providing play-by-play developments and adding a dollop of opinion. However, the Associated Press somehow engaged Alabama coach Frank Thomas to provide his own take on the results. He committed his thoughts to paper for readers.

"Stanford has the greatest football team we met all season," Thomas said. "I'll take that game as it stands and would prefer not to have to play those Indians again real soon because our unbeaten record certainly would be in jeopardy." Thomas praised Stanford defensive standout Monk Moscrip and runner Bobby Grayson, but he also did not pretend that Alabama was lucky. Instead, he noted, "The most we can say is we're thankful we could win." Thomas was happy with how Alabama responded to the less-than-marvelous first quarter with a devastating second quarter, coming from behind to alter the big picture. "This was the first game this season that they found themselves on the short end of the score, and I didn't know whether they were going to stand up or not."[5]

Thomas did not name names, did not shower compliments on Howell and Hutson, but it was no mystery whom he was talking about when he began ladling out some accolades.

"While our passing attack has worked well all year, it was at its best yesterday," Thomas said. "There can be no question about that. We knew

Caught by Don Hutson!

in advance we were going to have to throw the ball a lot if we hoped to win.... Then our passes worked so well it was natural we could find what holes we did for our running plays."[6] He never did mention Hutson by name, but did detour for a moment and praise Howell, whom he said might well have been as good as George Gipp, the old Notre Dame player who was memorialized in Rockne's "Win one for the Gipper" speech that is either fact or fiction, but does live on.

Stanford's coach, "Tiny" Thornhill, gave considerable credit to the efficiency of the passing game that ruined the Indians' aspirations. "I was very proud of my boys," Thornhill said. "They did everything they could possibly do, but they could not compete against the magic of that Alabama passing attack. No team that ever played could have stopped that passing. In all my playing and coaching experience, I never saw anything comparable to it."[7] Thornhill glimpsed the future of the game, and he wasn't prepared for it.

Alabama's football team was aboard a slow train home and spent much of the time reliving the highlights of its great highlights while friends and families in Tuscaloosa invested energy in planning a grand reception party. Newspaper reports of the win over Stanford made their way onto the train and were shared amongst the players, as were telegrams of congratulations. Besides the hearty well-wishes, the telegrams served as invitations for planned parties on the route homeward when the train chugged into different towns, New Orleans included. As it so happened, the Alabama basketball team was scheduled to play a game there, and several members of the football team also had card-carrying membership on the basketball team and were going to disembark for a quick change of uniforms.

The Rose Bowl was very much a special occasion, a special punctuation mark at the end of the college football season. Decades later, even after he won more games as a college football coach than any other, Bear Bryant remembered how excited he was when Alabama was chosen to play in that big game his senior year. Four decades later, he was still often asked if he remembered much about the Rose Bowl and he said, "I remember *everything* about it."[8] That's how big it was to Alabama, to Southern football, and the football world.

Bryant said even the practices were wild scenes, with so many celebrities, sportswriters, and hangers-on crowding the sidelines, it was difficult to get the necessary work in. Fed up, one day assistant coach Hank Crisp said he would give $2 to the first player who simply ran

7. The Rose Bowl

right over a bystander who got in the way. Bryant ended up having the opportunity when Howell threw a bit long to him. Bryant plowed into a smaller guy and knocked him flat. Collected his payment, too. Later, Howell badgered Bryant into giving him half of it. "Shoot, Dixie, I'm the guy who ran the guy over," Bryant said. "'Well, I threw the ball,'" Howell said. "'You couldn't have done it without me.'"[9]

Howell did find Bryant for a 15-yard completion during the game against Stanford, too. As an aside, young Paul Bryant did pose for a photo with a just-starting-out actress Lana Turner and said he kept that picture. In the lead-up to the game, Bryant said, a few of the players had a craps game going in Hutson's room. He did not mention how he would have reacted if later as coach he had walked in on some of his stars gambling just before a bowl game.

The Rose Bowl was the last football game Bryant and Hutson played together. Their lives would take divergent paths quite quickly.

Don Hutson, No. 14, dashes around right end at City Stadium in Green Bay (courtesy of Neville Public Museum of Brown County).

Caught by Don Hutson!

Bryant was about to begin working his way up the ladder to greatness in coaching and become a hero at his alma mater. Bryant became a leader of football teams. Hutson became a leader in football thinking. He would soon become renowned as the greatest pass catcher in the sport's history, shaping the passing game with his prowess for the next decade-plus and forevermore.

8

Off to Green Bay

The Green Bay Packers already had title to the leading passer in the National Football League with Arnie Herber on the roster. Curly Lambeau, owner/general manager/coach/former player, sensed that the passing game would be much deadlier if Herber had better targets who could catch the ball anywhere he put it.

Lambeau's conundrum was to find someone with the right skills who could enhance the attack. In 1935, the NFL had not yet created a draft of college players. That was on the cusp of becoming reality. The league introduced the draft that is still in effect today in 1936. The draft was established to equalize the spread of talent among teams, worst to first, to level the field of play and bring some order to the pursuit of young players.

The free-for-all pursuit of Don Hutson coming out of Alabama in 1935 may well have affected the thinking of NFL owners a year later, helping to convince them to become more organized in seeking graduating college seniors.

The NFL had been around for a decade and a half by then, but professional football was still not quite a thriving concern, and college men who spent four years earning degrees were often unimpressed by the salary offerings. They felt they could find more security in the private business world than they could in pro sports and make more money to support their families by doing something completely different. Wearing suits and ties to work instead of numbered uniforms offered more promise and solidified roots in the community.

Infamously, to illustrate the iffiness of a chosen life in professional football, when the draft was instituted in 1936, the first player selected declined to turn pro at all. The NFL's first draft was scheduled for February 8, 1936, at the Ritz-Carlton Hotel in Philadelphia. The plan was to beef up NFL rosters with new blood, with the teams running through nine rounds of selections.

Caught by Don Hutson!

These being the days before clubs had scouting specialists scouring the nation for appropriate players and when players were acquired on the recommendations of friends of the coaches, the list of some 90 players listed by the league as prospects was far from comprehensive, and it was not necessarily truly a list of the best prospective additions.

The all-time No. 1 draft pick was Jay Berwanger, whose full name was John Jacob Berwanger. He came from Iowa but was a running back out of the University of Chicago and was the Heisman Trophy winner as the acknowledged best player in college football in the fall of 1935. He was also an All-American and the Most Valuable Player in the Big Ten Conference. During his college days, when the Maroons still played major college football, Berwanger was involved in a contest that became better known later on. In a game versus the University of Michigan, Berwanger collided with a would-be tackler named Gerald Ford, leaving a scar on the opponent's chin. Ford, of course, became a long-time prominent congressman and ultimately the President of the United States.

The Philadelphia Eagles owned the first pick in the new draft and wanted to hire Berwanger to improve the squad. However, Berwanger made it clear he would not sign for less than $1,000 a game. This was no bluff of a holdout. He set his price and stuck to it. The Eagles did not have that kind of money. Instead of keeping up the negotiations, the Eagles traded their rights to Berwanger to the Chicago Bears. The Bears, operated by George Halas, thought they might be able to persuade Berwanger to sign, since they were essentially his hometown team.

Philadelphia obtained tackle Art Buss and bowed out of the picture. Talks were conducted between the Bears and Berwanger, but he was particularly reluctant to sign a contract at that time because he wished to preserve his amateur status for a shot at performing in the 1936 Summer Olympic Games in Berlin. He hoped to qualify as a decathlete with the American track and field team. The Bears could wait. Then Berwanger's track ambition fizzled. He did not make the Olympic squad. Halas was known for his penurious tendencies, but Berwanger was a stiff bargainer as well. He asked the Bears' kingpin for a $15,000-a-year rookie salary. Halas countered with $13,500, which was a high price and one many felt Halas would never offer. Berwanger wouldn't budge, and that was it. He never played a minute of pro football, going to work for a rubber company, though he also served as a part-time football coach for his old school. Such a scenario would never take place in the 2020s. The overall top pick in the NFL is always going to walk away from the draft

8. Off to Green Bay

as a rich man. Although Berwanger did later in life say he wished he had given pro ball a try, he remains the answer to a trivia question about the first player drafted. Also lurking in the background is the somewhat embarrassing fact that the NFL was so small-time at the time it could not convince the young man to compete in professional football.

That was long before the days when television so dramatically aided pro football's exposure and reputation that the sport offered high-paying jobs. Still, in 1935, Don Hutson was the object of a bidding war when no draft was in place. Lambeau's zeal for finding the right receiver played a major part in a series of incidents.

Lambeau may have been a Wisconsin guy, with his team and roots centered in the state, but as time went on, he became a bigger and bigger fan of California sunshine. Over the holiday season of 1934–1935, Lambeau was vacationing in California, and as a pro football figure with a serious interest in turning up potential worthwhile new Packers, he tried to drop by Alabama's Rose Bowl practices, but was banned from the premises for one of them because it was closed, for what was called a secret practice.

Still, Lambeau, who was prone to exaggeration, said that he climbed a fence, tearing a pair of pants, to get a good look at Hutson working out. "Hutson would glide downfield, leaning forward, as if to steady himself close to the ground," Lambeau said. "Then, as suddenly as you gulp or blink an eye, he'd feint one way and go the other,reach up like a dancer, gracefully squeeze the ball, and leave the scene of the accident, the accident being the defensive backs who tangled up their feet and fell trying to cover him."[1]

After Alabama's victory over Stanford, some sportswriters noted that Hutson had made pass catching look like a snap in pre-game practice. Lambeau may have had the same passing thought. If not then, he most assuredly was impressed by what he saw during the game itself.

One oddity about Hutson's second long touchdown catch from Howell's arm was that it was not supposed to happen. Alabama already led, 22–13, and Crimson Tide coach Frank Thomas was not looking for another distance heave when he put Hutson back into the game. Quarterback Dixie Howell saw Hutson coming to the huddle and assumed his presence meant a long pass was being called. The ball was hiked, Howell faded back, saw Hutson doing his free-ranging antelope thing downfield, and fired the ball to him. Touchdown. Thomas should have been happy but was apparently somewhat vexed, either because he did

Caught by Don Hutson!

not want to be viewed as a coach running up the score, or because his star players were ignoring his instructions. Following the 56-yard TD, Hutson said, "I had to catch it, coach. It was just too good a pass to drop."[2]

By the time the 60 minutes had elapsed on the clock in the Rose Bowl, Lambeau, rapidly falling in love with Hutson's receiving abilities, was completely smitten. He had to have Hutson for his Packers. Since this was the year prior to the initiation of the draft, Lambeau could do what he wanted, track down Hutson and make an offer.

At this point, with his Alabama football career complete, Hutson believed he had played his last down in the sport. He had no thoughts of undertaking a pro football career. If at all intrigued by making money from sports, playing baseball for cash was still in the back of his mind. A bit to his surprise, Hutson, an obscure player through his junior year, was suddenly in demand for his football skills.

Actually, one talent scout was ahead of Lambeau in making contact with Hutson. Long forgotten by younger fans is that there once was an NFL team named the Brooklyn Dodgers. They were located in the same borough as the baseball team and they had the same nickname. They were not as long-lasting, but they were in business at this time. The Brooklyn football club was founded in 1930, stuck around as the Dodgers through 1943, and played as the Brooklyn Tigers in 1944 before folding.

One of the owners was a colorful character named John "Shipwreck" Kelly. While Hutson was in college, Kelly was populating the backfield of the New York Giants, then for Brooklyn, where he became a player-coach-owner. Kelly made good money fast as an investment banker and spent some of it on football.

As Hutson was finishing up with Alabama, Kelly was on the prowl for players. A native of Kentucky, Kelly played his college ball at the University of Kentucky, where one season he rushed for more than 1,000 yards. Kentucky, of course, ended up in the same league as Alabama, something which may have raised his awareness of Hutson's prowess earlier than some other pro football figures.

Kelly was a good player who was featured in the Dodgers' punt-return game, but he was also a receiver himself, and in 1933 led the NFL in catches. He may well have recognized that Hutson was a better pass receiver than he was. Kelly developed into a savvy businessman, hobnobbed with the social elite in New York, and was a frequent visitor to

8. Off to Green Bay

such high-class hangouts as the Stork Club and the 21 Club. His wife, Brenda Frazier, was the supposed model for the comic strip character Brenda Starr. During World War II, as an FBI agent, Kelly spied on prominent Germans living in other countries who were suspected of helping the Nazis.

Although he never coached him or played with him, Kelly did have a significant role in Hutson's life when the player was wrapping up at Alabama. Kelly approached Hutson before the Rose Bowl and tried to cajole him into signing a pro pact. Hutson turned him down, but he did grant Kelly the right of first refusal in matching any other team's offer.

Eventually, once Hutson emerged as a star and became an All-American, he became a popular person for emissaries from professional teams. The highest bidders were Kelly and Lambeau, both of whom seemed to want his services so badly they pretty much brushed aside the rest of the competition. There was little standard by which to measure Hutson's worth, but he seemed happy when the bids reached $300 a game (never mind Berwanger's comparatively astronomical request later). He did not know that Lambeau could be as tight with a buck as Halas, and many of the Packers did not make more than $125 per game.

Lambeau made the pledge, and when Hutson sought out Kelly to match that price, he could not reach him. Hutson very much felt the moral obligation to give Kelly the last crack, as he had promised, but in crunch time, Kelly was nowhere around. Twice Hutson sought him out and could not make contact. Lambeau mailed a contract to Hutson for his signature, the player signed on the dotted line, and he deposited the paperwork in the mail, satisfied his future was arranged.

The next day, Kelly appeared on the doorstep of Hutson's house in Tuscaloosa, Alabama. He told Hutson he had been on vacation in Florida before he finally got word of Lambeau's offer. Kelly said he would be happy to equal Lambeau's offer. Very much feeling the pressure, with Kelly sitting right across from him, and feeling terrible that he had abridged the spirit of his own pledge, Hutson let himself be conned into signing a second contract. Kelly assured Hutson that he would take care of this problem.

The way the whole series of events played out was recounted by Hutson, who said that after other teams gave up, just the two most ardent suitors stayed with him.

Caught by Don Hutson!

A collage of Don Hutson memorabilia, including a football card signed by the Hall of Famer (author photo).

8. *Off to Green Bay*

> Finally, it was just Curly and Shipwreck. Each time, Curly would make an offer. I'd wire Shipwreck and he would match it. Well, it finally got up to $300 a game, quite a bit of money in those days. When Curly gave me the offer of $300 a game, I sent the wire to Shipwreck, but I didn't hear back from him. Curly kept calling me and after about a week went by, I sent another wire to Shipwreck, and I didn't hear anything from him again.[3]

Kelly said he came to Tuscaloosa because both of Hutson's telegrams had just reached him, and he still wanted Hutson for his team. Hutson told Kelly he had signed. Kelly replied, "Don, I think you at least owe me a chance to meet it." Hutson insisted he couldn't do that, but Kelly convinced him to sign the second deal "and let me worry about it."[4]

In theory, Hutson was then the property of both the Green Bay Packers and the Brooklyn Dodgers, the new wide receiver for both, an obvious impossibility. Lambeau received his signed contract from Hutson, turned around and mailed it special delivery to the NFL office of Commissioner Joe Carr. Kelly mailed his own version of a Hutson contract to the same place. Lore has it that Lambeau's contract arrived 17 minutes before Kelly's. In the end, Carr ruled that Lambeau's contract was the valid one, and his affiliation was with the Green Bay Packers.

In partnership with Herber (and other passers), Lambeau turned Hutson into a football hero, a groundbreaking performer who wrote history. There was no such first-rate quarterback awaiting Hutson in Brooklyn, so it is unclear how his career may have played out with that club, especially as it fell on difficult financial times and went out of existence before the end of Hutson's playing days.

Hutson commented much later that by going to Green Bay, things worked out the right way. "It was probably the biggest break I ever got in football," he said.[5]

The funniest thing was, once Lambeau got his man in the fold, he didn't want the rest of his Packers to know how much money Hutson would make. The $300-a-game level was so exorbitant that Lambeau went to the length of paying Hutson in two checks of $150 each, drawn on separate banks, so as to nip any brewing revolution if word leaked out about Hutson's high salary.

9

Starting with the Packers

When the coveted Don Hutson showed up to play for the Green Bay Packers at the start of the 1935 National Football League season, he was a newly married man. His responsibility was to make his wife, Julia Kathleen Richards, happy, but also make happy coach Curly Lambeau and Packers quarterback Arnie Herber.

Things worked out pretty well all-around. The couple was married for more than 60 years, had three children, all daughters, and Hutson helped the Packers become big winners over the next decade.

By the 1935 season, the Packers were pretty much the last of a breed. After the winnowing out process as the NFL matured from its crowd of wannabes in 1920, Green Bay was the last remaining small-town host of a big-time football team. Indeed, some 100 years after the founding of the NFL, Green Bay is the smallest community in North America to serve as home for a franchise in the NFL, Major League Baseball, the National Basketball Association, or the National Hockey League.

In against-the-odds perseverance, Green Bay, with just 105,000 people, has transformed its football team into a civic treasure. The Packers football club is the most important business in town, and the Packers keep Green Bay on the map of consciousness to a far greater degree than it would ever be minus the team. Green Bay is a county seat, not even the state capital of Wisconsin. It is the third-largest city in the state, behind Milwaukee and Madison, and it is a cold-weather climate situated on Lake Michigan.

The genius of the Packers' survival has its roots in the forward-thinking people of the community, who in 1923 incorporated. Green Bay Packers, Inc. was formed as a publicly held non-profit corporation. At that time, a share of stock in the Packers cost $5. Periodically, every decade, or few decades or so, a stock offering has been made to raise cash. By 2012, the total of stockholders topped 360,000, with

9. Starting with the Packers

the investors holding more than five million shares. No one owner is allowed to possess more than 200,000 shares, with the structure of the ownership plan guaranteeing that the team will always stay in Green Bay and not have its future subject to the whim of a carpetbagging owner wishing to move it elsewhere. The 2011–2012 sale was aimed at raising $143 million to pay for Lambeau Field renovation and expansion. At that time, 269,000 shares of stock were sold at $250 each. Investment brokers and financial whizzes who take such things seriously have suggested that Packers stock may be the worst of all stock investments. The reality is it is a hobby stock, for the most part purchased for fun.

All-around explorer, sailor, and French representative in the New World Samuel de Champlain, who ended up with a major-league lake named after him in Vermont, sent one of his minions, Jean Nicolet, westward to investigate the area, and Nicolet established a trading post at Green Bay in 1634. Three hundred years later, Lambeau and later Vince Lombardi would leave their own mark on the region.

Pretty soon, Hutson would do his mightiest to keep his adopted town in the headlines, too. Of course, the Packers had been good at doing so from the start of their existence. The Packers won league crowns in 1929, 1930 and 1931. They continued their superior play in 1932 with a 10–3–1 record but finished behind the Chicago Bears and the Portsmouth Spartans. A regular winner until then, the Packers dropped to 5–7–3 in 1933, the first sub-.500 record in club history. They were a little better in 1934. The team Hutson joined was coming off a 7–6 record.

Perhaps Hutson was the icing on the offense, but by the mid–1930s, Lambeau had a bevy of future Hall of Famers under contract such as Herber, Cal Hubbard, Clark Hinkle, Johnny Blood, and Mike Michalske. The Packers were about to bust out all over again when Hutson arrived. Another team great included Charles "Buckets" Goldenberg, a member of the NFL's 1930s All-Decade team, though not in the Hall of Fame, Lavvie Dilweg, who later became a United States Congressman and was in the same lack-of-recognition situation as part of the 1920s All-Decade team, and Paul Engebretsen, aka "Tiny," who, playing at about 240 pounds as an offensive lineman, wasn't really.

As was fitting with the 7–6 record of 1934, it was an up-and-down adventure, win one, lose one. The Packers' biggest loss occurred off the field. The team's home park was called City Stadium, and during the season, a fan took a tumble and suffered an injury. He sued the team and

Caught by Don Hutson!

was awarded $5,000 in damages. As an illustration of how close to the margins the team was living—and many other businesses during the Great Depression—after the insurance company paid out, it went out of business. The team coffers were running low, as well, and the unexpected expense led to local investors putting up an additional $15,000 to keep the club operating.

Unlike most other NFL teams that did not trust the passing game, the Packers gained almost the same number of yards through the air (1,165) as on the ground (1,183) in 1934. Herber was the premier passer in the league, but this demonstrated where Lambeau's head was at compared to his fellow coaches. The Chicago Bears, who fielded the top offense with 282 points scored, rushed for 2,847 yards while passing for 955.

That season marked the first time a ball carrier ever rushed for 1,000 yards in one campaign. The runner was Beattie Feathers—for the Bears—and his 1,004 yards had a kinship with Babe Ruth's 54 home runs of 1920 as an all-time offensive milestone. Feathers, who never had such success again, averaged 8.4 yards per rush that season. He had the great Bronko Nagurski running next to him in the same backfield—and blocking for him—while collecting 586 yards himself. No wonder coach George Halas did not want to invest too much money on the competition to sign Hutson. Besides, he may have been one of the NFL experts who thought Hutson would never physically hold up to the rigors of the pro game. It should also be noted that with his knees giving out and his focus more on the defensive backfield, Red Grange was only the sixth-leading rusher on the Bears in 1934.

The Packers opened the 1935 regular season on September 15 against the Chicago Cardinals. That was coming off a four-game pre-season against non–NFL teams, clubs that were semi-pro in nature who not so many years earlier would have been classified along with the Packers as company teams. Hutson was not available to the Packers quite as early as they would have liked because of the tradition of seniors from the past college season participating in the Chicago Charities College All-Star game that pitted the young players against the defending NFL titlist.

This was a fairly new venture, begun in 1934, one that lasted through 1976, as a fund-raising competition, with the exception of 1974, when pro players went on strike. It was still finding its way in 1935, when the champion New York Giants opted out. The runner-up Chicago Bears

9. Starting with the Packers

took their place against the collegians. The game had its roots in the same brain—belonging to *Chicago Tribune* sports editor Arch Ward—that birthed the Major League Baseball All-Star Game.

The first game in the series was a 0–0 tie. In 1935, the Bears prevailed by the unlikely score of 5–0. There wasn't much action for the 77,450 charitable ticket-buyers, but it was for a good cause. The game was not played until August 29, so Don Hutson was otherwise occupied when the Packers were working out the off-season kinks with a victory over the Merrill Foxes, 34–0. Hutson did make his first appearance in a Packers uniform a few days after the All-Star game, when Green Bay dumped the Chippewa Falls Marines, 22–0. The Packers, with Hutson, crushed Stevens Point and the La Crosse Lagers by huge margins, although Hutson was a non-scoring participant.

Given the missed Hutson practices, perhaps feeling it was the just thing to do, when the Packers opened versus the Cardinals (the linear descendants of the Arizona Cardinals) Lambeau started two other players, Milt Gantenbein and Al Rose, at the end positions. Hutson sat on the bench until mid-way through the second quarter, when he went in for Rose. Lambeau tried out the new toy immediately, calling on quarterback Bob Monnett, who shared that role with Herber, to throw to Hutson. He did so, the play went incomplete, and that was the only pass play to Hutson in the whole game.

Hutson's number was also called for an end-around play (shades of the Alabama offense), but it was halted for no gain by the Chicago defense. Hutson sat out the entire third quarter and was only reinserted in the lineup during the closing minutes of the contest. Playing both ways, he was in on a late-game tackle, but was also the focal point of another end-around handoff that went nowhere. Rather, it went backwards, losing 12 yards. There was little memorable for Hutson to take from the encounter except for the fact that regardless of the sport, everyone always recalls their first game. The main element for Hutson was that he did break a sweat. If not for his later fame, no one else would have the slightest interest in how he performed in Green Bay's 7–6 loss to the Cardinals.

Green Bay's second-week opponent was the other Chicago NFL team, though the Bears were never referred to that way, especially in derogatory fashion compared to the Cardinals. The Packers hosted the Bears at City Stadium in front of 13,600 fans in one of the early showdowns of the league's longest-standing and fiercest rivalry. The Packers

Caught by Don Hutson!

and Bears have met annually, regularly more than once a season, and sometimes more often if they tripped over one another in the playoffs. The Packers, who had won the last six meetings leading up to the 2022 season, held a 103–95–6 advantage in the series. The Bears won the first game in 1921, 20–0. The Bears did not win this September 22, 1935, match-up, and they got to meet Hutson in the bargain.

The final score was a rather simple 7–0 Green Bay win, and the game's only touchdown was scored by Hutson in the first quarter on an 83-yard pass from Herber, with Monnett kicking the extra point. In an interesting bit of symmetry, Beattie Feathers, he of the milestone 1,000-yard rushing season a year earlier, confessed that he was the one to blame when Hutson romped home.

"I had the distinction of defending against Don Hutson on his first touchdown as a pro," Feathers said, explaining how the Bears' defense was fooled. "Herber was back in the kicking position, but instead of punting he reared back and let go a long pass. I wasn't too concerned about it—thought it looked like a wild heave—but I kept an eye on Hutson as he came down the field. I'd played baseball against him during the summer, so I knew how fast he was. But still I misjudged it. I looked over my shoulder and there he was with the ball—and gone."[1]

It was far from the last time the Herber-to-Hutson combination would burn defensive players, and Hutson carried on doing so for much longer than they were a tandem. It could be embarrassing, and game-changing, but those optimists who populated defensive backfields quickly learned there was little they could do to fight back.

Feathers was speaking from the hindsight of a few decades when it was apparent to all that Hutson was a phenom. He referred to him with great admiration. "Don was Joe DiMaggio as far as football is concerned," Feathers said.[2]

Perhaps not in a single day, but it became obvious pretty quickly that Curly Lambeau had landed a gem, a major new weapon in his arsenal. The great believer in the effectiveness and threat of the passing game was in a sense getting the last laugh on coaches who were dissenters and doubters, those stuck in the past who failed to recognize the way passing could change the sport with lightning strikes like this one.

Perhaps it was symbolic, but the Green Bay Packers changed the look of their uniforms for the first time in team history for the 1935 season, just as Hutson and the forward pass were giving the club a new look on the field. It wasn't as if Lambeau went wild and commissioned

9. Starting with the Packers

Hawaiian shirts for playing jerseys, but he switched the team colors from blue and gold to green and gold. The green tops had gold sleeves, and the pants were gold with green stockings.

The Packers had only recently been three-time NFL champions. Some of the key men were holdovers for this refurbished outfit. Beating

Don Hutson (right) makes a tough catch with a defender draped on him (courtesy Pro Football Hall of Fame).

Caught by Don Hutson!

the Bears was always satisfying, and the win left Green Bay just 1–1, but the Packers had a fresh look all around, sartorially, on the field, and with key personnel on the 25-man roster. The win did herald good things and quickly showed the football world what Don Hutson was capable of doing if a team could put the ball in his hands through the air.

10

Making a Mark

It wasn't as if the Packers were short on talent when they added Don Hutson to the roster in 1935. The term "superstar" was not in use at the time, and it wasn't obvious to teammates and fans when he signed his contract, but they did make a superstar upgrade.

Soon enough, his rookie year, it became apparent that Hutson was going to be something special. The most obvious way he showed that was being uncoverable, as Beattie Feathers described on Hutson's first touchdown gallop.

The third game of the season, on September 29, pitted the Packers against the defending NFL champion New York Giants. That year, New York featured such future Hall of Famers as Red Badgro, Ray Flaherty, Mel Hein, and Ken Strong. Benny Friedman and his shotgun arm were already gone, though. Harry Newman, who had starred at Michigan, had only a short professional career, but excelled that year and the next. The former All-American, the 1932 College Player of the Year, was New York's leading passer and rusher in 1934.

Newman, like others of his time, felt he could make more money in private business than in sports and initially did not show up for the start of the 1935 season in order to spend more time with his liquor business. When he joined the Giants, he did not play nearly as well as in his two All-Pro seasons, and he wrapped up his professional career.

Newman was still a no-show for the Packers game—he played in just eight games in 1935—but it was a good sign nonetheless that Green Bay could handle the champs. It was a good show for the 10,000 in attendance at City Stadium. The score was 0–0 after the first quarter, and the Giants led, 7–6, at halftime.

Demonstrating their lack of consistency throwing the ball, the Giants lost this game on pivotal Packers picks. Green Bay's first touchdown was a 65-yard interception return by Hank Bruder. Trailing by

Caught by Don Hutson!

one point entering the fourth period, the Packers staged a 10-point rally to win, 16–7. Bob Monnett kicked a 17-yard field goal, and Cal Hubbard returned another interception for a touchdown, this one of eight yards.

Just as the country was starting to come out of the Great Depression, more startling national news roared across the headlines. As the Packers pounded their semi-pro neighbors to get ready for the NFL season, Huey Long, one of the most famous politicians in the country and someone who had been angling to become president, was assassinated in the state capitol building in Baton Rouge, Louisiana. Long, a United States Senator, was accused by many of being a demagogue, and his oratory was more colorful than any football coach of the time. He previously had been Louisiana's governor. He was shot on September 8 and died September 10. Blood stains were left on the walls of the capitol as a reminder of the tragedy.

A populist known as "Kingfish," Long was a harsh critic of President Franklin D. Roosevelt. If Long had lived, politics would have been messier leading up to the 1936 election. Long as president might have tried to wield influence over pro football. On behalf of Louisiana State University, he had beefed up the marching band, thrown his weight behind football coaches while telling them how to do their jobs, provided an airplane to help LSU with recruiting, and even appointed a star halfback to the state legislature. When the student newspaper blasted that action, he had staff members expelled from school. Long brought some of the best players on the Tigers into the governor's mansion for milkshakes and steaks.

If he hadn't been killed, Long may have promised to make pro football the National Pastime, some way, somehow, instead of baseball.

There was other troubling news breaking out as the NFL season began. Although it may not have been completely apparent at the time, Italy's behavior under dictator Benito Mussolini caused concern at the highest levels of American government, even if the average American ignored it. Italy was embracing an expansionist policy that dovetailed with Germany's ambitions, and it invaded Ethiopia. Mussolini lined up 200,000 soldiers to overrun the African country, starting in October of 1935.

The League of Nations, the forerunner of the United Nations, with backing from the United States and England, proposed plans for peace to avoid war, but they were snubbed.

This national and international news, combined with the lingering

10. Making a Mark

economic effects of the Depression, were harbingers of disturbing times ahead, but they seemed somewhat abstract to the daily lives of football players and football game ticket buyers. For most, the football games were as violent as daily life got.

Although Hutson was not a key factor to that point, following the confidence-building triumph over the Giants, the Packers were 2–1. Next up, on October 6, were the Pittsburgh Pirates. No, the baseball team representing the Steel City did not perform double duty. Hoping to attract extra fans through familiarity, for a time the Pittsburgh Steelers football team was called the Pirates as well.

The football Pirates were one of the newer teams in the league, created in 1933. Up until then, Pittsburgh blue laws prevented games being played on Sundays, and there was no way a local eleven could compete. When the law was changed, Pittsburgh obtained a team. From the start, Art Rooney, the revered future Hall of Fame owner, was in charge. He was a local sports promoter who paid a $2,500 fee to enter the league with a roster comprised mostly of local semi-pros. Pittsburgh may have had limited resources, but the Pirates were coming off a 3–6–2 debut season. Other expansion teams have displayed worse signs of hopelessness.

Football's Pirates did play their home games at Forbes Field, same as the baseball Pirates. By going 2–10 in 1934, the Pirates were worse their second season, and in their third campaign they showed only minimal improvement to 4–8.

The Packers treated Pittsburgh roughly in that early October game, as rudely as they knew how, beating the Pirates, 27–0, at City Stadium. Only 5,000 fans were interested enough to shell out, perhaps not taking Pittsburgh seriously as a foe.

After a scoreless first quarter, the Packers ran over the Pirates with 20 points in the second. Another of the team's newcomers, George Sauer, scored the squad's first touchdown on a three-yard run, followed by an Ade Schwammel extra point for a 7–0 lead. Sauer was an All-American halfback at the University of Nebraska under famed coach Dana X. Bible. Sauer was a solid player for Green Bay, but only for three seasons. Then he left the playing field to stand on the sidelines as a college coach, first at New Hampshire, then Kansas, Navy, and Baylor. He also coached college basketball at New Hampshire.

Sauer graduated to sports administration and became general manager of the New York Titans in the early days of the American

Caught by Don Hutson!

Football League before moving on to the Boston Patriots' front office through 1970.

His son, George Jr., played at the University of Texas and was a receiver for the New York Jets. A four-time AFL All-Star, this Sauer caught 309 passes in his career. He played alongside Joe Namath in the Jets' 1969 Super Bowl win over the Baltimore Colts. Sauer Jr. caught eight passes for 133 yards in that famous game. His dad caught nine in parts of three seasons for Green Bay.

Following Sauer Sr.'s opening TD against the Pirates, Joe Laws rushed for a score, too, before the rest of the day's offense was turned over to Arnie Herber and Don Hutson. The first connection was a 50-yard bomb capping the third-quarter scoring, and the second touchdown pass covered just one yard. In all, Hutson caught four passes for 109 yards, and he also played defense. Lambeau, taking the win for granted, benched some of his standouts for the whole game, letting them enjoy a Sunday of repose. Unlike in the modern game, where a kicking specialist trots out to the field for every extra point, three different Green Bay players made kicks, as if the whole exercise was an afterthought.

At 3–1, the Packers seemed ready for a rematch with the Chicago Cardinals, hoping to avenge the one-point, season-opening loss. Yet this encounter was worse. Green Bay was stung, 3–0, not scoring at all, falling again to a team it felt it should beat. Chicago's Paul Pardonner booted a 17-yard field goal in the second quarter, and that was the only scoring. The contest was played at Wisconsin State Fair Park, but it wasn't much of a showcase for the 13,000 fans who came out in West Allis. The park was new, just a year old, and it was an opportunity to show off the team in spanking new quarters. The idea kind of fizzled.

The masthead of the *Green Bay Press-Gazette* boasted, "Everybody Reads It," but the Packers would have been better off if no one picked up the paper the day after that game.

Still, the Packers tried it all over again at the same location on October 20. Although fewer spectators, 9,500, bought tickets, the result was more satisfying, a 13–9 win over the Detroit Lions. Although the Lions would gradually evolve into a major divisional rival of the Packers, that was not true yet in 1935. The club started as the Portsmouth Spartans, based in Ohio, in 1928, before moving to the bigger city for the 1934 season.

10. Making a Mark

There was some notable leftover history connecting the Packers and Portsmouth, however. During the 1932 season, the Spartans engaged the Packers in what came to be called the "iron man" game. Portsmouth coach Potsy Clark played the same 11 men on offense, on defense, and on special teams, throughout the whole contest, and Portsmouth won, 19–0. By the end of that season, though, points for bravado aside, Portsmouth was close enough to bankruptcy that instead of their usual salaries, the players were paid in team stock shares.

The Spartans were bought by a radio magnate named George Richards. He did not imitate the Pittsburgh football team by adopting the Detroit Tigers name, but issued his own roar by choosing Lions as the club nickname. He also liked the idea that the lion was the king of the jungle, and he was planning to develop them into kings of the NFL. The thought was nice, anyway.

The Lions were quite good in their Detroit debut season, finishing 10–3, and with 238 points became the second-highest-scoring team in the NFL. The Bears still outdid them, though, going 13–0 and scoring 286 points. The Lions were thinking big for 1935, and this Packers game figured to be a tight one.

The struggle was a worthy spectator production. Detroit scored first on a 43-yard Earl "Dutch" Clark field goal. Clark, who was inducted into both the College and Professional Football Halls of Fame, did everything in the sport. He was a six-time All-Pro back for Portsmouth and Detroit, a college and professional coach, and a member of the league's All-Decade team. That was a very good distance to cover for a field goal during that era, and the lead held up through halftime.

Green Bay made its move in the third quarter, taking the lead with a 10-point spurt. Hutson's speed and explosiveness were on display when he grabbed a blocked punt and returned it 41 yards for a score. Ernie Smith kicked the extra point for a 7–3 margin. Ade Schwammel, responding to Clark's best foot offering, retaliated with his own 39-yard field goal before the fourth quarter.

The Lions closed the lead on a 12-yard TD rush by Ernie Caddell to make the score 10–9 in favor of the Packers. Schwammel closed the scoring in the fourth period with a 40-yard field goal. Green Bay was now 4–2 and thinking it had as good a chance as any team to capture the Western Division title and advance to the NFL championship game.

On the last Sunday in October, the Packers had a rematch with the Bears at Wrigley Field in Chicago with an attendance of 29,386. Decades

Caught by Don Hutson!

later, Green Bay sportswriter Lee Remmel, who was later the team's public relations director, and followed the Packers for 62 years, ranked the greatest games in team history. No. 8 on his all-time list was this Bears game, which given the length of Green Bay football history at more than half a century was notable. The Packers had already captured a long list of titles, and this was a mere regular-season game.

One reason Remmel gave for including the game was that it was part of Hutson's rookie season. The description appeared in a 1975 game program, and a sub-headline on the story included the phrase "The Year of Don Hutson."[1]

This was a tight game and particularly low-scoring in the first half. It was scoreless in the first period, and the Bears got on the scoreboard for the first time with a Schwammel 18-yard field goal in the second quarter. The Bears-Packers rivalry may have been young in 1935, but it was already intense. In one newspaper story, there was a reference to the Packers playing "their favorite enemies." Also, leading up to the second game, the local *Press-Gazette* included an inflammatory headline as a reminder of Hutson's 83-yard touchdown catch. It read, "Here's Don—Remember, Bears?" A photograph of that big play was re-run.[2]

The Bears took the lead in the third quarter on a 44-yard pass from Bernie Masterson to Gene Ronzani, topped by a Jack Manders extra point. Advantage, Bears. Chicago went up 14–3 in the fourth period when Johnny Sisk darted free for a 55-yard score, with Manders again kicking successfully. It was looking good for the Bears before Arnie Herber went to work. Over the game's last two-and-a-half minutes, the Packers bounced back with two touchdown passes for the Herber-Hutson partnership, the first a 69-yard strike followed by a Schwammel extra point to make it close. The Packers got the ball back and rammed it downfield. This time Herber completed a four-yard pass TD to Hutson, and the Packers won, 17–14.

Green Bay sportswriters had hyped the game significantly enough that Packers fans took a $3.95 per ticket round-trip ride by train to swell the Wrigley Field crowd. They were the ones who got to celebrate.

This Hutson–led rally followed a stretch mid-game when he was dinged by some kind of contact from the Bears, sending him to the sideline for a bit. He recovered enough to make the big scores. "I got hit sometime in the game," Hutson said. "I was dizzy and I was out of the game for a while, sometime after the second half started. Then Curly put me back in with two-and-a-half minutes left."[3] Just in time, it could

10. Making a Mark

be said. The 69-yarder was a matter of looking for short yardage, but Hutson's speed turned it into the game's biggest play.

"Herber threw a little flat pass to me, and I went the rest of the way for a touchdown," Hutson said. "I ran to the left sideline, then cut back to the middle, went back to the sidelines and then back to the middle before I got into the end zone."[4] Several Bears had shots at Hutson as he sped past, including Ronzani, who nearly nailed him, and Masterson, who got at least one hand on him, and then he zipped past Keith Molesworth closer to the end zone. Molesworth nearly brought Hutson down, but after being hit, Hutson fell over the goal line, thrusting the ball ahead of him.

The Bears, wary of Hutson's skills, had shifted into a "prevent defense," and Hutson said it actually helped open up the field and give him running room when he needed it. "The Bears were playing back deep for a long one," he said.[5]

As big a play as that was, the Bears gift-wrapped the last opportunity with a fumble by Masterson as time was ticking off the clock. The Packers took over on the Chicago 13-yard line. Green Bay didn't move the ball much on a couple of tries, but in the huddle, Hutson informed Herber he knew he could get open.

"I can out-run Molesworth, in case you want to try '15' left," he said. "Fifteen, it is," Herber decided.[6] The play worked as diagrammed and represented the winning points in the great comeback, made all the sweeter because it came against the Bears.

In reminiscing about the game many years later, Hutson said there were a few ironies. "There are two things I remember about that game," he said. "The rest of the game we didn't do much on offense. The other thing I remember is that most everybody had gone home by the time we started our comeback. We hadn't done anything and we were behind, 14–3."[7]

The Packers took the train home to Green Bay after the game, and their company was shared by many fans who had been at Wrigley Field. However, many of the people Hutson said he talked to had left early and missed the team's great rally. Although there was no instant-replay or other technology in place at the time to zoom Hutson's efforts around to those not already inside the stadium, word got around quickly enough that he was a dangerous new component in the Packers' offense. Teams had to game-plan against him doing damage.

This win gave the Packers a 5–2 record and a very satisfying

Caught by Don Hutson!

triumph over the Bears. Although the rivalry would not quite reach the proportions of the one versus the Bears, the annual meetings with the Detroit Lions began growing in importance, too. The November 10 second game between the clubs in 1935 drew 12,000 fans to City Stadium, and it in no way resembled the rugged battle witnessed in the first contest of October 20.

Riding the momentum of their recent play, the Packers drubbed Detroit, 31–7, one of their biggest wins of the year. This was a wipeout over one of the best teams in the league, unlike the runaway over Pittsburgh.

This was a gradual slaughter, not a clear-cut one from the opening kickoff. Clarke Hinkle kicked a 30-yard field goal in the first quarter for a 3–0 lead. George Sauer, Sr., rushed for a touchdown, and Ernie Smith punctuated that with the extra point for a 10–0 second-quarter lead before the Lions inched back in with their only TD that quarter, so it was only 10–7 at halftime.

But the Packers gained deed to the second half. Taking his cue from Hutson's specialty, Johnny Blood caught back-to-back touchdown passes from Herber, one of 26 yards and one of 70, before Hutson, not to be left out, added the last touchdown in the fourth quarter on a 44-yard grab. Blood caught another pass in the end zone from Herber for the two-point conversion.

Johnny Blood, whose real last name was McNally, made it a bloody day for Detroit. *Press-Gazette* sports editor John Walter took one long look at this performance and wrote that the "bombardment that left the 12,000 spectators just about convinced that the 1935 edition of the Green Bay football team is one of the best gridiron outfits of all time."[8]

This may have been a premature coronation, but hype was breaking out all over. It was not as if the *Milwaukee Sentinel* disagreed with the sentiments. One writer jotted down, "Bring on the adjectives; bring on the exclamation points; the Packers deserve 'em. Especially that ace of passers, Arnie Herber."[9]

Hutson collected another long TD pass, but this was Blood's show more than anyone else except perhaps Herber. Blood obtained his last-name-nickname from a movie marquee. Years earlier, McNally and friend Ralph Hensen were on their way for a tryout with a Minneapolis semi-pro team and wanted to use fake names because they were affiliated with St. John's University of Collegeville, Minnesota. They saw the

10. Making a Mark

movie *Blood and Sand* playing and chose those two last names for their very own.

McNally/Blood graduated from high school at 14 as a top student, without playing football at all. He was a natural at the game. Just one of his many gifts. He was acknowledged to be quite handsome, quite athletic, and quite smart, but also a wild man and usually unpredictable in choices he made. His two wives said so. Blood once jumped between two rooftops six stories high, and another time he took refuge on the outside of a moving train to avoid being caught by teammate Lavvie Dilweg after a wet towel fight. He once played football for 10 days with a ruptured kidney.

Although he transferred from tiny St. John's to Notre Dame, Blood never suited up for the Irish. Later in the 1920s, he was on the move often between teams in the new NFL, earning a second nickname, "The Vagabond Halfback." He stuck longer with Green Bay, where he made his pro reputation. Blood was popular enough in town, then a community with some 37,000 people, to pen a local sports column with the Vagabond Halfback tag.

Curly Lambeau always worried about Blood's drinking habits and late-night carousing. Blood played for the Pack between 1929 and 1933, but he drifted to Pittsburgh for the 1934 season. Lambeau asked him back for 1935 because he was so talented. Blood was a top-notch player, and when Herber began throwing more often, Blood drew some of the defensive backfield coverage away from Hutson, allowing the newcomer more room to roam.

Blood, who played for the Milwaukee Badgers, Duluth Eskimos, and Pottsville Maroons before Green Bay, had a well-developed sense of self-worth and wanted to be paid well. Once, under the belief of the fiction put out about how much Hutson was earning, being unaware of the two bank accounts Lambeau used, he made a comparison. "I was getting $150 a game and Hutson was getting $175," Blood said. "I figured I deserved to be paid as much as he did. Curly didn't see it that way, but he came around after I missed the first three games."[10]

Lambeau admired Blood's ability but doubted his seriousness. The guy was an off-the-field flake by nature with an in-bred sense of rebelliousness. Yet he also huddled with Lambeau privately many a time the night before a game to talk strategy in an era when the head coach did not have an abundance of assistants with whom to debate X's and O's.

Blood was a good enough player to be enshrined in Canton, Ohio,

Caught by Don Hutson!

in the first class, and when he pondered his past it pretty much jibed with the reputation he had established when he was active with the Packers. "I zigged and zagged on the field," Blood said, "and I've zigged and zagged off of it, too. I wouldn't trade anything, not one of my experiences in football."[11]

And presumably, on the periphery. Sometimes Blood raced sprints against Hutson. He did not beat him in the foot races, but he did make it close. Another time, probably when he was younger, he out-ran a police dog in a race. Blood didn't think that was such a great achievement because the dog didn't know the rules of the match. "I knew the dog wasn't trained to race, anyway," he said.[12]

In a bit of unusual scheduling, the Packers and the Lions played again the next week, November 17, this time in Detroit. The site was the University of Detroit, in front of 12,500 fans, and after a week stewing about the sound defeat, the Lions showed their mettle. To the surprise of many connected to Green Bay, Detroit turned around the result, this time containing the explosive Packers offense and winning, 20–10.

Green Bay led 3–0 after a quarter thanks to Ernie Smith's foot. He clicked on a 22-yard field goal. The Lions went ahead on a pass play. The Packers pushed back in front in the third quarter, utilizing the pass, but not relying on the usual suspects. Milt Gantenbein registered a nine-yard TD catch thrown by George Sauer, Sr. After that, the Lions held and posted two fourth-quarter touchdowns on runs by Bill Shepherd. Instead of controlling the division lead, Green Bay allowed Detroit to inch closer. The standings stood at 6–3 for the Packers and 5–3–1 for the Lions.

Things were about to become more disconcerting for the Packers prior to a second blowout of the Pirates, 34–14. That was an easy enough win, but there were other matters of import clouding the circumstances. Sauer Sr., scored two touchdowns, including one on a 75-yard interception return, and so did Blood, his coming on a 41-yard touchdown pass from Bob Monnett and also on an interception runback, this one of 11 yards. Clarke Hinkle also contributed a TD. Hutson's name was not found in the box score because he was not a contributor in the November 24 contest held before 12,902 fans at Forbes Field.

Between the loss to Detroit and the win over Pittsburgh, Hutson entered St. Vincent's Hospital, where he was treated for appendicitis. Apparently, Hutson had been feeling ill all day during the Detroit game and ran a fever of 100 degrees, though that did not sideline him.

10. Making a Mark

Monday, the day after that game, Hutson felt worse, and consulted Dr. W.W. Kelly.

"Hutson came to me yesterday with very definite indications of appendicitis," Kelly noted of his meeting with the Packers' left end. "The symptoms were sufficiently prominent for him to be placed in the hospital for observation."[13]

This was an ill-timed pain in the belly, for sure. Arnie Herber had his own woes with a right hand swollen to roughly the size of a football. George Sauer, Sr., had a torn muscle. So at this critical juncture of the season, the Packers had several key guys hurting.

Early-in-the-week analysis downplayed the seriousness of Hutson's condition, but he was not well enough to play. The game was as easy as the Packers could have hoped for in the second one-sided match-up with Pittsburgh, raising the team's record to 7–3. But the rest of the schedule would not prove so easy to handle.

The next opponent, on November 28, was the Chicago Cardinals for a second time. The Packers felt their first loss to the Cards was a should-have-won contest, but the second game played out much the same, with Chicago taking a 9–7 victory. Although the Packers tasted first blood, it wasn't anything Johnny Blood did. Green Bay scored its only touchdown in the first quarter on a Monnett 60-yard run, followed by an Ernie Smith kick. The Cardinals retaliated and choked off any scoring response, although the Packers came close to pulling the win out. A late field goal attempt by Ade Schwammel sailed wide from the 16-yard line that would have won the game, 10–9. The boot just missed. Or so it was determined by the officials.

Arnie Herber, who had as clear a view as anyone in the stadium of the kick, even if he was biased, always insisted the effort was good. "I know the ball was right in the middle of the goal post," Herber said, "because I held the ball for the kicker, and it was as perfect as any kick could ever have been."[14]

Not many people took notice, with just 5,500 fans in Wrigley Field, but the Green Bay championship prospects took a hit.

The last game of the 1935 season was played on December 8 against the Philadelphia Eagles in the Baker Bowl in Philly, and it did not drum up much excitement locally. The Packers prevailed, 13–6, after a scoreless first quarter and helped by a Hinkle touchdown and field goal.

That gave Green Bay a final record of 8–4. The West was much stronger than the East. The Cardinals and Bears both went 6–4–2, and

Caught by Don Hutson!

that was a tie for third, behind the division-winning Lions at 7–3–2 to the Packers' 8–4. Detroit had a higher winning percentage since ties didn't count, and the Lions advanced to the championship game versus the Giants, who went 9–3. New York had the East's only winning record. Detroit showed its toughness by topping the Giants, 26–7, to win the title.

Don Hutson's rookie year was eventful in several ways. His statistics were not as impressive as his impact. He appeared in just nine of the Packers' 12 games, missing the last two due to the appendicitis problem. He started only five games and caught 18 passes, six of them for touchdowns. His average per catch was an eye-catching 23.3 yards, a flashy number indeed.

However, with his speed and moves, and the way he manufactured those big gains, Hutson woke up the NFL. One sports scribe, writing decades later, compared Hutson's break-in year to a scientific breakthrough in educating the rest of the world. "Hutson was football's Copernicus, proving that the universe did not revolve around the sun."[15]

The layman's translation was that Hutson introduced a new way of thinking about offensive football, demonstrating that the passing game was here to stay, and the heretofore pre-eminent ground game was not the only bright spot in the solar system.

11

Baseball Still Beckons— For a While

Even after his professional football debut in the 1935 season, Don Hutson had not completely forsaken baseball. He still loved the game, and although he probably knew it was unlikely that he would make the grade in the majors, he still had an itch to scratch. Besides, what better summer job could there be than getting paid to play baseball?

He returned to Pine Bluff, Arkansas, a place where he hadn't spent much time since he graduated high school, and signed up to play the outfield for the local minor league team, the Pine Bluff Judges, in a revival version of the Cotton States League.

A welcome-home story in the *Pine Bluff Commercial* highlighted Hutson's athletic past with the local high school Zebras in hailing his commitment to the Judges (a St. Louis Cardinals affiliation) in the spring of 1936. It actually served as a reminder story for the local sports fans who had not seen Hutson perform on any athletic field for several years, reading, in part, "Hutson was a multi-sport athlete for the Pine Bluff Zebras, excelling at basketball, baseball, football and track. As a teenager, he played baseball for the local town team."[1]

The Judges' manager, L.L. "Cowboy" Jones, admitted he did not know Hutson personally, but was aware of the reputation he established as a college grid star. "But if he can snag that baseball the way he did that football for Alabama, he should have no worry. I understand he's a good hitter, too."[2]

Neither did Jones have to worry about the caliber of player he was getting. Hutson was not some local yokel trading on past exploits. He could still play baseball. The previous summer, Hutson batted .380 for the Troy team in the Dixie Amateur League. Hutson had kept up with his baseball, but after graduating from Alabama, he could surrender his

Caught by Don Hutson!

amateur status without fear of repercussions on his eligibility standing with the school's football team.

Baseball ruled the sports landscape, and although there were only 16 major league teams spread across the eastern half of the country, it was two decades shy of when the first California teams broke into the National League. There were minor league teams galore from Class D, the lowest classification, on up the alphabet.

The most aggressive team in signing vast numbers of minor leaguers was the St. Louis Cardinals, under the domain of Branch Rickey. Rickey pioneered the farm system, and it seemed it was his goal to sign every able-bodied player to a club hoping to overturn hidden gems, but at the least locking up talented players so other teams could not sign them. Rickey was so hard-nosed in this regard that ultimately Commissioner Kenesaw Mountain Landis broke up his attempt at monopoly and freed many young players from obligations to the Cardinals. Essentially, since Hutson possessed some talent, was still keen on playing, and had recorded some recent success, it was not difficult for him to hook on with a team. As long as he showed some development, clubs would not cut him loose, but give him chances to shine. This may have been especially likely now because he had a name, even if it had been publicized in another sport.

Hutson was slated to play for Knoxville, Tennessee, in 1936, but there was a high-level administration friendship between the Knoxville and Pine Bluff teams, and it was requested that he be assigned to his hometown club since it might boost attendance. Indeed, that angle seemed to pay off, since Pine Bluff drew more than 50,000 fans to lead the league in spectators that year.

Hutson was indeed an asset, the team finishing 77–62 in the Class C Cotton States League for third place. Hutson appeared in 132 games, collected 167 hits, and batted .312. He put his speed to good use, stealing 25 bases and scoring 95 runs. He was also chosen for the circuit's All-Star team.

This was not the end of Hutson's flirtation with professional baseball, either. In 1937, Hutson started the season in the Class A New York-Penn League, a stay that lasted just 14 games. He was sent to the Class B Southeastern League, splitting 48 games between the Selma Cloverleafs and the Jackson Senators. Although facing stiffer challenges from the mound than he had in the Cotton States League, Hutson compiled a .297 average. Still, time was running out on Hutson's baseball

11. Baseball Still Beckons—For a While

aspirations as he became more important in the NFL. He concluded his minor league play with a .301 average in 194 games.

Hutson's days in baseball were more productive than basketball star Michael Jordan's, and if he had stuck with it while lacking any other sports alternative, he might well have risen to the top ranks of the sport. It didn't take long, though, for it to become clear that Hutson was a budding legend in his other game.

Ironically, Hutson the football player influenced one of the greatest baseball players of all time without ever teaming with him or sharing a field. In an unlikely marriage of renowned football and baseball figures, the great Willie Mays, a native of Alabama, many years later mentioned that how Hutson caught a football helped teach him how to best catch a baseball.

Mays, who turned 90 years old in 2021, was born in Westfield, Alabama, in 1931, His father, Carl, was a very good local baseball player, and his mother, Annie Satterwhite, played basketball and ran track. His parents split up when Mays was three, and he was raised by his father. The boy sat on the bench of his father's Birmingham company team starting when he was 10 and was always around the sport. Mays played baseball, football, and basketball at Fairfield High, graduating in 1950. However, it was 1948 when Mays made his professional baseball debut for the Chattanooga Choo-Choos, a Negro Leagues minor league squad, and then played for the Birmingham Black Barons.

Although this was long after Don Hutson competed for the University of Alabama, and even after he retired from the NFL, Mays' Alabama ties throughout his youth made him aware of one of the state's most famous athletic performers.

Mays was sought after by several major league teams the moment his high school class graduated, making his mark with the New York and San Francisco Giants before finishing his playing days with the New York Mets. A brilliant all-around player, Mays was renowned for his hitting, running, and fielding. The most famous catch he ever made took place during the 1954 World Series against the Cleveland Indians.

A legendary baseball photograph documents the moment Mays, his back turned to home plate at the Polo Grounds on Vic Wertz's smash, gathered in the hard-hit ball over his shoulder, grabbing it just as a football receiver would catch a quarterback's downfield pass. That was no accident. Some years later, in a chat with syndicated columnist Jimmy Cannon, one of the nation's most famous sportswriters, Mays made the

Caught by Don Hutson!

surprising comment that he learned how to catch baseballs like that from watching Don Hutson catch footballs like that.

"You know Don Hutson?" Mays began his explanation.

> I learned how to play fences watching Don Hutson. I saw him in the movies [likely newsreels]. A friend of mine showed me him. I watched the way he caught a football. He would catch a football and stop real fast. Go one way, go the other way. I watched what he did. I said, "If he can do that with a football, why can't I do it with a baseball?" I studied what he did. Then I went out and would run hard at the fence and stop. I kept doing it until I could do it good. I twisted just like he did. He'd catch the ball and twist away from a guy going to tackle him. I catch the ball and twist away from the fence.[3]

That was certainly a difference between catches made by Hutson and catches made by Mays. The football player had to be alert to being instantly leveled by a tackler. The baseball player had to be careful not to slam his body into a ballpark wall.

At the time he was speaking, Mays' home field was Candlestick Park, which was renowned for being afflicted with wild wind currents that affected the trajectory of a fly ball. It has to be blowing a wicked, full gale for a football's flight to be too affected beyond the reach of a receiver because the ball is weightier and larger than a baseball. Yet Mays said he was able to ignore the nasty wind at Candlestick. "It don't bother me none," he said of the perch he had in center field. "I have no problem with that wind. Suppose the ball is hit to left. I pause. I just stand there a little while. Then I make my move. It's like you're leading a band. You beat one, two, three, and then you go. You play in a park, you got to study all kinds of things like this."[4]

Wind velocity was not that much of an issue for Hutson, but Mays did not have to contend with members of the opposing team seeking to cut him off at the pass. The opponent was not trying to outrace him to the ball either, or make sure he couldn't catch up with it. It was not as if Wertz, the slugging first baseman, took lessons from Arnie Herber in placing that baseball in that Series where Mays could somehow, unbelievably catch up to it.

One of Hutson's chief skills was being able to get open in the first place. He had the built-in 100-yard dash man speed, the type of sports speed that is a bonus for a competitor in any athletic endeavor. However, Olympic gold medalists have had NFL wide receiver tryouts in the decades post–Hutson and could not make the grade. They either could

11. Baseball Still Beckons—For a While

not apply their speed to football or could not hold onto the ball when it was thrown their way.

Sometimes track sprinter speed did translate to the gridiron. Henry Carr, who won gold medals in the 200 meters and relay in Tokyo in 1964, was drafted by the New York Giants and had some good moments in the defensive secondary before his career was cut short by a knee injury.

Far excelling Carr from the same Olympics was Bob Hayes, aka "Bullet Bob," who set the world record at 100 yards and won two golds before becoming an 11-year NFL player, mostly for the Dallas Cowboys. Hayes caught 371 passes in his all-star career, 71 of them for touchdowns. He was inducted into the Pro Football Hall of Fame.

This seemingly successful experiment led to one with sprinter Jim Hines in 1968. Hines, one of the United States' greatest track men, held the world record in the 100-meter dash for 15 years and won Olympic gold, too. The Miami Dolphins drafted Hines and gave him a tryout as a pass catcher, but it did not work out. His lighting speed could get him open, but he dropped so many passes he was insulted with the nickname "Oops." Hines ended up catching just two passes in his NFL career. He could not make the crossover.

Hutson was fast for his time, though not as fast as those later track runners, but he had football ability, the knack for playing the game, and was able to mesh his track speed with football plays in a manner which had never before been accomplished as the forward pass came of age in the NFL.

What Hutson could do, as was evident even in his slightly limited rookie year, but which became increasingly obvious starting with the 1936 season, was get himself open and wiggle free of defenders, so he could practically wave back to Herber in the backfield, signaling, "Here I am. Throw the ball."

There is an old black-and-white sliver of film on display at the Green Bay Packers Hall of Fame that summarizes Hutson's extraordinary ability to get open. It only lasts a few seconds, but it screams about what it was that set Hutson apart. Captured on camera is Hutson downfield, a defender trailing by so much territory he is barely on the screen. Hutson catches a pass and dashes to daylight, all the way to the end zone. Easy enough when you build a 10-yard lead before gathering in the ball.

It did not take very long for Hutson to make an impact for the Packers that rookie year, which surprised even him. When he showed up that

Caught by Don Hutson!

season, he engaged in a quiet conversation with lineman Cal Hubbard, who later had the distinction of being a Pro Football Hall of Famer and being enshrined in the Baseball Hall of Fame following a second career as an umpire. When it was all beginning, Hutson confided in Hubbard, "I'm scared to death. I did all right in college, but these fellows are so much bigger and better. I'm not even sure I belong." Hubbard offered a very succinct pep talk in reply. "Don't worry, kid," he said. "You belong."[5]

He did. Hutson learned that quickly enough, as did defenders and all football watchers.

"He had all the moves," said Packers teammate Tony Canadeo. "He invented the moves. And he had great hands and speed, deceptive speed. He could go get the long ones, run the hitch, the down-and-out. He'd go over the middle, too. And he was great at getting off the line because he always had people popping him."[6]

Canadeo offered a laundry list of what made Hutson special, what

Pre-game strategy. Don Hutson (left), quarterback Cecil Isbell (middle), and coach Curly Lambeau go over the X's and O's before a Packers game (courtesy Pro Football Hall of Fame).

11. Baseball Still Beckons—For a While

makes the best receivers the best receivers. But the most critical aspect of his statement was the beginning, when he spoke of Hutson inventing the moves. That was the key element. No one else had ever done what Hutson did.

Those shimmies and shakes as Hutson ran downfield trying to shed defensive backs didn't even have names at the time. Long before any receiver was said to "shake and bake," Hutson did his own shaking, baking, and leaving opponents in the dust. Long-time Pittsburgh sports editor Pat Livingston echoed Canadeo's comment, writing, "Single-handedly, Hutson, the receiver, who invented such routes as the z-in and z-out, the button hook, the comeback and the hook-and-go, brought sophisticated passing to football."[7]

Simply put, Hutson boggled minds, minds that did not believe what they saw because it was all new to them.

"He was the only man I ever saw who could feint in three directions at once," said Greasy Neale, who played pro football and major league baseball, as well as coaching the Philadelphia Eagles during Hutson's playing days.[8]

12

First Championship

The 1935 season showed the Green Bay Packers what they could be, and in the 1936 season they showed what they could do. The Packers swept to a 10–1–1 record and won the franchise's first NFL title since 1931. It had not been a long wait, but it was long enough for the impatient Curly Lambeau.

After his gradual, yet notable, break-in season, ended by illness, Don Hutson had established confidence and knew he could play at the professional level. There was no reason for the nervousness he had displayed to Cal Hubbard.

This season, Hutson caught 34 passes for 536 yards and eight touchdowns through the air. Those statistics not only led the league but established National Football League records. During the 2020s, those would be modestly successful numbers for a wide receiver, but in an era when hardly any team trusted the forward pass, they were stunning totals. Opposing coaches were not used to setting up defensive alignments that guarded against an offensive formation forging quick-strike opportunities. When Hutson shook free and Arnie Herber could find him with the ball, the foes were usually left in the dust, shaking their heads in response to a long score.

The new season began on September 13 at City Stadium against the nemesis Chicago Cardinals. Only 8,900 fans were interested enough to invest their emotions in a new campaign, but the Packers found the answer to the pesky visitors this time around after dropping two close ones to Chicago in 1935.

This was much the same type of defensive struggle as the teams engaged in the year before, but instead of losing a close one, the Packers triumphed, 10–7. Chicago scored first on its own touchdown pass, 38 yards from Phil Sarboe to Charlie McBride, but did not score again all day. Green Bay tied the game in the third period on a George Sauer, Sr.,

12. First Championship

rush and won the game in the fourth quarter on a 25-yard Ernie Smith field goal. This was long before the field goal became an extensively used weapon, and long before field goals were routinely kicked from longer than 40 yards. But they had their place from inside the 40 and were employed as difference-makers even if those who kicked them had not spent a lifetime training for the role.

This was a satisfying victory over the Cardinals, but lest the Packers get too high on the early-season accomplishment, the next week, September 20, that other Chicago team, the hungry Bears, gave Green Bay a very sound thrashing. Given the popular history against the opponent and no doubt the good feeling left by the opening win over the Cardinals, fans were enticed to City Stadium in larger numbers, some 14,312, for this encounter. They were severely disappointed as the Bears ran roughshod over the hosts, bashing the Packers, 30–3.

An Ade Schwammel 26-yard field goal represented the only points by Green Bay. The Bears scored in all four periods, including 14 points in the fourth, with some of their stalwarts, Jack Manders, Gene Ronzani, Carl Brumbough, and future Hall of Fame end Bill Hewitt, who played without a helmet, ruling the Packers. The margin of defeat left Green Bay battered and bruised and 1–1.

There was a definite need to regroup, and surprisingly the schedule was written in such a manner that the Packers played the Chicago Cardinals again rather than seeing them a second time at the end of the year. Whether it was anger, familiarity, or exactly what, this time the contest was not close. The Packers uncharacteristically dominated, 24–0, on October 4. Maybe the change of venue, to Wisconsin State Fair Park, helped.

After a scoreless period, the Packers ran out to a 14–0 halftime lead. Swede Johnston and Clarke Hinkle ran for scores, and both times Green Bay converted the extra-point kicks. The Packers added another six-pointer in the third quarter on a 41-yard Joe Laws dash, and a final field goal. The thoroughness of the victory was needed to demonstrate that the offense could do more than slumber. After that it was finally time to play against teams from somewhere besides Chicago.

Little-remembered, even in the city itself, is that the NFL Washington football team that for decades was called the Redskins before going in search of a new nickname to make amends to Native Americans offended by the old one, once represented Boston. The creation of the Boston Patriots, later called New England, was not the first time pro

Caught by Don Hutson!

ball was played in the "Hub of the Universe." The Boston club began play in 1932 under the ownership of George Preston Marshall and was still located in Massachusetts during the 1936 season. Marshall, an explosive and mercurial character who ran the club for years and was the league's most embarrassing and harshest critic of integration, got sick of poor attendance at his team's home games and moved the Redskins to Washington in 1937. The 1936 season was turning into the Redskins' first winning year, which may have accounted for the previous lack of interest by fans.

That early in the season, it was not clear whether Boston would be a winning team. The Redskins proved to be a get-well elixir for the Packers, who crushed them, 31–2. Green Bay went up 10–0 in the first quarter and only allowed Boston a safety on a Packers fumble out of the end zone. Johnny Blood notched a touchdown, as did Hutson, who scored his first TD of the year on a 38-yard pass from Herber. This was the opening touchdown of the game and the first major indication of the season that the duo was getting sharp. For variety, Green Bay scored on an interception, and Joe Laws tossed a TD pass to Paul Miller. Ernie Smith inserted his foot into the mix with two extra points and a field goal. At that point, Boston had a mediocre 2–3 record.

The Packers could not know they had reached a turning point in the season, but they were now on a winning streak lasting the rest of the year. They had to dig down for the next opponent, the dangerous Detroit Lions. Green Bay learned the year before that any meeting with Detroit was bound to produce either-way results. This game was no different. The Packers jumped ahead early when Tiny Engebretsen boomed a 40-yard field goal and Milt Gantenbein caught a 22-yard touchdown throw from Herber. That gave the hosts a 10–0 lead at halftime, but that margin was in jeopardy after a 9–0 third quarter by the Lions on a touchdown and a safety.

Detroit took a 15–10 lead in the fourth quarter when Ernie Caddell hauled in a 14-yard touchdown pass from Dutch Clark. The Packers seemed to be in trouble, but they regained the lead when Johnny Blood came through with a big catch on a throw by Herber, a 46-yard heave that gave Green Bay a 17–15 lead. That did not solve the matter. The Lions rallied again, and Clark gave the lead back to Detroit on a 28-yard field goal. Although Herber's two touchdown passes were critical, the game came down to Engebretsen's toe. His 18-yard field goal

12. First Championship

won it, 20–18. The 13,500 fans in City Stadium whooped it up over the result, and the Packers were a healthy 4–1.

Herber was gaining more renown the more the Packers relied on the forward pass. It wasn't just his connection with Hutson, but he could spread the ball around. Sometimes other Packers receivers found daylight because defenses keyed on Hutson.

Herber was less heralded when he joined the team, being paid just $75 a game at first. Once, he accidentally was handed the wrong player's paycheck—it belonged to star lineman Mike Michalske—only to read that the offensive guard and sometime fullback was making $175 a ballgame. One might wonder how he felt about that, although Michalske was an older veteran with stature.

Since salaries didn't get talked about much in those days, and Lambeau certainly didn't want his guys comparing notes, they were left to think they knew what other guys were making, or read some newspaper report, or heard later what might have been. By comparison, Herber believed Hutson was getting wealthy. "We didn't have that much money in those days and we had to watch it," Herber said. "The teams weren't rich. I remember in 1935 we signed Don Hutson for $5,000, and it was an unheard of salary."[1]

On the field, the most unusual aspect of Herber's throwing style was something that quarterbacks never do and are never taught. Passers always nestle the surface of the ball in their hands, with their fingers on the laces. Herber did it the opposite way, backwards, with the laces held against his palm, a cardinal no-no. "No reason, particularly," he said. "Just that it was something I had been doing since my days in high school. I felt I could get more on the ball by palming the laces."[2]

As time passed, Herber and Hutson became more comfortable with one another. Sportswriters regularly used the phrase, "Herber to Hutson," and Herber steadily gained appreciation for what Hutson could do to twist defenses and how that also benefited the passer. "He had speed, brains and deception," Herber said. "Any [player] who would try to follow him downfield or pick him up in a pattern was foolish. He'd drive you nuts. We always had spot passing plans with Don. No matter where he was, I knew where he was supposed to be and I'd just uncork 'er, that's all. He usually got there, too."[3]

In 1936, Herber was on his way to career highs of 11 touchdown passes and 1,239 yards. This is when he first received notice as "a long passer." It was Herber's coach, Lambeau, who burnished his reputation

Caught by Don Hutson!

for throwing deep. "A lot of guys today can throw the ball as far, or maybe as even farther," Lambeau said of his man decades ago, "but none as well for distance. The guy was phenomenal."[4]

It should always be remembered that when guys like Benny Friedman and Herber were in the league, the forward pass was not only just feeling its way in coaches' heads, but the rules were stacked against their success, too. There was no roughing-the-passer rule in place to protect the quarterback when Herber came into the league. The practical effect was that it was open season on passers, including after they released the ball. The ball may have been sailing downfield to its intended destination, but pass rushers still followed through and clobbered the passer. They didn't pull up short to avoid contact, they ran right through the QB.

"I never threw a pass without getting knocked down," Herber said. "Never."[5]

After their tough contest with the Lions, the Packers moved on to face the cream puff Pittsburgh Pirates, who were no better in 1936 than they had been in 1935—and the Packers were better than they had been. Green Bay romped, 42–10, to move to 5–1. It was already 28–3 by halftime, and the Packers had all their points by the end of the third quarter.

It was a festival of touchdowns for Green Bay. Joe Laws and Johnny Blood scored once each, Blood's TD coming on a 58-yard interception return. Paul Miller scored twice, on a rush and a pass reception, and Hutson helped out in a major way with two scores through the air, on receptions of 21 and 11 yards, both from Herber. As respected as Blood was running out of the offensive backfield, he was a quadruple threat, also catching passes, running back kicks, and in the secondary. If he got the ball in his hands, he would pile up some yardage, one way or another.

The eighth game of the season, November 1, brought the eagerly awaited rematch with the Chicago Bears. Thumped, 30–3, early in the year, the Packers had not lost since. The Bears were undefeated, 6–0, coming into Wrigley Field. The game attracted considerable fanfare, as the rivalry always did, but perhaps more so since both clubs were riding along at the top of the Western Division. Some 31,346 fans turned out. The Packers wanted to show that the first result was a fluke, and the Bears wanted to prove they were as good as they had appeared to be.

This game began as the other had played out. The Bears pounced on the Pack and ran up two quick scores to take a 10–0 lead in the first

12. First Championship

quarter. Chicago's Jack Manders kicked a 23-yard field goal. Playing both ways, on offense and defense, as most players did in those days, Chicago end Bill Hewett demoralized Green Bay with a 53-yard fumble return for a touchdown capped by a Manders extra point. But the Packers shrugged off the poor start as the home fans howled and Bears boss George Halas looked on with satisfaction.

Fittingly, it was the Herber-Hutson combination that sparked the Packers. Hutson ran in a 9-yard pass for a touchdown in the second quarter, Ernie Smith kicked the extra point, and Clarke Hinkle burst free for a 59-yard touchdown run with Smith kicking again for a 14–10 Packer lead at halftime. By then Green Bay had Halas' attention. He was definitely not paying heed to the marching band during the intermission.

The third quarter was a scoreless struggle, but the Packers were the only team to score in the fourth, George Sauer, Sr., crossing the goal line on a 2-yard TD. Final score: 21–10, Green Bay. The teams were tied for first place.

News of the world took precedence over football two days later. FDR was up for re-election against Republican challenger Alf Landon, the governor of Kansas. This was a referendum on how Roosevelt had been handling the country's shambles of an economy during the Great Depression, and in one of the most lopsided results in presidential election history, he won 523 electoral college votes to Landon's 8. Roosevelt and vice-presidential running mate James Nance Garner captured 60.8 percent of the popular vote. The early reports, long before there was electronic voting and tabulation, indicated there was a high turnout.

The 1936 schedule had been drafted in an odd manner. The Packers played at home every week from September 13 through October 27 and played the rest of their regularly scheduled games on the road, starting with that second Bears meeting. Back in Green Bay, Baum's Dry Goods store jump-started its own bandwagon after the Bears victory.

Established in 1888, Baum's was a well-respected major downtown business. Wanting to associate itself with a winner and offer encouragement to the hometown boys, Baum's took out a full-page advertisement in the *Green Bay Press-Gazette*, wishing the Packers well on the road and urging them to come home with a title.

The missive, signed by Cecil Baum, president of the company, announced, "Coming to Green Bay, The Football Championship of the

Caught by Don Hutson!

World. An Open Letter to the Green Bay Packers from Baum's." The letter read in part:

> You're going away tomorrow. To four of the nation's greatest cities, Boston, New York, Brooklyn and Detroit. You are going as the representative of the smallest city in professional football—and the greatest football town in America. You are going to bring back to Green Bay, just before Christmas, that Christmas present that city wants most of anything obtainable—the National Professional Football Championship. And your Green Bay will be the only city ever to win a fourth championship since the league was formed.[6]

Then the letter truly began gushing, praising the team and players, the city and fans, for their mutual loyalties and declaring that the squad had what it took to go all the way and win the crown. Accompanying President Baum's signature were the words, "Good health and good fortune, from Wisconsin, Green Bay, and everyone at Baum's." There was a tag line reading, "Baum's: Which Has Also Served Its City Well."[7]

Three days later, the Packers took on the Redskins for a second time. The improving Redskins were a different outfit than in the early-season 31–2 loss. The second time around was much more of a battle, but the Packers still prevailed, in totally different fashion, 7–3. Naturally enough, the only Green Bay touchdown, in the third quarter, came on a pass from Herber, 20 yards to Hutson. That was just enough to get the W, even though it counted the same in the standings as the much more emphatic victory.

There was no such close shave the next game, at the Brooklyn Dodgers, in Ebbets Field, the same locale occupied by the major league baseball franchise. More than 25,000 attended, and Hutson showed his stuff again, heating up as the schedule continued. This was a runaway all the way, with the Packers banking all of their points in the 38–7 triumph by third quarter's end. Hutson collected touchdown passes from Herber of 5 and 12 yards, and many back-ups got into the act.

The Polo Grounds beckoned for a November 22 match with the New York Giants, always a formidable opponent and often the best in the East. This win took work to seal. The Packers outscored the Giants, 26–14, but led only 3–0 at halftime. New York pulled within 17–14 in the fourth quarter, but a safety and a Sauer Sr., run gave the Packers their final points as they inched away.

The schedule didn't get any easier with the next stop, Detroit to face the 7–3 roaring Lions, who were not giving up on catching the

12. First Championship

Packers. Green Bay settled that question, but it was again not an easy tussle. After going ahead 20–14 at halftime, Green Bay fended off the Lions with strong defense.

Becoming increasingly dangerous with more experience, Hutson shocked the Lions in the first quarter on a 58-yard scoring play with Herber's cooperation. Detroit star Dutch Clark retaliated with a one-yard score, but Green Bay runner Clarke Hinkle answered back. Hutson provided the big play on special teams before the half, running a blocked punt back 40 yards for a TD. That play ruined Detroit. The Lions only mustered a field goal in the second half.

By then, Cecil Baum should have been happy, convinced that his pep talk paid such great dividends on this extended road swing. Whether he was misinformed by his underlings or had misread the schedule, Baum overlooked one last regularly scheduled road game in Chicago to face the pesky Cardinals a second time. Although it did not matter in the big picture, the mojo seemed to have worn off from the advertising page. The Packers and Cardinals played to a 0–0 standoff, a moral victory for 3–8–1 Chicago against 10–1–1 Green Bay.

The Packers were the easy champs of the West, ahead of the Bears, 9–3, and Lions, 8–4. The East was the weak division in 1936. After their slow start, the Boston Redskins gained momentum, and their 7–5 record turned out to be good enough for first place and a spot in the title game against the Packers. No other team in the East finished above .500, and of all clubs, it was the perpetually losing Pirates next with a 6–6 mark.

After the final Sunday of the regular season, the pairing was set for the championship game in a season that ended much earlier than it does in the 2020s. The league finale took place in mid–December, the 13th of the month. In between the last regular-season game on December 6 and the championship tilt a week later, there was stunning international news grabbing headlines. The big story occurred when England's King Edward VIII abdicated his position on the throne to marry an American commoner. The 36th king of England, ostensible ruler of 500 million subjects of the British Commonwealth worldwide, chose love over power in declaring devotion to Wallis Simpson.

The British royals still regularly command headlines in newspapers and on television, but this was one of the most significant disturbances within the royal family concerning the whole world. Simpson grew up in Baltimore and was going through a divorce, also severely frowned on

Caught by Don Hutson!

in polite society, and the king's decision triggered a constitutional crisis. He renounced his status as head of state, leaving the kingdom to the rule of his brother, the Duke of York. Simpson became the Duchess of Windsor, and Edward became the Duke of Windsor.

Edward made his announcement to the British people via radio on December 11, while the Packers and Redskins sought to keep their minds on the big game that would declare the victor kings of the football world, which was followed closely by considerably fewer than 500 million fans.

The game was played at a neutral site, not like the modern-era Super Bowl at a place selected by the league years ahead of time, but because of the pique of Boston owner George Preston Marshall. He gave up on the city as home for his franchise and thought the contest would draw better elsewhere. Marshall said he had lost $100,000 over five years trying to establish the Redskins in Boston, and he was licked by the lack of interest.

The championship shifted to the Polo Grounds in New York. In a huff, the temperamental Marshall said he was never bringing his team back to Boston—and he did not—moving to Washington, D.C., for the 1937 season.

Weather cooperated for mid-December, with the temperature hitting 36 degrees at kickoff and just a 6-mph wind stirring the air. There was sunshine, too, when there could have been snow. The cachet of the game was strong enough that nearly 30,000 fans came out despite New York having no allegiance to either team. That crowd did include 5,000 children admitted for 40 cents each.

The Packers received the opening kickoff, and although they did not score on that possession, the next time with the ball, Green Bay did exactly what scouting reports must have warned the Redskins about. The Packers took a 7–0 lead courtesy of a 48-yard touchdown pass from Herber to Hutson followed by an Ernie Smith extra point. Those words may have been copied directly from Curly Lambeau's playbook.

Boston did not roll over. The Redskins fought back in the second period, when Pug Renter made it across the goal for a six-pointer. No extra point was registered, however, leaving Green Bay with a 7–6 halftime lead. This was very much still a contest entering the second half, Boston giving favored Green Bay a serious scare.

Things began to change in the third quarter. Herber completed another touchdown pass, this time to Milt Gantenbein from the 8-yard

12. First Championship

line. Smith made good on the kick again, and the Packers were up, 14–6. The Redskins were out of steam and didn't mount much more of a challenge, while the Packers added another TD on a 2-yard run by Bob Monnett in the fourth period for the final score of 21–6.

More than once in the ensuing press coverage, the game was referred to as a "rout" although the final spread was not that tremendous. Many sportswriters lavished praise on the Packers' passing game. Indeed, the *Green Bay Press-Gazette* seemed to do its best to gather up compliments penned by New York writers on just how wonderful the Packers were. There were enough flattering words to please even Cecil Baum. Edward VIII had no comment.

Stanley Woodward, the esteemed columnist and future sports editor of the *New York Herald-Tribune*, did, however. He said the decisiveness of the Packers' victory (no doubt also coupled with the state of the standings), proved the superiority of the West over the East, and that if things stayed that way, it might hurt the professional game financially. "As the league is now," Woodward wrote, "the West has at least 60 percent of the manpower. In the course of a whole season the only worthwhile intersectional victory scored by the East was that of the New York Giants over the Detroit Lions. Green Bay and the Chicago Bears were not beaten by an Eastern team."[8]

At the very end of November, when the Packers had clinched the Western Division crown, they returned to Green Bay by train and were welcomed by 3,000 fans. The celebration was even more raucous when they got home after the NFL title triumph. As they returned by train again late in the evening of December 14, a pathway of red flares, simulating fire, lighted the way along the rails. A scheduled banquet feting the champs had almost immediately sold out.

By then, the Packers themselves had been celebrating before reaching Green Bay. Dinner on the train was announced on a hurriedly printed menu with the introduction reading, "The Milwaukee Road Menu; Green Bay Packers World's Champion Professional Football Team; Dinner, Monday, December 14, 1936."

This was served: Cotuit oysters on the half shell, cocktail sauce, crisp golden celery hearts, Burr gherkins, Rose Bud Radishes, and Consommé Julienne. Then came: Fillet of Wall-Eyed Pike with lemon butter; combination grill Hiawatha, baked potato, roast young turkey, cranberry sauce, candied sweet potatoes. Also, Brussels sprouts, head lettuce salad with Olympian or 1000 Island dressing, and assorted bread.

Caught by Don Hutson!

For dessert: mince pie, hot or cold, with cheese, cherry parfait wafers, or a cheese crock. Coffee, tea, or milk was available. The cost of the meal was $1.25.

It should be noted that at least one member of the roster had a different game plan for celebrating. Clarke Hinkle got married right after the championship. While he most likely enjoyed the companionship of his Packers teammates, he probably did not wish the 25 or so others, plus coaches, trainers, equipment helpers and the like to join him on his honeymoon.

13

Aiming for Another Title

Green Bay was so good in 1936, there was every reason for coach Curly Lambeau to think the Packers could repeat in 1937. He was always hungry for a winner, and he seemed to have the ingredients needed to keep going.

It was not beyond Lambeau to try to gain every inch he could over an opponent, legal or not. At that time, the National Football League had a rule in place that precluded coaching from the bench. It extended so far that a player who came into the game as a substitute could not bring in the next play to be called. That may sound silly, but it was a restriction. However, Lambeau developed a series of secret hand signals to relay information to his men on the field. The man was a micro-manager, and ceding any type of authority came hard to him.

This extended to all aspects of his role. Lambeau was in charge of the Packers, on and off the field, and wielded his authority with a sledgehammer more often than gently. He was the boss and flexed that power. This was especially true during contract discussions. Lambeau, much like the Chicago Bears' George Halas, was restrained in his spending. Maybe these two gruff old-timers had this in common because they were there at the beginning with their franchises and witnessed first-hand the disappearance of many fellow owners whose clubs went under. Lambeau wanted the best talent he could find, but he wanted to ink contracts as cheaply as possible.

"Contract negotiations with Curly were like a three-act play," said Charles "Buckets" Goldenberg, one of the team's stalwarts at guard and running back during this period. Goldenberg, whose birthplace was listed as "Odessa, Ukraine, Russian Empire" in 1911, was a member of a Jewish family that departed Russia when he was four. After that, he was Wisconsin all the way, attending high school in Milwaukee, college at the University of Wisconsin in Madison, and playing for the Packers.

Caught by Don Hutson!

"You started out full of hope. Then Curly started to talk down your demands. At the end, you felt like a bad guy trying to rob the Packers." Goldenberg said Lambeau would bring out a fake copy of a contract belonging to stars Clarke Hinkle and Don Hutson, to ask another player if he thought he was worth more than them.[1]

As an individual, though, Lambeau did not mind spending his own loot. He drove a Cadillac, bought a boat, and dressed in high fashion. Lambeau was a tremendous judge of talent and a stern leader, a tough guy to the players in almost all ways. He maintained separation of player and coach and could act imperially. His first allegiance was to the Green Bay franchise, but then, above all else, to winning.

"He was Mr. Green Bay," Goldenberg once said. "Curly was a great coach and his vision and foresight made the Packers and the National Football League what they are today. If you won for him, and this is what he wanted most, you could ask for the world and the moon. If you lost, you stayed away from him. In addition to being a great coach, he was a great salesman. He could sell oysters to a fisherman. It was this salesmanship that helped him develop many stars."[2]

By that, Goldenberg, who was an All-Pro player and a member of three championship teams, meant that Lambeau's stamp of approval helped build confidence in a Packer and acknowledged his ability to convince players pre-draft to sign with Green Bay.

The Packers were still winners in 1937, but they were not champions. Whether Lambeau failed to prepare them properly to defend the crown, the players were too full of themselves from their prior accomplishment, the Bears were simply the better team that year, or a combination of all those reasons, Green Bay had a good season, but not a great one.

Things began poorly. The Packers started 0–2, with losses to both Chicago teams right away in September, 14–7 to the Cardinals and 14–2 to the Bears, both defeats even more annoyingly occurring at City Stadium in Green Bay. It was not a grand way to celebrate a championship achievement. It appeared that the offense failed to suit up.

One reason was quarterback Arnie Herber. Herber made it into just nine games in 1937, and his statistics were far below the level of the season before. He completed 47 of 104 passes for 684 yards and seven touchdowns. Bob Monnett, a talented player, saw considerable action, gaining 580 yards through the air and heaving eight touchdown passes. Yet the snap seemed gone from the Green Bay offense in the early going.

13. Aiming for Another Title

There was an even earlier hint of problems when the Packers, as defending NFL champs, faced off against the College All-Stars in that annual charity exhibition game. Not only did the Packers lose, they were shut out, 6–0.

Champions who are assigned the task of competing against the all-stars take time away from training camp, but in theory are superior because they are pros and teammates, better organized even if their hearts aren't really into competing in this game. That was the impression the Packers made.

"It was no secret that Lambeau was far from pleased with his club's state of readiness," a Chicago newspaper stated in the lead-up. "He could not get them up for an exhibition game against a bunch of college seniors. The attitude of the men leaves much to be desired. They have evinced no concern over Wednesday's contest."[3]

Lambeau, ever the fashion plate, had outfitted his players in new uniforms, but it turned out they were made of some material that made them hotter on the humid and high-temperature afternoon. Some 85,000 fans watched the Packers essentially embarrass themselves. Lambeau did not bellow at reporters in the wake of the loss, but he did ditch the uniforms.

Opening day of the regular season was September 12 and the Cardinals took an early lead. Green Bay's only retaliation was a four-yard touchdown run by newlywed Clarke Hinkle, whose wife's cooking didn't put sufficient poundage on him to slow his churning legs.

Between the All-Star debacle and the season-opening defeat, fans were restless by the time the Packers fell to the Bears without a touchdown. The lead paragraph recounting events in the *Milwaukee Journal* summed things up bleakly. The story read, "It wasn't enough that the college all-stars and Chicago Cardinals should mistreat our once proud Packers. Chicago's Bears rubbed it in further here Sunday afternoon, 14 to 2. A crowd of 17,000, the largest in Green Bay's history, saw the sad show."[4]

The score was 0–0 at halftime, but it was 14–0 Bears in the third quarter when Green Bay notched its only points. The scoring came on a safety after Don Hutson blocked a punt, and that was it for the game. The *Journal* was not subtle in its doom-and-gloom analysis of the situation before all the autumn leaves had fallen from trees, a sub-headline noting "Title Hopes Nearly Blasted by Second Trimming."[5]

If Lambeau were the star of a cartoon like a Bugs Bunny figure or

Caught by Don Hutson!

the like, he would have had steam coming out of his ears on a movie screen. This was one time when a team welcomed a bye in the schedule. The Packers had a week off before resuming play on October 3, back at City Stadium.

As became evident by the statistics and the increasing reliance on Monnett, Lambeau began losing confidence in Herber as the solution at quarterback. He was only 28 years old, so age should not have made him over the hill, and he had established himself as the best in the league, yet Lambeau, trusting his instincts, sensed that Herber was no longer the long-term answer in that key position.

The feeble start to the season confirmed Lambeau's suspicions, and Herber, once a Packers hero and a future Hall of Famer, was out of favor. Lambeau spent much of 1937 working around him rather than counting on him. Fair or not, that's how the season played out. Whatever type of torture in workouts Lambeau visited upon the Packers during the bye week, when they had not completely come around after the all-star mess, they did respond to the demoralizing losses to the two Chicago teams. The players believed they were better than they had shown and that it was not too late to show it. It was only October.

This 0–2 start did not seem to completely crush Green Bay fans because when the team played October 3 against the Detroit Lions, some 17,553 showed up. They saw a rejuvenated group of Packers who dominated, 26–6, though the Lions had been 2–0 coming in. Green Bay scored in the first quarter, the second quarter, and added two more touchdowns in the fourth quarter. Detroit's only visit to the scoreboard occurred in the third period. Hinkle, Paul Miller, Milt Gantenbein and Monnett each scored a touchdown. Nothing for Hutson. Monnett hit Gantenbein for a 77-yard score.

This was the beginning of a salvage campaign. For the first time the 1937, Packers resembled the 1936 Packers. A 1–2 record did not call for bragging, but it was a signal. What followed surprised the rest of the NFL. The Lions victory was the first of seven in a row by the previously moribund Packers.

The comatose offense was revived. From zeros and single-digit totals, Green Bay began running up high scores. In the coming weeks, the Packers rolled. In a revenge match against the Chicago Cardinals, the Packers triumphed, 34–13. That game was 24–7 at the half. Running and kicking, Hinkle went on the board twice, Tiny Engebretsen kicked a field goal, Gantenbein caught a 12-yard TD pass from Herber

13. Aiming for Another Title

(remember him?), and Bernie Scherber grabbed an 18-yarder from Monnett. Ed Jankowski scored on a 46-run run.

Hutson made up for his absence from the scoring column in the October 17 crushing of the Cleveland Rams. The 35–10 win lifted Green Bay over .500 with a 3–2 record, and the Packers were definitely on the move. Hutson woke up the echoes with three touchdown catches of five and 35 yards from Herber and another 35-yard toss from Monnett. Everyone feasted on the Rams.

In a fortunate bit of scheduling for the Packers, they turned right around the next week and played the Rams again, with the same overpowering result, this time beating Cleveland, 35–7. This was an elixir for Green Bay and must have been depressing for the Rams to have their inferiority reinforced. Neither Hutson nor Herber had much to do with this victory. Neither showed up in the scoring summary at all.

Hinkle scored on the biggest play, a 49-yard rush, and Herb Schneidman, Hank Bruder, Ade Schammel, and Joe Laws each added touchdowns. The margin of the decision allowed Lambeau to give playing time to some guys who didn't often get off the bench at crunch time in closer games.

The W added the following week, October 31, was much more dear. The rematch with the Detroit Lions, at the University of Detroit Stadium, was nothing like the first game except in result. The Packers won their fifth straight, but the final score was just 14–13, hardly an easily-earned triumph. Dutch Clark, the Detroit star, scored both of his team's touchdowns, but failure to convert an extra point in the first quarter was the difference-maker. Green Bay received TDs from Clarke Hinkle and Ed Jankowski, and Ernie Smith booted two extra points. The crowd of 21,311 was a big one for the time, and the tightness of the affair made the viewing worthwhile.

On November 7, the Packers met the Bears for the second time in the 1937 season. Chicago brought a 5–0–1, record into the showdown at Wrigley Field. As always, the rivalry was hyped. The Packers had lost the first round, but now the teams were almost even in the West standings. A victory by Green Bay would make up for the early-season loss and provide additional optimism that the Packers could run the table and capture a place in the NFL title game again.

Forget the Detroit attendance. There were more than twice as many fans in the stands in Chicago for this contest. The fans comprehended the import of the moment. So did coaches Lambeau and Halas.

Caught by Don Hutson!

They knew one another well, and there was always said to be some bad blood between them. They never bothered to shake hands with each other after these high-tension rivalry games. Theirs was a relationship of one-upmanship, always seeking to outmaneuver the other. They did not trust one another and competed to sign the same players, especially prior to the draft. Halas had wanted Hutson, just not as badly as Lambeau. Later in life, they became friends of a sort, long after they had established mutual respect.

Insiders said the men wanted to beat each other's teams more than they wanted to beat any other team in the league. Bob Snyder, who played some quarterback for the Bears starting in 1939, although he was a member of the Rams when the Packers steamrolled them this season, said Halas would practically lose his mind in a frenzy, making preparations during the week leading up to Packers games. "We practiced twice on Monday, twice on Tuesday, twice on Wednesday, twice on Thursday, twice on Friday," Snyder said. "We had meetings every night. We called it 'Green Bay nut week.' All the guys bitched, but Halas would just go crazy. Then I go up to Green Bay as an assistant coach and I'll be goddamned if it wasn't the same thing with Lambeau."[6]

This was a Green Bay day. The first quarter was a stalemate, 0–0, with defenses prevailing. The Packers turned things their way with a 17-point second quarter, and it was the reliable duo of Hutson and Herber silencing the crowd when they connected on a 78-yard touchdown bomb, capped by a Hinkle extra point kick. Smith kicked a field goal, and Jankowski ran back an interception 23 yards for another touchdown, this time with a Smith extra-point boot. That provided enough of a cushion to withstand a Bears touchdown interception return in the third period. Green Bay's clinching points came on a four-yard Hinkle reception from Monnett in the fourth quarter. When the game ended, 24–14, Green Bay's record was 6–2, and the Bears stood at 5–1–1.

There was no doubt the Packers were on a high after the win. They were on a juicy roll that seemed likely to pay off with another Western Division crown and a spot in the championship game. They reinforced their positive emotions and sterling play on November 14, a 37–7 rout of the Philadelphia Eagles. The game was back home at Wisconsin State Fair Park, with more than 13,000 happy attendees.

Green Bay led early, late, and throughout. The Packers had a 16–0

13. Aiming for Another Title

lead at the half and piled on 21 points in the fourth quarter to clinch things. Once again, the passing game was in vintage form, the duo of Hutson and Herber combining for key plays. One touchdown catch was a two-yarder, the other, the last score of the day, a 34-yarder. Monnett tossed a TD pass, too. Buckets Goldenberg scored on a 27-yard interception return, his first touchdown since 1934.

With a 7–2 record and so much momentum, it seemed nothing could stop the Packers short of the title game. That was the thinking from Lambeau down through the roster, and around town among the citizenry. And they were all wrong. After such a tremendous and tantalizing run, the Packers fell apart at the end. They bookended their two early-season losses with two late-season losses.

Traveling to the Polo Grounds on November 21, the Packers were completely stifled by the New York Giants, 10–0. Same problem as in September, Green Bay just couldn't score. The Packers' juggernaut offense of the preceding weeks evaporated. It wasn't as if the game ever got out of hand. It was 0–0 after one quarter, 3–0 New York at halftime, and New York added a touchdown in the third. There was plenty of time to come back, if Green Bay could mount something.

That was a crucial loss, a pothole that perhaps could be patched. But no, on November 28, the Packers fell to the Washington Redskins at Griffith Stadium, the ballpark owned by the Washington Senators baseball team that had become the old Boston Redskins' home. Hutson caught an early touchdown pass from Monnett for the early Green Bay lead, but that was all the points the Packers tallied. Washington scored all of its points in the second half. The final score of 14–6 sealed Green Bay's fate for the season.

After their loss to the Packers, the Bears kept winning and rolled to a 9–1–1, record while Green Bay and the Lions tied for second with 7–4 marks. It was the Redskins who emerged from the East as the winner and took down the Bears for the championship.

Washington was led by the latest passing phenom, one of the greatest NFL players of all time, a rookie named Sammy Baugh out of Texas Christian University, who succeeded Herber as the king of throwers by leading the league with the most completions, attempts, and passing yards gained for the 1937 season.

Hutson, at 24, still led the league in catches with 41 and TD receptions with seven. But the days of Herber-to-Hutson as a significant weapon were done. Herber had been replaced at the top of the NFL stats

Caught by Don Hutson!

list by a new face, and he was being phased out in Green Bay, too, by Curly Lambeau, the same man and coach who had presented him with his big chance. Lambeau the scout was searching for Herber's long-term replacement, which clearly would have a long-term impact on Don Hutson, as well.

14

Close to Winning It All Again

One of the most challenging accomplishments in sports is repeating as a champion, and the 1936 Green Bay Packers could not do so in 1937. Coach Curly Lambeau saw enough from his players to recognize that there was still abundant talent on his team, but for a man who wanted to win all the time, coming close wasn't good enough.

The core of Green Bay's offense was quarterback Arnie Herber throwing the ball to receiver Don Hutson. This was the Packers' edge. But there was depth and ability spread all up and down the roster. Football was a young man's game, and this was especially true in the late 1920s and into the 1930s, when the pro model was not always the choice for a long career.

Lambeau had supplemented the top talent on the team over the years, filling spots and counting on veterans less heralded than the big names. Players like Clarke Hinkle, Buckets Goldenberg, Bob Monnett, Tiny Engebretsen, and Milt Gantenbein were especially valuable. But Johnny Blood, Cal Hubbard, and Mike Michalske were no longer around in 1938.

Sports history is littered with tales of coaches who misjudged players' hearts and staying power, though many say those men who reward loyalty count on favored players too long when they should have replaced them. As harsh as his judgment sounded, Lambeau wanted to find a first-class quarterback worthy of throwing to Hutson, though keeping up with Hutson was no easy task. Lambeau knew from the start, and had it proven to him, that Hutson was a singular talent. It was not going to do the player, the coach, the team, and the fans much good to squander his value. Green Bay had to have a quarterback who could handle the responsibility of getting the ball to Hutson.

Caught by Don Hutson!

As always, the pressure was on the front office to find the fresh blood needed to sustain success. The thing of it was that Lambeau was also the front office. He had to discover his own new players. By 1938, the National Football League draft was a few years old, even if scouting methods seemed prehistoric.

Whether Lambeau ensured the Packers' immediate future with his brains and judgment, with common sense, or just got lucky, when it came Green Bay's turn to make its No. 1 draft choice, the team did the right thing. Picking seventh in the first round, the Packers watched future Supreme Court justice Byron "Whizzer" White go to the Pittsburgh Pirates as a running back and future Pro Football Hall of Fame center Alex Wojciechowicz go to the Detroit Lions.

Green Bay made Lambeau's feelings clear when it selected quarterback Cecil Isbell, out of Purdue University. Isbell, 6-foot-1 and 190 pounds, was definitely brought to Wisconsin to compete with Herber for the starting job. Isbell was not ready-made to take over, but during the 1938 season, he was given considerable playing time. Lambeau started Herber at QB most games, started Isbell some games, and played the two of them together in the same backfield, Isbell as a ball carrier, some of the time. It was a learning curve for Isbell and a learning curve for Lambeau, to determine what he had. So-called quarterback controversies became much more common on NFL teams in the future, but this was perhaps the first in league history.

Plus, when it came to supervising the "Notre Dame Box" offense Lambeau preferred, the Packers still had Monnett available. That year, Isbell completed 37 of 91 attempts for 659 yards and eight touchdowns, Monnett completed 31 of 57 passes for 465 yards and nine touchdowns, and Herber completed 22 of 55 passes for 336 yards and three touchdowns.

Even if Hutson could only guess who might be throwing him the ball, he caught 32 passes for 548 yards and nine touchdowns. His yards gained and touchdowns caught still led the league. There really was no receiver from that time period who could compete with Hutson. He was the best by a huge margin despite Lambeau serving up a quarterback of the day much like a catch of the day in a restaurant.

Isbell made a strong impression on Lambeau early, and years later, the Packers coach rated the Boilermakers alumnus the best passer he had ever seen. It may have hurt Herber to have Isbell rated higher than himself, but Lambeau was so smitten with Isbell that he ranked him as

14. Close to Winning It All Again

being better than other all-stars, something a more objective observer would not.

"Isbell was the best," Lambeau said, "with Sid Luckman of the Bears a close second and Sammy Baugh of the Redskins a long third. Luckman wasn't as versatile and Baugh couldn't compare on the long ones. Isbell was a master at any range. He could throw soft passes, bullet passes, or long passes."[1]

Isbell, a rookie in 1938, only played in the pros through 1942. If he was able to do as many tricks with his arm as Lambeau recalled, it was rather amazing because Isbell said he played part of his college days in West Lafayette, Indiana, and all of his pro days in Green Bay with a protective device holding down his left shoulder after he separated it twice in one college game.

"After that, they decided I should have a chain on my left arm, so I couldn't raise it too high," Isbell said. "That way, the shoulder never went out again. I wore the chain in practice and in games, both at Purdue and with the Packers. Sure, it hampered me some." He also punted and played defensive back, which was routine for quarterbacks in those days. "When I was punting, I couldn't extend my left arm all the way out, so I had to learn to drop the ball one-handed. And I played defense all the time (we didn't have two platoons) and it wasn't good for tackling. Not that it was so tender, but because it hindered the grasp. My reach didn't have the range it would have had."[2]

Although the Isbell-Hutson link gradually blossomed, when the season began on September 11 against the Cleveland Rams at City Stadium in Green Bay, and the Packers rolled over the visitors, 26–17, it was Herber and Hutson, as usual, who excelled with touchdown passes of 7, 53, and 18 yards. None of the 8,247 fans in the stands would have guessed that Herber was soon to become an after-thought in the Packers' offense.

That's how the 1938 regular season began for the Packers, everything seeming peachy, as if they would overwhelm all teams in their path. The previous season should have been a lesson that one week's victory meant nothing the next week, but they lived it all over again in painful fashion on September 18.

It was an absolutely miserable day for the Packers. Green Bay was shut out, but it wasn't only that which hurt so much. The day's loss came to the Chicago Bears—bonus points of pain. And the final score was a ridiculous 2–0, as if it was a pitcher's duel, not a football game. The

Caught by Don Hutson!

game was a scoreless tie for three quarters, and the losing (or call it the winning) points were scored in humiliating fashion. Pinned deep in their own territory, the Packers planned to punt. The snap went awry, bounced into the end zone, and became a safety by the Bears.

That was a nightmare result. Just one week after Hutson himself tallied three touchdowns through the air, Green Bay completed just three passes. It was make-or-break time with a 1–1 record. The third game could be critical for how the season would play out. It was not as if the Packers had been free of aggravation in previous meetings with the Chicago Cardinals, but this was one time the Cards appearing on the schedule came at the right time.

On September 25, the Packers were rejuvenated by a resounding win at Wisconsin State Fair Park as 18,000 locals rooted hard for a turnaround. Green Bay pushed the Cardinals around, winning in a walk, 28–7. The Packers scored two touchdowns in the second period and two more in the third to grab control. One of the most surprising agate-type lines of the football season caught the careful reader off-balance in a summary of the game. The Packers' third touchdown, providing a 21–0 lead, read this way: "Arnie Herber, 15-yard pass from Cecil Isbell." How about that? Isbell to Herber. Weird on all counts.

In another of those early-days quirks of scheduling, the same two teams faced off again a week later, this time in a galaxy far, far away. As sometimes happened, the two games seemed as if they were produced by different contenders. The Packers did survive, 24–22, but just barely. In another oddity to the interested historian, the game was played in Buffalo, New York, while listed as a Chicago home game.

The clicking combo of Herber and Isbell fooled the Cardinals the first time, but who would imagine the same trick could be successful again so soon? And on September 28, a game played on a Wednesday instead of a Sunday, too? This was a tough event for the Packers. They had to work to get out of town with the W.

The first quarter was 0–0 and then, beginning with an Isbell-to-Herber scoring pass (followed by a Tiny Engebretsen kick), the action not only picked up, but went back and forth. It was 7–0 Green Bay when the Cardinals retaliated on a Buddy Parker 1-yard run. Parker, a future NFL head coach, was not helped in his quest to tie the game when the Cardinals failed to convert the extra point. Before halftime, Clarke Hinkle added to the Packers' lead, though caught from Monnett, not Isbell or Herber. Then Hinkle, not Engebretsen, kicked the point

14. Close to Winning It All Again

after. Lambeau must have thought he was confusing Chicago by how he deployed his personnel.

Green Bay inched a little farther ahead when Isbell hit Hutson for a 15-yard touchdown pass with Engebretsen kicking. The Cardinals charged back after that with two touchdowns and a field goal to take a 22–21 lead. In late clutch play, Green Bay drove deep into Cardinals territory, and Engebretsen kicked a 20-yard field goal to win the game, 24–22.

The famous Academy Award-winning movie starring Humphrey Bogart, *Casablanca*, ends with the comment about his character and another figure being at the beginning of a beautiful friendship. It might be said that Isbell's and Hutson's friendship truly began in this game with that touchdown pass. Isbell was still learning and Herber was still in the picture, but the score showed what an Isbell-Hutson duo could do.

"Don Hutson once called me the best passer in Green Bay Packers' history," Isbell wrote later. "I'd like to say something about him. Don Hutson was the greatest player in the history of football."[3]

Isbell said in older age that he and Hutson would have been an unreal passing-game combination when it became common for NFL quarterbacks to throw more than 30 times a game. He could only imagine the damage they could have done.

> If I got the ball close to him, he never missed the catch, whether it was high or low. He never gave a damn about the pressure of running into the middle on those button hooks, although usually he was running down-and-out patterns. He had finesse. He could freeze a defensive back better than anybody I've seen. He'd come out of there slow, head down, watching their feet. Once he saw that defensive back make a move with his feet he'd "bob" him, get him off balance, make the cut and be off to the races. He had triple speed. The man could do the most amazing things.[4]

Things were going pretty smoothly in Green Bay-land with the Packers' record at 3–1. Then they ran up against the Detroit Lions. Just when fans were getting truly excited about the Pack again, they were let down. Nearly 22,000 showed up at City Stadium and saw the Lions' defense control the day. The final was 17–7 Detroit, though Isbell had another touchdown pass, this one covering 12 yards to Carl Mulleneaux.

It was another crossroads for the Packers. Five weeks in, the season could go either way. The Packers could prove they were as good as

Caught by Don Hutson!

people thought they could be, or they could fizzle and falter. There were six regular-season games remaining.

On October 16, Green Bay dismantled the Brooklyn Dodgers, 35–7, and the way the offense operated provided a feel-good boost. Five different Packers scored touchdowns in a true share-the-wealth day. Not only did Hutson and Isbell work well enough together for a 33-yard touchdown pass, but Hutson kicked an extra point on rookie Andy Uram's 18-yard rushing TD. Uram had been taken in the sixth round of the draft, well after Isbell, and played six seasons with the Packers.

Hinkle had an active day with a touchdown and three extra points. Isbell tossed another touchdown, 11 yards to Joe Laws. Monnett also threw a touchdown pass. Herber was absent from the scoring summary, but the team got what it needed.

That triggered a five-game winning streak with hardly any close contests, as the Packers took command of the West. They got past their early malaise to follow up the Brooklyn triumph with wins over Pittsburgh, 20–0, the Cleveland Rams for a second time, 28–7, and the Chicago Bears, 24–17, adding in revenge over the Lions, 28–7. The Packers' defense mostly ruled, pitching one shutout and, counting the Brooklyn game, with three other showings in which it allowed just a single touchdown.

Besides the shutout, a highlight of the Pirates win was Isbell scoring on a 38-yard run. He had not shown off his wheels much yet in the pros, something he was adept at doing at Purdue. Laws also scored, but on a 38-yard interception, a reminder of how in those days the same players scored on offense and defense.

The Packers defeated the Rams even more resoundingly the second time, and Don Hutson was far and away the star of the show, dazzling with his breaks into the clear, glue-like hands, and fancy moves. He caught three more touchdown passes, of 53, 31 and 50 yards, unheard-of production in those days. Interestingly, he caught the longest one from Isbell and the other two from Monnett. Hinkle also caught a 15-yarder from Monnett that day, giving the ostensible third-string quarterback a three-TD game.

Green Bay's victory over the Bears was the closest during that skein, but likely the most satisfying, because, simply, it came over the Bears. Hutson gathered in another touchdown, also from Monnett, this one from 20 yards out. Hinkle contributed a touchdown and a field goal. The Packers went up, 14–10, in the first quarter, and it was 21–17

14. Close to Winning It All Again

at halftime. The Bears were blanked in the second half, and the Packers added only a field goal, but they maintained their margin.

If the Bears victory did not provide the most pleasure, the rematch against the Lions on November 13 might have. Playing before 45,139 fans at Briggs Stadium, home of the Detroit Tigers baseball club, Green Bay moved its record to 8–2 and sealed its claim as the best squad in the West. It was 0–0 after one quarter, but the Packers pushed ahead 14–0 on two touchdowns by Clarke Hinkle. The first six-pointer came on a 14-yard toss from Isbell. Isbell scored himself later on a 23-yard run—and Hutson kicked the extra point. The final touchdown was provided by Andy Uram on a 70-yard interception.

That left just one regular-season game. It was a cross-division match with the New York Giants in front of 48,279 fans in the Polo Grounds. The New York defense smothered the Packers' offense, and the Giants managed their 15–3 margin for the win, stifling Green Bay's winning streak, on a 75-yard run by Tuffy Leemans and a 50-yard interception grabbed by eventual Hall of Famer Mel Hein.

Green Bay completed the campaign with an 8–3 record, and New York was 7–2, but the season was not quite complete. The Giants had two games to play, and they won one and tied one. That was good enough to put them at 8–2–1, better than the East's second-best team, the Washington Redskins, who went 6–3–2. The Packers were one game better in the West standings than 7–4 Detroit.

That set the Packers and Giants up for a rematch on December 11 in New York, with the NFL crown at stake. They were back at the Polo Grounds, and the attendance of 48,120 was a league playoff record at the time.

The Packers had enough experience splitting games during regular seasons to realize that just because the Giants had edged them the first time, they still had a very respectable chance in the big game. The Packers were right where Lambeau counted on them being—with a shot at another title.

This game was a much more entertaining war than the regular-season encounter. The Giants got off to the better start with Ward Cuff kicking a 14-yard field goal and Tuffy Leemans scoring on a 6-yard rush for a 9–0 first-quarter lead. The weather, at 31 degrees with an 8 mph hint of wind, was not ideal for passing, and the Giants' defense was geared to halting the Green Bay throwing game. The Packers had to give it a try anyway, and lo-and-behold, the early star was nearly forgotten

Caught by Don Hutson!

quarterback Arnie Herber unleashing a 40-yard touchdown throw to Carl Mulleneaux in the second period. The Giants argued back with their own touchdown throw, and the Packers rallied to within 16–14 at halftime when Hinkle scored on a short run.

In the third quarter, Tiny Engebretsen booted a 15-yard field goal for a 17–16 Green Bay lead. It did not stand up. Hank Soar caught a 23-yard pass from Ed Danowski to win the game. Soar later became a well-known Major League Baseball umpire. The score was 23–17 after the extra point, leaving the Packers with an entire quarter to catch up.

They could not do it. Lambeau relied more on Herber than Isbell to try to pull things out. Isbell led one series in the fourth period, but Herber was pitching before and after him. The Giants' defense was stellar, but Herber did have the Packers threatening as the game clock ran out. For their last try, the Packers got the ball on their own 20-yard line. Herber faded back, wanted to throw, but was pressured into running. The play turned into a 16-yard gain for Green Bay. From their own 36, the Packers went for an offbeat, tricky play. Herber completed a pass to Mulleneaux, who gained 14 yards and then tossed a lateral to the trailing Hutson, who was brought down on the New York 40. Time was ticking off fast when Herber got the ball, but he was quickly under siege by the New York defenders. As he was heavily rushed, Herber threw downfield incomplete.

That's how the game ended—and the season. There was little mystery about how the Giants did it. They allowed just 79 points all year in 12 games. The Packers came close but could not defend the title Curly Lambeau so strongly felt his team deserved.

15

1939—Another Crown

Although it seemed that the great phase-out of Arnie Herber had begun in 1938 with the arrival of Cecil Isbell and the continuing, looming, valuable presence of Bob Monnett, by the start of the next season it was Monnett who was an ex–Green Bay Packer. Herber was still around and actually threw more passes during the 1939 season than Isbell.

Herber was 57 for 139 for 1,107 yards and eight touchdowns. Isbell was 43 for 103 for 749 yards and six touchdowns. Neither man could go wrong by heaving the ball to Don Hutson. Hutson made 34 receptions for 846 yards and six touchdowns. Carl Mulleneaux's 12 catches were second-best on the team. Hutson led the National Football League in catches, yards gained on passes, and with a stupendous 24.9 yards-per-catch average.

This was a season when the Packers' defense was as nasty as they come, with results showing one shutout and three other games with no more than a single touchdown allowed.

The season began well enough with a rugged home game against the Chicago Cardinals. Green Bay won, 14–10, with all 14 points coming in the second quarter. Mulleneaux grabbed a 26-yard pass from Herber for the first score, and nearly 12,000 Packers fans watched Chicago's offense stifled. A week later, the Packers downed the other Chicago team, the Bears, 21–16, with more than 19,000 Green Bay supporters watching another tense game. Isbell scored on an 11-yard run, and Clarke Hinkle, the veteran back, kept producing, adding another TD. The passing game was controlled by the Cardinals, who held the Packers to 90 yards through the air. These games were close enough that the Packers could have lost either one, but instead sported a 2–0 start.

The offense got going the next week, October 1, with Herber running for a TD, Hutson kicking an extra point, and Hinkle scoring on a field goal. But unlike in recent years when the Packers held sway over

Caught by Don Hutson!

the Cleveland Rams, this time the Rams gained revenge with a 27–24 victory.

So it was a somewhat shaky 2–1 record the Packers brought in against the Cardinals in a rematch that seemed too soon after the previous meeting. When it came to his big-play status, Hutson had been quiet these few weeks into the season, but he startled the Cardinals in the first quarter, and the rest of the league, when he caught a 92-yard touchdown pass from Herber, one of his two TD grabs in the game.

It was an electrifying play, but it was needed because although the Cardinals were under .500, they played the Packers to a near-standstill before falling, 27–20. Hutson scored on another touchdown pass later in the game, also thrown by Herber. Andy Uram actually topped Hutson by scoring on a 97-yard run. Old reliable Hinkle added a six-pointer that was much shorter, from one yard. Sportswriters did not enter locker rooms for player interviews in those days and rarely even interviewed coaches in the immediate aftermath of a game. Mostly, they wrote game play-by-play that fans in the house had seen with their own eyes. The writers were the first line of information for others, and their analysis came from within, from their own typewriters, not from the mouths of the participants.

Hutson was a beloved player in Green Bay and a man about town, but he was not a showman, not someone who gave glorious accounts of the games to writers, who did not realize how lucky they had it when Johnny Blood was around making news. Or maybe they did.

"He wouldn't say two words in an A-bomb attack," Hutson's mother, Mabel Hutson, said much later. "Don just doesn't talk unless he has something important to say."[1] That apparently did not include talking about his own football exploits as an active player, although he occasionally indulged after retirement.

Always-tough Detroit was next on October 22 after a bye week, and the Lions were 4–0. This was a good yardstick to see if the Packers were for real. They aced the test, belting the Lions, 26–7. The aerial game was cooking. Herber hurled two touchdown passes and Isbell one. The Packers took over the game in the second period with 17 points. Uram caught a TD toss from Herber, and so did Hutson, Hutson's a back-breaking 60-yarder. In the fourth quarter, with the Packers pulling away, Hutson hauled in a 51-yard pass for a score from Isbell. Hutson was an equal opportunity quarterback employer. The last scoring was of the insult

15. 1939—Another Crown

variety, Mulleneaux blocking a Detroit pass out of the end zone for a safety.

The following contest, on October 29, was a statement game. The Washington Redskins had emerged as a steady power in the East, and they brought a 4–0–1 record to Wisconsin State Fair Park. They provoked enough excitement for more than 24,000 fans to turn out to check them out. This was a pretty good struggle. Hinkle put the Packers on the board first with a 2-yard run. Isbell threw a 9-yarder to Hank Bruder for the only score through the air (Hutson was silent this game), and Joe Laws helped out on the ground. Green Bay prevailed, 24–14, capturing the win but not establishing clear supremacy.

There was no reason to believe the November 5 game, a rematch with the Bears before 40,537 fans at Wrigley Field, would be easy. In fact, there did not seem to be many breathers on the schedule in 1939. These were the new-look Bears. George Halas had found his dream quarterback and signed Sid Luckman out of Columbia University, and the Bears moved to the T-formation style of offense. Luckman was a rookie and being eased into action slowly throughout the season. Soon enough, he emerged as a future Hall of Famer and one of the finest quarterbacks of the era, if not the best, alongside Sammy Baugh.

This game was full of drama and big plays. The Packers came out of the first quarter ahead 13–7, a 72-yard punt return for a TD by Joe Laws the highlight. But Isbell also hit Milt Gantenbein for a 32-yard touchdown. A Luckman touchdown throw gave the Bears the lead in the second period, but the Packers led at halftime, 20–17, after Isbell fired another touchdown pass of 29 yards to Ed Jankowski. The second half was lower-scoring, but with lead swings. Herber and Hutson, working together as they often had, combined on a 20-yard touchdown. But the Bears scored last in the fourth period on a three-yard Bill Osmanski rush for a 30–27 Chicago win. That pulled the Bears to within a half-game of the Packers in the standings, so there was considerable remaining regular-season suspense.

For the Packers, it seemed almost every opponent on the schedule was good, or at least a threat. An exception was the Philadelphia Eagles. The Eagles were 0–5–1 entering the November 12 game at Philadelphia Municipal Stadium that attracted 23,832 fans. The Eagles didn't know they were supposed to roll over, though, and battled throughout before Green Bay edged the hosts, 23–16. It was closer than that until Tiny Engebretsen kicked a 27-yard, fourth-quarter field goal. Uram caught a

Caught by Don Hutson!

touchdown throw from Isbell, and Hinkle scored on the ground. It was a survival victory rather than a beauty pageant victory. It wasn't a clunker, and it went into the W column, as it was supposed to do.

The season was about two months old and heading into the homestretch, but it was being played out against a background of international angst. It would be incorrect to suggest that the people of Green Bay cared more about what was happening in Europe, or fans of other NFL contenders were focused beyond their home stadiums in the fall of 1939. But among government officials, military experts, wise academics, and nervous followers of foreign affairs, the September 1 invasion of Poland by Germany with 1.5-million troops and ceaseless bombing from the air was not easily dismissed. Poland's defenses crumbled quickly, and Germany partitioned Polish territory with the Soviet Union. Germany had spent years beefing up its Army and its military equipment, and Poland was saddled with outdated equipment. France and Great Britain declared war on Germany within a day.

Across the United States, many wanted to stay clear of European politics, and where the memory of World War I, which had only ended in 1918, lingered strongly, the prevailing sentiment seemed to be mind-your-own-business isolationism. President Franklin D. Roosevelt felt the U.S. was not yet prepared for a world war, and there was significant political opposition to embroiling the country in the conflict at the time. Believing in the inevitability of American involvement, FDR did order a rapid build-up of military might.

Soon enough, the evil and expansionist tendencies and determinations of Nazi Germany, directed by Adolf Hitler, in conjunction with forces from Italy and especially Japan in the South Pacific, would become the paramount issue across the world and ignite unimaginable havoc and conflagration. Soon enough, there would be no ignoring war raging in ever-more places. Respite through this 1939 season was still in place, where the main form of American combat took place on the gridiron. But not for long.

For the time being, the games could still be enjoyed in the big cities of the NFL and in comparatively tiny Green Bay. On November 19, at Ebbets Field, nearly 20,000 fans observed the Packers dismantle their Brooklyn Dodgers, 28–0, a dominating result that gave the Packers a 7–2 record and helped propel them to the Western Division championship. Green Bay scored regularly through the first three periods, starting with a shake-'em-up big play by the old Herber-to-Hutson act to

15. 1939—Another Crown

first illuminate the scoreboard. This time the pass covered 69 yards for a touchdown. Bud Svenson rumbled with a fumble for 37 yards for a TD, and Isbell completed a 19-yard touchdown pass to Harry Jacunski, scored on a 1-yard run and then kicked an extra point as if he was determined to win a punt, pass, and kick contest.

The next game was an intriguing challenge, to make a point. After losing to the Cleveland Rams, the Packers wanted to balance the ledger in the return game on November 26.

As an example of how thoroughly Hutson ruled the receiver lists, he had only been playing for a few seasons when he established a new career yardage record for gains on pass receptions, and he set a new season mark well before the season ended. Modern-era football fans might laugh at the totals, but this merely illustrates how far ahead of his time Hutson was and how little the forward pass had been previously used in the NFL. Going into the Rams game, Hutson had accumulated 794 yards receiving for the season and 2,838 as a career total.

The Rams had previously been horrible, but in 1939 brought a .500 record into this late-season encounter. Green Bay could still win a championship, with or without a win, but the Packers wanted to take care of this unfinished business. Cleveland sports fans were interested in what might happen and turned out 30,691 strong at Municipal Stadium. The game was scoreless at halftime, and the Packers were also shut out in the third period. Cleveland's Jim Benton scored on an 18-yard touchdown pass, but the Rams did not make the extra point. Still, it was 6–0, a frustrating score for several reasons to the Packers. It was not until the fourth period that the Packers breached the Cleveland end zone. Isbell heaved an 18-yard strike to Joe Laws for a score, and when Tiny Engebretsen boomed the extra point, Green Bay owned a 7–6 lead.

That was where the scoring stopped. It was a "whew" for the Packers. The result was described this way in one Green Bay newspaper: "The Green Bay Packers raced the Cleveland Rams to the tape in a photo finish football fracas. It was just as close as it sounds."[2]

Green Bay should have won by a larger margin after outgaining the Rams, 329 to 202. But the Packers committed three turnovers and that hurt. There was an intense race for first place going on in the East between the New York Giants and the Redskins. The Packers were in first in the West, but the Bears were still hovering.

This was an all-around, first-rate Packers team. While the Packers

Caught by Don Hutson!

had reached the title game in 1938, and fell just short in 1937, because the two losses at the start of the regular season and two at the end were costly, this time Curly Lambeau and the players thought they had the goods to go all the way.

"Our '39 bunch was very versatile," Hinkle said.

> We had four good punters in Arnie Herber, Cecil Isbell, Frank Balasz and myself, four placement kickers with Tiny Engebretsen, Don Hutson, Ernie Smith and yours truly. And two of the greatest passers in football history—Cecil Isbell and Arnie Herber. While there were 33 players on the roster, we relied on 16 men who played a lot of the game, 60 minutes each game. These 16 fellows stayed healthy through a tough, 11-game schedule. What contributed to our success? We had an intense desire to get the job done, pride and loyalty to the team and supreme confidence that we could win.[3]

A few years into his NFL career, Don Hutson was not any kind of secret to defenses, which had to game-plan for his skills, though it had taken some of that see-it-with-my-own eyes skepticism out there until individuals played him up close.

"I remember the first time I played against him," said defensive back Dwight Sloan, a three-year NFL competitor who played for the Lions in 1939. "He came out for a pass and I had no trouble keeping up with him. 'This isn't too hard,' I thought to myself, and then I couldn't find him. Suddenly, I looked behind me and he was far up the field taking in the pass. He had shifted into high gear and left me standing there."[4] Sloan had the nickname "Paddlefoot," but it is not certain if he was saddled with the moniker because Hutson burned him.

The Packers and Lions met the last weekend of Green Bay's regular season at Briggs Stadium, and Detroit produced a good crowd of guests with attendance logged at 30,699. It was rainy and wet and the ground was muddy, making the football difficult to grip. The Packers fumbled way too often but retained possession on most of them. It was too late for the Lions to mount a run for the division crown, but any showdown with the Packers was meaningful. It was hard work getting past the Lions this time, but with a field goal, safety, and one touchdown, notched by Hinkle on a 1-yard run, Green Bay won this one, 12–7. Detroit's touchdown was scored by Paddlefoot Sloan himself, on a 15-yard run.

That concluded the regular season and sent the Packers ahead to another NFL title game versus the New York Giants, who finished with a 9–1–1 record, ahead of the breathing-down-their-necks Redskins,

15. 1939—Another Crown

who were 8–2–1. It would be Green Bay against New York on December 10, 1939, at Wisconsin State Fair Park. The Packers had brought the championship game to their home state, and 32,279 responded by buying tickets. The frantic fans wanted to witness the crowning of the objects of their affection in person. They were hungry for a fifth NFL championship.

Early indications were against the Packers prior to the title tilt at Wisconsin State Fair Park. It was noted that practice was so sour an angry coach Lambeau brought the players back for a second run-through later on Wednesday night. Compounding the aggravation surrounding the game, Leland Johannes, president of the Packers Corporation, made a public announcement that some 1,500 bogus tickets for the championship game were circulating, and he warned buyers beware lest they get cheated. The team offered a $250 reward to anyone providing evidence leading to the conviction of anyone who made fake tickets. The message was to avoid buying tickets from strangers and to stick to authorized sales agents.

Excitement pervaded Green Bay, and a day before the scheduled kickoff, a group of 16 businesses purchased a full-page advertisement in the *Green Bay Press-Gazette* to cheer the Packers on. With Christmas about two weeks away, the businessmen adopted a holiday theme for the ad, picturing Santa Claus passing on the appropriate message. "It's in the old sock," the ad read. "Santa Claus, Prophet of Good Times, Forecasts a WORLD CHAMPIONSHIP FOR GREEN BAY'S PACKERS."[5]

Also cited were the years of previous titles won—1929, 1930, 1931, and 1936—and wishes for every Packer to have a Merry Christmas.

Still another advertisement paid for by the same large group of businesses featured a powerful-looking football player with a football tucked in the crook of his right arm. This message read: "ONE MORE GAME. Make It the Best Game You've Ever Played!" The writing continued: "You've written football history again, Packers. You've made Green Bay known and respected in the far corners of the country. You've given us thrillers that will be told and retold when you and we are gone. More than that, you've made Green Bay proud."[6]

The Menominee Sugar Co. of Green Bay proclaimed, "The Packers Are a Sweet Ball Club." This was a double-meaning ad, taking note that Giants coach Steve Owen had labeled the Packers in that manner the year before. The firm promised that the sweet club would "turn out to be a bitter pill" for New York this time around.[7]

Caught by Don Hutson!

While also participating in the group advertising statements, the Gordon Bent Co. took out its own super-confident message: "WORLD CHAMPIONS." The ad included a team photograph of the Packers, beneath which were listed 1929, 1930, 1931 and 1936, signifying past titles earned, but added, "and 1939" in larger type. The icing was a note instructing fans to "Hang This in Your Window Tonight," Saturday evening, December 9, before the game. "It would be conservative to wait until Monday. But it wouldn't be GREEN BAY to wait 'til Monday. Start the celebration tonight! You'll be proud it is there Monday."[8]

The hype was loud in Green Bay, and the Packers took all of those good wishes to heart as 32,279 fans showed up, an impressive total given that Green Bay's total population was about 40,000. Many fans took special trains. The post-game advertising could have read this way: "How Sweet It Is," because the Packers roasted the Giants, overwhelming them in every way.

Final score: 27–0 for Green Bay's fifth championship. A shutout for the defense. A statement for the offense. In 35 rushes, New York gained just 70 yards on the ground. The Giants were just 8-for-25 for 94 yards through the air. New York threw six interceptions. The *Press-Gazette* did not call it gloating, but the game report did gush over the all-around effort by the home team, and the headline in part read, "Play Magnificent Football...."[9] A sports columnist may have sounded as if he was exaggerating, but the statistics did not lie. He wrote, "Only out of politeness to the visiting Giants could it be said that they were in the ball game. They were out-thought, out-rushed, out-passed, out-run, out-fought and completely out-played from start to finish."[10]

The Packers scored once in the first quarter and kept the lead before adding 10 points in each of the last two quarters. Hutson did not score, but Herber and Isbell each threw a touchdown pass to other guys. Milt Gantenbein caught a 7-yarder from Herber, and Joe Laws collected a 31-yarder from Isbell.

When the team reached Green Bay by train after capturing its fifth championship between 1929 and 1939, thousands of fans fought their way to the station to fete them. Only a few days later, some 1,500 people bought tickets to a victory banquet to continue the celebration. Organized by the Lions Club and held at the Columbus Club, the party included the issuing of an official invitation from *Chicago Tribune* sports editor Arch Ward for the Packers to compete in the next charity game against the College All-Stars.

15. 1939—Another Crown

The ceremonies, the festivities lasted four hours. Carl Mulleneaux said aloud that the banquet was such a great show it made him want to win the title every year. The loudest ovations were accorded to Clark Hinkle, the long-standing star, and to Don Hutson, in recognition of his greatness.

A look at an old-style sign advertising Lambeau Field, home of the Packers, in Green Bay (author photo).

16

The Biggest Little Town

Even by 1940 standards, Green Bay was a marvel compared to other cities fielding professional sports teams across North America. This was an era prior to organized professional basketball the way we know it with the NBA, but the city in northern Wisconsin differed in many ways from the other big towns of the NFL and the home cities of Major League Baseball.

Two decades into its run as the pro football league, the NFL had shaken loose the former small-town clubs that had populated its ranks, such as Portsmouth, Canton, and so many others, leaving the landscape dotted by the Chicagos, New Yorks, and Philadelphias. The same had long been true in big-league baseball. Even in the six-team National Hockey League, the teams represented New York, Boston, Detroit, and Chicago in the United States and only Montreal and Toronto in Canada, the teams classified as "The Original Six."

Green Bay, with its population of 45,000 by 1940, was an anomaly. Green Bay, with its fans owning stock in the team, was different from all other operations. Yet Green Bay owned five world championships. Green Bay practically busted its buttons with pride over the success of its home team. The players were treated as gods, and while there were great expectations, built up by team founder and coach Curly Lambeau, his were no less than the fans'. He wanted them to expect titles, and he expected titles. Whether they cared more about their team than supporters did in other communities might be difficult to measure, but it felt as if they did. There were so many other things to do in those metropolitan areas and prominent college towns. They had theater, museums, and art galleries beyond following the fortunes of sports teams. In Green Bay, from the start, in 1940, and even now, another 80-plus years later, the Packers were kings.

It would have been one thing to note the differences, but the

16. The Biggest Little Town

success, winning all those titles, magnified them more so. It was as if the place was a Shangri-La for football, a magical kingdom. Five championships in a decade. How did they do it? Even during an era when the media did not include the Internet or national television, and newspapers and radio were the main media to spread the sports news, those who kept track of the doings in the sport wanted to know more about the little city that was not a travel crossroads and its special relationship with its pro football team.

The *Saturday Evening Post*, a magazine that was a significant player on the national print scene, ventured north to try to get at the root of why the Green Bay Packers were so consistently good and why Green Bay was so enamored of them. Appropriately enough for the locale that would much later give the National Football League "The Ice Bowl" and routinely have its turf described as "the frozen tundra," when the magazine writer showed up, he was caught in a November blizzard. Happy Thanksgiving! That was the first lesson. Winter came to Green Bay earlier than it typically did to other clubs in the league.

The author noted that "jubilant children" listened to the no-school announcement on the radio station provided by St. Norbert College and "huge plows fought a losing battle to keep the streets open."[1] That was clearly a familiar scenario to many a visitor to Green Bay when the dead of winter sneaked in before it was proclaimed on the calendar.

A brisk business in ticket sales proceeded, advance requests being firecracker hot for the Bears game and the Lions game, the chief Western rivals, but not bad, either, for the other contests to be played in Wisconsin. The banter was such that the Bears would be very tough, but Lambeau's men could take them if it didn't rain and the ball stayed dry for quarterback Cecil Isbell's throws. Snow was left out of the conversational equation. Despite a heavy storm raging, no one seemed to take particular note. They were used to snowfall in northern Wisconsin, and the people never tired of discussing the Packers' chances to win.

The visiting writer did quickly conclude that everyone "feels he has a voice in the management." That included Mayor Alex Biemeret, but no more so than the traffic cop on the corner or those in other positions who had not been elected. In a rather humorous observation, the writer noted a traveling salesman who showed up in a store at an inopportune time—when those present were arguing the status of the team. He could not get a chance to endorse his product, and he made the faux pas of indicating that he knew nothing about any Packers. The owner replied,

Caught by Don Hutson!

"Never mind coming back. If you've never hard of the Packers, I've never heard of your company."[2]

So it goes. The uninitiated must tread lightly in Green Bay (even now), lest he deliver what is the equal of an insult to someone's fair-haired child.

The Packers overcame financial troubles competing against the big, bad opponents, restructured their stock plans, and that only rekindled and deepened faith in the squad. Proving his allegiance during a trying time, Eric Karl, a musician from Milwaukee who was a true blue fan, wrote a song of encouragement for the Packers.

It went like this:

> "Go you Packers, go and get 'em;
> Go, you fighting fools, upset 'em;
> Smash that line with all your might,
> A touchdown, Packers, fight, fight, fight.
> Fight on, you green and gold, to glory;
> Win this game, the same old story;
> Fight you Packers, fight,
> And bring the bacon home to old Green Bay."[3]

As great American classics go, it does not rank up there with "White Christmas" or "God Bless America," but Packers fans may look at that differently in their personal rankings.

It should be noted that while Green Bay held tenaciously to the Packers in general, the Packers were truly all of Wisconsin's team. For decades, the Packers played some home games in Milwaukee, the state's largest city, though that largesse eventually ran its course, and after that, if anyone wanted to see a Packers home game, he had to travel to Green Bay. Still, for some time, the wealth was shared.

Lambeau had the skill to replenish rosters as they aged. The magazine story listed some of the successes of Lambeau's good eye but gave the highest praise to his capture of Hutson. "Hutson, of course, was the prize catch of them all," the story continued. "He has been ranked with the great offensive ends of all time." That was just before the title was granted Hutson by acclamation—THE greatest. "No one has ever set a defense that can stop him," said New York Giants star Mel Hein. "When you play Green Bay, you have to play them with 10 men because two of your players have to devote their entire attention to Hutson."[4]

Hutson got his catches and he got his points, but there were many times during the course of games when defenders were draped on him

16. The Biggest Little Town

that did leave teammates open for the tosses of Arnie Herber or Cecil Isbell. That was how Green Bay scored its first touchdown in the 1939 championship victory over the New York Giants. Hutson was surrounded by a gang of defenders, and Milt Gantenbein was the lonesome end who scored. In fact, during that decisive title game, the Packers only threw once to Hutson. They were proving Hein's adage, and the Giants could not beat the Packers that way.

Those inside the game and those who followed the game realized Don Hutson's value, even when he wasn't running up numbers. Still, by 1940, he was a full-fledged star, and his name was increasingly mentioned in connection with statistics that proved the point. That season, scoring seven touchdowns and kicking 15 extra points, Hutson led the NFL in scoring—by one point over Cleveland Rams back Johnny Drake. Before the end of September that year, Hutson had reeled in his 38th career touchdown pass. That set a new league record, surpassing Johnny Blood by one. These were the embryonic days of growing reliance on the pass, and Hutson was out front in establishing it so it would never be in the shadows again.

Lambeau was very much a key figure in this growth of the pass, and his scouring the marketplace to bring in first Herber, and then Isbell, was a demonstration that teams would be left behind if they didn't join in. The sight of Hutson dashing behind defensive backs and disappearing over the horizon with the ball illustrated what would happen if teams did not respond.

Some did in a big way. There were now more good quarterbacks in the league. It was indisputable that the Washington Redskins' Sammy Baugh and the Chicago Bears' Sid Luckman had become the two best passers. They built on what the Packers had accomplished, although neither of them had as a reliable a man as Hutson to catch the ball, or who was as much of a game-breaker.

Baugh was a Texan who not only seemed like a transplanted cowboy in the nation's capital, he was. He was a rancher who had dabbled in rodeo, and though his first love was baseball, he blossomed into a superstar in football after excelling at Texas Christian University. In accordance with the times, he played both offense and defense, and he was a finer defensive back than most of his dual-position contemporaries. Furthermore, Baugh was a triple threat, the best punter in the league. During the course of his NFL career, he was voted an all-star as a quarterback, defender, and punter.

Caught by Don Hutson!

As a passer, Baugh came on strong fast. He led the NFL in completions and yards gained as a rookie in 1937 and led the league five times in all in completions, four times in yards, and twice in touchdown passes. Tellingly, he topped the league in accuracy eight times, bringing an unheard-of measure of precision. Whereas Herber had completed just over 40 percent of his passes at times, Baugh hit 70 percent one season, one season was over 62 percent, and routinely completed 55 percent or more of his throws.

Baugh delivered the ball where he aimed, and on his watch the Redskins became champions and repeat title contenders. He played hardball over salary with owner George Preston Marshall, and unlike most of his teammates, he won in negotiations. Marshall understood how important Baugh was to the team. The Redskins won the crown in 1937 and again in 1945, and three other times with Baugh reached the championship game.

Baugh became so famous, Hollywood cast him in movie Westerns. Hutson much more so had the looks of a leading man, though there were no reports of movieland seeking him out. Baugh acted for the money, not the pleasure of it, and for a guy who even hated leaving his ranch in the off-season, likely participated only because the flicks were Westerns. "Hell, I'm a football player," he growled.[5]

So was Luckman, though he didn't plan to be. When he completed his Ivy League education at Columbia, he wanted to enter the business world. George Halas wanted Luckman's business to be football. Luckman said he didn't want to play. Halas invited himself to dinner with Luckman and his new bride and talked him into it. Halas read the future and saw that Luckman was the missing piece for his otherwise loaded team. Luckman was a rookie in 1939, retiring in 1950, and like Baugh ended up in the Pro Football Hall of Fame. He led the NFL in accuracy once, touchdown passes three times, and yards gained three times. With him at quarterback, the Bears won four championships.

Luckman basically learned the T-formation on the job during his first two seasons with the Bears, so he did not make as immediate an impact as Baugh did with the Redskins. But then he got rolling. One season Luckman hurled 28 touchdown passes. Previously, Baugh had hit for 25 in a year. Those numbers far exceeded anything seen in the 1920s and the early 1930s.

During one of his sprees, Luckman set the NFL record for most touchdown passes in a game with seven. That mark has been tied several

16. The Biggest Little Town

times, but remains the league standard after decades. Luckman was at the helm when the Bears won the most decisive victory in NFL history. The stunning, humiliating shutout of the Redskins in the 1940 title game came by the score of 73–0. There has never been anything like it before or since in an NFL contest.

The Redskins had defeated Chicago in a low-scoring, close game a couple of weeks prior to the title game at Griffith Stadium in Washington, D.C., and Marshall, the Redskins' owner, rubbed it in. Halas, the master strategist, may have coined the term billboard material, posting newspaper stories contained Marshall's belittling remarks. The all-time worst drubbing followed, the Bears leading 28–0 at halftime and 54–0 after the third quarter. Officials were even running out of footballs for extra points as the game neared its end.

As the new decade dawned, the Packers were the reigning champions, and they may have owned the best pass receiver in the world, but Baugh and Luckman showed that Green Bay no longer had the NFL monopoly on star quarterbacks.

That did nothing to diminish Green Bay's ardor for its Packers, nor cap expectations. Packers fans never quite came down from the giddiness of winning that fifth world title, and with big names back they clearly believed Green Bay would defend the honor of the small community and win a sixth pro championship.

Were the fans spoiled? Delusional? It was sometime later, in 1961, when Green Bay businessmen gave the place the self-proclaimed "Titletown, USA" nickname, but residents believed it from roughly 1929, and thought it applied, informally, from then on.

As a team that only a few seasons earlier had won three crowns in a row, and quickly rebuilding on the backs of Hutson, Herber, and Isbell, the Packers had fooled their fans into believing they could win it all every year.

17

Trying to Repeat

Pro football was better than ever by 1940 with the influx of such new all-time talents as Sammy Baugh and Sid Luckman, but the world at large was going to hell. Outside of the United States, there was no time for sport, only survival. There were no Olympic Games conducted under the guise of sportsmanship. Numerous countries were fighting for survival under the onslaught of Germany and Japan, with assistance from Italy.

World events seemed certain to overtake daily life in the U.S., but the question was when. In the meantime, the watchword was to play on and hope for as much normalcy as possible. The English people did likewise, although under much more trying circumstances after the Battle of Britain began in July and German planes blitzed London and elsewhere in the country almost ceaselessly.

The finest oratory of the time was delivered by Winston Churchill, who became prime minister of the United Kingdom in May of 1940, not Curly Lambeau, football coach, during a halftime pep talk on what it would take to come back against George Halas' Bears. On May 13, when Churchill first convened his cabinet, he said, "I have nothing to offer, but blood, toil, tears and sweat."[1] Many a football coach has asked for the same from his team, though never was the occasion as critical as in wartime. Mostly, Churchill recognized he had mere words to offer for inspiration because he could not fly the planes in defense of the homeland any more than the coach could take the field to repel an opposition squad short of the goal line.

Only weeks later, on June 4, addressing the House of Commons, after the rousingly successful evacuation at Dunkirk, which Churchill called "a miracle of deliverance," he once again employed words as weapons. He spoke of facing the enemy against the bleakest of odds and never giving up. Churchill said, "We shall fight on the seas and oceans.

17. Trying to Repeat

We shall fight with growing confidence and growing strength in the air. We shall defend our island, whatever the cost may be. We shall fight on the beaches. We shall fight on the landing grounds. We shall fight in the field and in the streets. We shall fight in the hills. We shall never surrender."[2]

By then, the United Kingdom had been rationing food for months. Japan had sent 10,000 more troops to China. Finland had at first repelled Russian tanks. Germany began preparations to invade Denmark and Norway. Then Germany invaded Belgium, France, Luxembourg, and the Netherlands. By June, Germany was bombing Paris. Russia took over the Baltic States. General Charles de Gaulle formed a free French government in exile. In September, one of Adolf Hitler's motivational sub-plots became clearer to the world. German Jews were ordered to wear yellow stars on their clothing in public so they could be singled out and identified. The full extent of the Holocaust, as his attempt to exterminate Jews would be called, was not known to the world until it had claimed some six million lives.

The war was spreading everywhere as the National Football League began a new season in the fall of 1940, the Green Bay Packers in defense of a sporting title, while so many countries were defending their way of life. While he knew the inevitability of American involvement loomed, Franklin D. Roosevelt kept trying to buy time to speed up the manufacture of weapons and equipment. This occurred even as Roosevelt's second term as president was expiring and he had to battle for re-election and an unprecedented third term. The Democrats renominated FDR at their convention in Chicago.

Roosevelt did not think the United States was ready to take on a powerful enemy yet. Hitler was focused on devastating Europe, and Japan was focused on Asia. But on May 26, in one of Roosevelt's Fireside Chats broadcast on radio, he referred to "this moment of sadness throughout the world ... we are shocked by the incredible eyewitness stories that come to us."[3] Stories from other nations told of the horrors inflicted on civilian populations.

In Green Bay's tiny corner of the world and in the United States, the main area of concern as a new school calendar began was the fortunes of the Packers. The town was still on a high coming off the 1939 world championship, and no one cared to hear any malarkey about how difficult it might be to repeat. After all, the Packers had only recently won titles three years in a row. But sports teams are never static, even if

Caught by Don Hutson!

the roster appears to be much the same from one year to the next. Injuries are different, skills erode at different paces, and the weather on any given Sunday is different from what it was the last time you played that team. Heck, that team's personnel, or coaching, or both, are different.

Rebuilding is an art form, a talent some coaches possess and others don't. There is also the matter of luck from one season to the next. It was not as if the Packers were short on many of the staple players who enjoyed the victory banquet. Don Hutson was still present and accounted for, along with Arnie Herber, Cecil Isbell, Clarke Hinkle, Tiny Engebretsen, Buckets Goldenberg, Milt Gantenbein and others of the old gang. Some recent additions who played key roles, like Andy Uram, Joe Laws, Carl Mulleneaux, and Ed Jankowski, were back as well. Beattie Feathers, a transfer from the Bears who had established that the 1,000-yard marker was no longer inviolate for runners, was now a member of the Pack, though he never approached his breakthrough campaign.

A decent number of those fellows were 30 or older, which may have led to suspicions about how much quality time they had left in the game. But there were more questions about Herber than anyone else. Herber turned 30 in the off-season. He once had been Curly Lambeau's shining star, the personification of the coach's love affair with the forward pass, but 10 years into his career, Lambeau more than ever seemed to trust Herber less and count on Isbell more. The pro sports cliché has long been, "What have you done for me lately?" But the real meaning is, "What can you do for me today? What can you do for me right now?"

In Lambeau's mind, those theoretically rhetorical questions were very real. When applied to Herber, they came across as: Not much. Not now. Or at least definitely not as much as he used to. This was Herber's last season with the Packers. Undoubtedly, he and Lambeau believed it was going to be his final year in pro football, too, though that turned out not to be the case. A later chapter in Herber's career provided a twist and a surprise. But in 1940 he was still somewhat in the mix as a regular, alongside Isbell, as they had dueled for a few years now, with a young Hal Van Every, just 22, thrown into the fray periodically. Herber completed 38 of 89 passes (just 42.7 percent) for 560 yards and six touchdowns that season. Isbell was 68 for 150 for 1,037 yards (45.3 percent) and eight touchdowns. Van Every was far less active but did throw four touchdown passes.

17. Trying to Repeat

Herber was as popular as any athlete in Green Bay. He was homegrown, played high school ball there and spent some of his college days suiting up for the University of Wisconsin, as well as the last decade in the Packers lineup. Going back to the beginning, when Lambeau was wooing Hutson, one selling point he wielded was that Herber, a first-class quarterback, was in the fold. "I remember Curly Lambeau telling me over the phone that Green Bay had the best long passer in pro football," Hutson said.[4]

As in any reliable quarterback-receiver combination, Herber and Hutson could read one another's thinking when the action swirled around them. They developed a telepathy and a rhythm. Hutson had fabulous instincts that allowed him to break free from coverage, and Herber got used to what Hutson brought to the offense and how he maneuvered around those defenses in a way no pass catcher had done. It was Hutson's job to get free downfield, and it was Herber's (and Isbell's) job to find him with the football. They found him often enough. Hutson caught 45 passes during the 1940 season. Ironically, and as evidence that some other members of the league were catching up in the passing game, he did not lead the NFL in receptions that season after doing so the year before with 34.

The Packers experienced a couple of especially satisfying moments leading up to the regular season. One came early. As the defending NFL champion, the Packers faced the College All-Stars in the annual charity game. In 1937, they had not acquitted themselves well, losing by a shutout. This time the Packers won, 45–28, against the collection of young talent.

Much later, and in a surprising answer to a question posed by a sportswriter, Curly Lambeau announced that this exhibition win was one of the most significant of his long coaching career.

> The most satisfying game we ever won was the All-Star game of 1940. Maybe this sounds funny for me to say, but I believe pro football, all of pro football, turned the corner in that game. You see, pro football had not yet caught on all over the country. There were a lot of detractors, especially among college people. They called the pros lazy and uninspired. There were even some, including a few good college coaches, who kept insisting that a well-coached college team could beat a pro team any day.[5]

It was the early days of the All-Star game. The college grads had won twice with three ties, and the NFL had won twice. After this Packers win, the pros won almost all of the time.

Caught by Don Hutson!

That game took place August 29, and a few days later the Packers polished off the Washington Redskins, 28–20, in a league exhibition. Hutson never failed to astonish with critical touchdown grabs, one reporter noting, "The mystifying Hutson again stole the show. With burning speed to elude defensive men, and with glue on his fingertips to catch passes which just seemed couldn't be caught, he gave the fans a thrill almost every minute of the short time he played."[6]

One of those highlights was a 65-yard pass from Isbell, which was slightly overthrown. Hutson lunged, half-falling, juggled the ball, and cradled it into his arms as he hit the ground. It certainly seemed as if the Packers were ready for the season.

The new season opened for the Packers on September 15 against the Philadelphia Eagles. The Eagles, who came into the league in 1933, were in the midst of one of the worst stretches in franchise history. The year before, they finished 1–9–1, and 1940 did not promise to be much better (nor was it, with Philadelphia ending up 1–10). But this was hardly a pattycake game. Perhaps the defending champion Packers took the Eagles lightly.

Philadelphia was coached by Bert Bell, who later became NFL commissioner. The Eagles played hard and rallied late, but the Packers pulled out the game, 27–20, at City Stadium. Some 11,657 fans paid their way in to celebrate a new football season. Although it happened in haphazard fashion, by the time the points were totaled, most of Green Bay's key offensive individuals figured in the scoring.

Isbell scored the team's first touchdown of the season on a 39-yard run, and Hutson, who took on more of such duties that year, kicked the extra point. The second Green Bay TD came on a six-yard heave from Isbell to Carl Mulleneaux, with Hutson again kicking the extra point. The Packers ran out to a 21–0 lead in the first period when Mulleneaux caught a second touchdown pass, this one thrown by Herber. And as if Hutson's foot was tired, Lambeau called upon Engebretsen to boot the extra point.

The Eagles did score before the half, but the Packers improved their margin to 27–6 in the third quarter when Hinkle kicked two field goals of 45 yards. Philadelphia made the game seem closer by scoring two touchdowns in the fourth quarter. Philly's Davey O'Brien, who was a star quarterback at Texas Christian University, winning the Heisman Trophy in 1938, but who played just two years in the NFL, threw for 225 yards, but his four interceptions hurt. O'Brien was second-team All-Pro

17. Trying to Repeat

both seasons with the Eagles, then gave up football to become an FBI agent.

If there was any alarm about the Eagles' late comeback, it was muted. After all, the Packers were 1–0. The excitement the following week was generated by the annual visit to Wisconsin by the Bears. Twice as many fans, more than 22,000, turned out at City Stadium for the rivalry match, but left groaning. Chicago overwhelmed the Packers, 41–10. This was not a pretty picture. The Bears thrashed Green Bay from start to finish, running up 27 points in the second half.

The Bears stunned the Packers twice on long kickoffs, embarrassing Green Bay's defense when George McAfee strode 93 yards for one touchdown and Ray Nolting dashed 97 yards for another. McAfee also scored on a 9-yard run and threw an 8-yard touchdown to Ken Kavanaugh. Kavanaugh scored on another TD pass from Bob Snyder (Sid Luckman was still working his way into becoming the No. 1 signal-caller). McAfee, who missed four seasons of play while in the Navy during World War II yet made the Hall of Fame, pretty much had a Hall of Fame game this day. The Bears also plucked seven interceptions, turning the Packers' aerial game into a nightmare.

Happily for the Packers, the next Chicago team they faced was the Cardinals on September 29, and they did unto the Cards what the Bears had done unto them. Green Bay whomped the Cards, 31–6. Isbell was a bigger factor than anyone else, rushing for touchdowns of 39 yards and 1 yard. Hutson grabbed a 35-yard TD pass from Isbell and kicked one extra point on a day when three different Packers kicked one-pointers.

Almost as if nothing had happened against the Bears, the revived Packers romped over the Cleveland Rams, 31–14, on October 13. This was a showcase for the passing game in all its splendor. Green Bay collected 327 yards through the air, Isbell tossed three touchdown passes, and Herber threw one. Hutson notched one of the TDs from Isbell, and Mulleneaux caught the other two. Uram caught the touchdown from Herber. The Packers were 3–1, still in the hunt for the division title in the West.

If the Packers were under the impression that all they had to worry about was to take it to the Bears in a rematch, they were surprised when they ran up against their other rival, the Detroit Lions. Even at home, with 21,001 fans screaming for them, the Packers could not contain the Lions. Detroit won this one, 23–14, and scrambled the standings. Isbell and Herber threw one touchdown pass each, and Hutson kicked

Caught by Don Hutson!

one extra point, but after falling behind briefly in the second quarter, Detroit mostly controlled this one. That left the Packers at 3–2 and the Lions at 3–2–1. The Bears were 4–1. That was a costly loss.

A feel-good opportunity presented itself October 27 at Wisconsin State Fair Park when the Packers faced Pittsburgh. These guys were no longer the Pirates, but the Steelers. The 1940 season was the first one the club played under that nickname, which brought far more glory to the city than the football Pirates. Except for an early field goal, the Packers smothered the Steelers, 24–3. Hutson made an extra-point kick and scored the last touchdown on a 19-yard throw from Van Every in the fourth period, after the result was decided.

The Packers had a chip the size of the Rock of Gibraltar on their shoulders when they embarked for Chicago for a rematch against the Bears on November 3, and motivation coursed through their veins for revenge and defense of property—their title. Wrigley Field was hopping with more than 45,000 hyped fans eager for destruction of the Packers, convinced another whipping would bury them for this season.

Those fans likely dreamed of a repeat of September 22, when the Bears rose up and smote the Packers by that 31-point margin. That was not to be. This game was a struggle, for both teams, for the whole 60 minutes. The Chicagoans got what they wanted, but they had to sweat for it. Joe Maniaci's 3-yard rush into the end zone, followed by Jack Manders' kick, made it 7–0 Bears in the first quarter. But Green Bay tied the game before halftime. It was Hutson, the touchdown machine, who put his team on the board, catching a 5-yard throw from Herber. Yet that lead did not last until the band played. Chicago added another touchdown on a short run and led 14–7 after 30 minutes. And after 45. And after 60. The score never budged from there, and the Bears succeeded in holding off the challenge, winning 14–7 and moving their record to 6–1. At 4–3, the Packers were teetering on the edge of a cliff.

It can be assumed Curly Lambeau sought to soar in oratory the way Winston Churchill did, to inspire his own troops. Maybe that played a role in what occurred next, another dismantling of the Chicago Cardinals. There were 11,364 souls at Comiskey Park, home of the White Sox baseball team, when Green Bay invaded on November 10. The situation was not hopeless for the Pack, but every win was crucial.

Green Bay treated the Cardinals as pushovers, stomping them, 28–7. It might as well have been a Clarke Hinkle holiday. He entered the end zone from 12, 1 and 9 yards, the first on a pass, the others on

17. Trying to Repeat

runs, for 18 of the Packers' points. Hutson contributed a couple of extra points. Hinkle, a seven-time All-Pro selection, was a sturdy 5-foot-11 and 202 pounds, and during his 10 seasons he was a constantly versatile performer for the Packers. He could run and kick and was hard to bring down, perhaps not as flashy as Hutson, but the perfect backfield complement to the receiver. Hutson had three extra points that game.

Hope was still alive in the Green Bay locker room after this win, but not after the next week's game, when the always-tough New York Giants won out in a 7–3 contest at the Polo Grounds. This ruined the Packers' season as surely as any other game. Lee Shaffer's 8-yard pass from Len Barnum was the only touchdown. Hinkle's 32-yard field goal represented the Packers' only points. They were 5–4 on the season and were floating dead in the Hudson River as far as any chance at the playoffs remained.

They still had to play, however. November 24 brought the Detroit Lions. The earlier loss to Detroit had been annoying, and payback was more delicious than Thanksgiving turkey. The contest was at Briggs Stadium, and optimistic fans showed up numbering 26,019. There was little reason for them to stay beyond halftime, when it was 27–0 Packers in a game that ended with Green Bay on top, 50–7.

Hutson scored early on an 8-yard pass from Isbell, and his foot chipped in three extra points. Eight Packers contributed points, including Andy Uram with two touchdowns and Ed Jankowski with two more.

That left one last game, on December 1, at Cleveland's Municipal Stadium to face the Rams. Whether the Packers were just going through the motions is not clear, but the game ended in a 13–13 tie. Hutson recorded the team's last touchdown of the season on an 11-yard pass from Van Every, and Hinkle scored the last points of the season on a 26-yard field goal.

The 6–4–1 final record was not horrendous, but it was less than satisfying, especially when the organization and community hoped for another world title.

18

1941

By 1941, the sight of Don Hutson streaking downfield all alone, no defender within 10 yards of him, pigskin tucked under his arm, his No. 14 Green Bay jersey receding in the distance from tacklers, was commonplace. Fans in all National Football League cities were used to seeing that green jersey with the gold numeral and shoulder slabs headed into the end zone.

Above all, it seemed, despite his unprecedented achievements, despite setting new standards as a pass catcher, Hutson was getting better and was still able to accomplish new and better things. He was the fastest with the mostest, and as long as Curly Lambeau also had hired help who could get the ball to him, Hutson was a singular weapon.

The Green Bay fans were let down by the 1940 team, but they never held a grudge against their boys. They always believed that come next fall, the Packers would be able to pick off another world championship. They cared too much not to think that way. For that matter, Lambeau thought the same way. He was practical enough to realize the Packers would always face new and different threats (or in the Bears, seemingly, the same old threat) each autumn. But he was of the "Why not us?" approach to the sport. The Packers were his baby, and he wanted only the best for them—and himself.

The Bears concluded the 1940 season by smearing the Washington Redskins, 73–0, in the most lopsided game in NFL history. The first step in any season for the Packers was almost always to be better than the Bears, because they had to finish ahead of them in the West to compete for the title.

While it was unlikely that the perfect game carried out by the Bears over the Redskins would be repeated (and it never has been), the ominous statement of such power had to cast somewhat of a shadow over

18. 1941

the 1941 season. Clearly, the Bears were the team to beat for another team to capture any hardware for its trophy case.

Hutson's trophy case was becoming overstuffed. His 1941 season was better than ever. He led the National Football League in catches, receiving yards, and touchdowns. Adding two on the ground, he finished with 12 six-pointers. His totals for the 11-game season were 58 catches, 738 yards, and 10 TDs through the air. This marked the first time in league history anyone caught more than 50 passes in one season. It was another breakthrough.

"For every pass I caught in a game, I caught a thousand in practice," Hutson said.[1] That was probably true, especially since football games are played just once a week and teams may practice the other six days.

Hutson wrote the record book at his position, and then he rewrote it several times. He would have just added to his records if he had played longer. He was so far ahead of his time, many of his records lasted decades. Almost never mentioned, because the day of the two-way player long ago gave way to the era of the specialist, is that Hutson also intercepted 30 passes as a defensive back. He excelled at covering men like him who played his position on offense.

Hutson's prime dates back so far, few are alive who saw him play in person, but in 2017, Hall of Fame executive Gil Brandt, then midway through his 80s and having been around the NFL for 60 years, produced a personal ranking that included a list of the greatest wide receivers of all time. Brandt, who spent nearly 30 years building and rebuilding the Dallas Cowboys from their inception as an expansion franchise in 1960, put Hutson second on his list, behind only Jerry Rice. Hutson was the only old-timer in the top 10, unless one counts Raymond Berry, who played from 1955 to 1967. Since the list was populated with such well-known recent figures as Randy Moss, Terrell Owens, Larry Fitzgerald, and Marvin Harrison, it demonstrated the great respect Hutson maintained.

Besides his long tenure in the NFL and later as a broadcaster, it so happened that Brandt grew up in Wisconsin, graduated from the University of Wisconsin, and although he was just a kid at the time, Hutson retiring by the time Brandt was 13, he did watch him play live for the Packers.

"He was without question, one of the great players of all-time," Brandt said. "His pass catching, his technique of catching, was totally different for his time. He caught the ball in his hands. He didn't trap the ball. Nobody knows how great Hutson was [based on] passes caught."[2]

Caught by Don Hutson!

Hutson's fan club grew during his time in the NFL, his reputation by 1941 no longer regional in the South or limited to the college game. Those pro teams represented big cities, and they were served by big-city newspapers with great reach. The sportswriters who covered the clubs in New York, Philadelphia, Washington, and Chicago saw Hutson's magic on a regular basis, sometimes twice a season, and sometimes, if a championship was on the line, three times in one year. You didn't have to see much of him to experience his greatness.

Alfred Earle "Greasy" Neale was an early convert. Neale, who played major league baseball for the Cincinnati Reds and the Philadelphia Phillies, played pro football with the Canton Bulldogs and coached the Philadelphia Eagles for fully half of Hutson's Packers career, starting with the 1941 season. "Hutson is the only man I ever saw who could feint in three directions at the same time," Neale said.[3] No wonder defenses couldn't stop him.

Brandt said the modern fan doesn't understand the difference in the way the game was played during Hutson's career and how it is played now. For someone to catch 50 passes in a season now is somewhat routine, as opposed to unheard-of until Hutson did so. Arnie Herber made the Hall of Fame by completing about 41 percent of his passes. Even Joe Namath barely completed 50 percent of his tosses. There are no NFL quarterbacks (at least not for long) in the game now whose accuracy rates are not far superior.

"You look today and you see completion rates are 60–66 percent," Brandt said a few years ago. "In those days [the Hutson period], if teams completed 30 percent of their passes, that was good. For him to catch the number of passes he caught was a true exception."[4]

Teams threw less frequently, completed fewer passes, relied on running more, and ran less sophisticated offenses altogether, while players competed without nutritional or weight-lifting programs and had less developed medical care at their disposal. They also played 11 or 12 games per season, not 14, as the schedule later expanded to, or now 17. Sometimes, in the 2000s, it seems teams have almost completely forgotten about the run and devoted themselves to clever, nearly unstoppable passing games. In 2020, Packers quarterback Aaron Rodgers completed 70.7 percent of his pass attempts, and he attempted 526 of them as compared to the 283 tried by three Packers quarterbacks combined in 1940 and 253 in 1941.

As an aside, Brandt is one long-time NFL official who believes the

18. 1941

slightly cuckoo 1935 race to sign Hutson by the Packers in competition with the Brooklyn team, Lambeau versus Shipwreck Kelly and the role of the post office, convinced other league owners to institute the player draft. "Don Hutson was probably responsible, more than anything, for the draft," Brandt claimed. "We won't have any more instances of guys signing with two different teams."[5]

Celebrityhood attached itself to Hutson easily in Green Bay, but he did not seek it, it just naturally accrued to anyone who wore the home uniform. But Green Bay was hardly Broadway with its bright lights. A guy could raise his family, the three daughters Hutson had with wife Julia, in relative peace. Not anonymity, but without being besieged. Hutson was not aloof but pretty natural, not full of himself, but more one of the guys than someone who considered himself special.

"He was approachable," said Art Daley, a Green Bay sports reporter who wrote about the Packers for nearly 70 years starting in 1941.[6] Daley, a community institution, was no relation to Arthur Daley, the Pulitzer-Prize-winning sports columnist for the *New York Times*, who wrote the "Sports of the Times" column from 1942 to 1974. Art Daley was born Lukenheimer but took his stepfather's last name.

Inside the dressing room, teammate Tony Canadeo, a rookie in 1941 who spent his entire career with Green Bay, said Hutson was just one of the gang, subject to the same pranks and jokes as other players when the atmosphere was light-hearted. "He was a regular guy in the locker room," Canadeo said.[7]

It is likely that the late Steve Sabol watched more video tape of NFL play from the ancient league play, through the decades, and up through the modern era, than any other human being. The co-founder of NFL Films in New Jersey with his father Ed, and chosen for the Pro Football Hall of Fame, Steve Sabol raised football filmmaking to an art form. Ed was elected to the Hall of Fame nine years prior to Steve's selection in 2020, and in 2003 they shared a Lifetime Emmy Award. Steve won 35 Emmys and helped found the NFL Network.

What struck Steve Sabol most about Hutson was his body movements. While he heard such a description applied to many athletes, he said the first time he heard the appellation "poetry in motion," it was said of Hutson. "He was capable of scoring from anyplace on the field at any moment of the game."[8]

When the 1941 season began, the Chicago Bears had the title, and the Green Bay Packers wanted it back. None of those participating in the

Caught by Don Hutson!

NFL campaign that autumn, players, coaches or owners, could imagine how the season would end just a few months later, but as always, when play began, there was optimism in several training camps.

Nothing had eased up in the wars across foreign borders, Germany and Japan still casting imperialistic eyes to all corners of the earth, their might being advertised in carnage in numerous locations, with horrors extending to and engulfing many areas. England was holding tough but was regularly bombed by the Luftwaffe, the Old Bailey taking hits in January. General Erwin Rommel took over German land forces in Africa. Adolf Hitler began expanding his concentration camps out of sight of mainstream politicians and foreign eyes, herding innocent men, women, and children to their deaths by the millions. Buckingham Palace was hit by bombs in March.

American involvement ratcheted up on the periphery. President Roosevelt endorsed and Congress passed the Lend-Lease Act, which allowed for Britain, China and other allied nations to purchase materials from the United States and not make payment until peacetime. It was one way to supply equipment to the likeminded without declaring war on the enemies of American allies.

Rudolf Hess, one of Hitler's chief Nazi aides, apparently went crazy, parachuted into Scotland talking of brokering a separate peace, and was taken into custody and imprisoned. Great Britain held him until after the war, when he was repatriated to Germany for the Nuremberg trials and convicted of war crimes. He remained in prison until committing suicide in 1987.

Australian, Free French, British, and Indian allies fought the Vichy-French in the Middle East in June, while in the United States, the Tuskegee Airmen, the all-Black 99th Fighter Squadron of pilots, was formed. In September, as the football season was starting, the USS *Greer* was fired upon by a German U-boat, the first time the neutral American Navy was struck in an incident that increased tensions between the U.S. and Germany. That month, too, Liberty Ships began rolling off American manufacturing lines to fill orders to replace sunken British ships. The first of the 2,710 American-made cargo ships to haul supplies began sailing. Desperate to conquer the Soviet Union, Hitler hurled massive numbers of men and amounts of equipment into capturing Moscow and Leningrad. The siege of Leningrad began in September, and before the end of October, FDR approved more than $1 billion in Lend-Lease aid for the Communist country. As if anyone did not realize one of Hitler's

18. 1941

nefarious goals, on October 19, Germany announced that Luxembourg had been "cleansed of Jews."

During World War II, the Bears' Sid Luckman was one of the most prominent and elite Jewish athletes in the United States. He was football's answer to baseball's Hank Greenberg, the Detroit Tigers' slugger. This was a period rife with anti-Semitism, and the world circumstances brought more attention to the plight of Jews in other nations as Hitler sought their extermination.

Luckman was born in Brooklyn, New York, in 1916 to father Meyer and mother Ethel, who depending on the source, emigrated from Germany, Russia, or Lithuania. By 1941, it was easy to wonder whether his would have been an early tragic ending if he were raised in Europe. Luckman was not an outspoken athlete and was not intensely interviewed about off-the-field matters much, but he was also hiding a secret.

Meyer Luckman was a member of the Jewish mob headed by Louis Lepke. Luckman's father was convicted of murder, of killing his brother-in-law, and the young quarterback, then attending Columbia, watched the trial and was tortured by the outcome. He visited his father in Sing Sing prison until Meyer's death in 1944, but believed he was innocent and never spoke of this family skeleton in the closet to newspapermen.

Still considered the best of all Bears quarterbacks and viewed as a son by Chicago owner George Halas, post-playing days, Luckman manifested his Judaism in various ways. He performed fund-raising for the Maccabiah Games in Israel and said of his own observant religious nature, "I go to the temple regularly, and I observe the High Holidays [Rosh Hashanah and Yom Kippur], and I never go to bed at night without saying a little prayer."[9]

The 1941 season began for the Packers without Arnie Herber, who retired and went into business in Wisconsin. The quarterback job belonged outright to Cecil Isbell now, with Hal Van Every as the backup, but seldom-relied-upon pitchman. After learning while playing and sharing the rest of the time, being turned loose by Curly Lambeau gave Isbell more confidence, as well as responsibility, and he lived up to expectations. This was his finest season to this point. Isbell led the NFL in completions with 117, attempts with 206, passing yards with 1,479, and touchdown passes with 15. He threw more than ever as Hutson caught more than ever.

September 15 was the first day of the season for the Packers, and

Caught by Don Hutson!

they looked terrific dismembering the Detroit Lions with a thorough 23–0 smackdown. They were still paying the Lions back for the previous season's early loss. The two follow-up wins came by a 47–7 margin. This margin seemed as if it could have been bigger as the Packers became more comfortable in their offense. Ed Jankowski hit a 40-yard field goal for the team's first points of the season, Clarke Hinkle booted a three-pointer from 39 yards, and Tiny Engebretsen put one through the uprights from 36 yards. Three different long-range kickers? Strange times. When the Packers finally got around to scoring a touchdown, it was Hutson who came through on an 8-yard fling from Isbell. Familiar sights for fans. Green Bay put a bow on the scoring with a Tony Canadeo touchdown run. Frank Balasz hit the extra point, making the fourth member of the team to score with his foot that day.

A week later, Green Bay pounced on the Cleveland Rams, 24–7, inviting 18,463 fans into Wisconsin State Fair Park. The Rams didn't score until the Packers had 24 points in the bank. Canadeo was looking like a useful addition. First, he threw a touchdown pass to Joe Laws, then he scored on a short run. Hutson kicked one extra point. Hinkle scored on a 7-yard pass from Isbell and kicked an extra point.

Hinkle, at 32, was approaching the end of a football career that carried him from Bucknell University, through the Packers, and into the Pro Football Hall of Fame. This season he carried the ball most often during his pro career, 129 rushes. A reputation for remarkable toughness followed him around the league, enhanced by his sometimes brutal encounters with Chicago's Bronko Nagurski, whom other players considered to be the toughest player they faced. Nagurski said the same of Hinkle, and once, in what might be summarized as a head-on car wreck, Nagurski incurred a broken nose and had to leave a Bears-Packers game after colliding with Hinkle.

Yes, but that was the result of hard-earned lessons being dished out by the 230-pound fullback-defender Nagurski on other occasions. "I made a mistake that day," Hinkle said of one 1930s game between the bitter rivals. "I waited for him to come to me. From then on, I always tried to get to Bronko before he got to me. After that, I played Bronko pretty even, nose to nose. [So to speak.] But I learned never to stand still and wait for him because he would have killed me."[10]

It is interesting to note that Buckets Goldenberg, who teamed with Hinkle for years and watched him up-close weekly, thought he was the best pro football player of all. In an interesting symbiotic relationship,

18. 1941

when Hinkle was enshrined in the Pro Football Hall of Fame in 1964, the institution's second class, it was Nagurski, a member of the inaugural class of 1963, who was his presenter.

Hinkle was as good as ever, and Hutson was Hutson, for the third game of the 1941 season when the Packers met their first real test against the defending champion Bears. On September 28, the Bears were opening late, and Green Bay already had played two games. It couldn't save the Packers, though. Nor could jamming 24,876 fans into City Stadium.

Chicago scored first, in the first quarter, on a 63-yard pass from George McAfee to Ken Kavanaugh, and the Bears booted two field goals to go up, 15–0. Fans had to be worried they were seeing the juggernaut Bears who had demolished the Redskins in that 73–0 blowout. But the Packers battled back in the second quarter when Hutson yanked down a 45-yard touchdown pass from Isbell and kicked his own extra point, and Hinkle added a 40-yard field goal.

That left things 15–10 at the half, and Green Bay responded to Lambeau's exhortations at halftime with a 1-yard touchdown run by Hinkle with Hutson adding the point after. The Packers led, 17–15. But the Green Bay offense ran out of steam, and the Bears were in command in the second half. McAfee scored a touchdown on a run, Bob Snyder kicked a field goal, and Chicago won, 25–17.

This could have left the Packers in a shaky situation in the team race. The Chicago Cardinals came to Wisconsin as the next foe, and this was at least the struggle of the Bears match. Green Bay prevailed, 14–13, for the critical win. Hinkle scored a touchdown and Hutson nailed two extra points, but the key score was notched by an unlikely source.

Lou Brock (not to be confused with the Hall of Fame baseball player of the same name) was a halfback drafted out of Purdue in 1940. His cousin was Green Bay center-linebacker Charley Brock, who became a five-time All-Pro. The Packers trailed, 13–7, in the fourth quarter before working the ball close to the goal-line. Isbell hit Lou Brock for the game-winning pass that gave Green Bay a 3–1 record. Lou Brock played six seasons for Green Bay before injuries drove him out of the game, increasing his value as time passed. "Brock is too valuable a man to be left on the bench too often," Lambeau said. "He's a good punter and a better than average passer."[11]

Following a loss and a tight win, the Packers slipped into an impressive rhythm. They crushed the Brooklyn Dodgers, 30–7, on October 12. Hutson opened the scoring on a 32-yard touchdown pass from Isbell.

Caught by Don Hutson!

Hutson also collected a rare rushing TD that game, on an 18-yard run. Uram rubbed things in with a 90-yard punt return, again showing off his knack for racing into the clear when coverage overran him. Hinkle added a field goal and extra point, and Canadeo put up a rushing touchdown.

From there, the Packers kept winning. Some games were nail-biters, some were routs. Green Bay edged the Rams next. In a rare usage, Lambeau sent Hutson onto the field to try a 13-yard field goal in the fourth period. The kick was good and represented the winning points. All of a sudden, Hutson was Mr. Clutch with his toes.

The October 26 game against the Lions was a repeat of the first game. The Packers were ascendant, Detroit descendant, dropped to 1–4–1 following Green Bay's 24–7 beating. Hutson was the main nemesis. Touchdowns were his friends this season. He began the game with a 12-yard score from Isbell, who was on fire. He also grabbed a 6-yard TD from Isbell later in the game. Isbell threw three touchdown passes in this one, including a 26-yarder to Carl Mulleneaux.

In a trivia tidbit, the only Detroit touchdown of the day was registered on a 77-yard punt return by Steve Belichick. This was Belichick's only season playing professional football. He appeared in six games and scored two touchdowns for his career. After World War II, Belichick embarked on a long college coaching career, including 1956 to 1989 at the United States Naval Academy. However, when he passed away at 86 in 2005, he was better known to the average football fan as the father of Bill Belichick, the long-time coach of the New England Patriots, regarded by some as the greatest NFL coach of all time.

On November 2, the hungry Packers were ready for the game the entire National Football League wanted to see, including 46,484 paying customers at Wrigley Field in Chicago. The Bears gave Green Bay its only loss, and now Green Bay inflicted the Bears' one loss, dropping Chicago to 5–1 with a 16–14 victory.

The Packers played fired-up from the start. The Bears did growl their way back into contention in the fourth period, scoring their 14 points. Lou Brock made another of the biggest plays of his season, running into the end zone on a 36-yard pass from Isbell. Isbell also scored on a short run. Hinkle kicked a 43-yard field goal, and Hutson mixed in one extra point. It was just enough to survive.

Already playing life-and-death with the theoretically much weaker Chicago Cardinals, the Packers entertained them in Green Bay on

18. 1941

November 16, and this contest was no easier even if the Cards brought a 2–4–1 record into the meeting. Green Bay got 'em again, this time 17–9, and Hutson did most of the damage, catching a touchdown pass of 25 yards from Isbell, kicking that extra point, and scoring in the fourth period on an 11-yard run. All of a sudden, Hutson was taking handoffs to trick other people. Oh, he kicked that second extra point, too.

Jimmy Conzelman, who played for the Decatur Staleys in 1920, George Halas' inaugural NFL club, the Rock Island Independents, Milwaukee Badgers, and Providence Steam Roller, and more, then coached the Cardinals for three years prior to World War II and three seasons after World War II, saw enough of Hutson to act as a press-agent for him in a 1943 magazine article.

Look, the popular national magazine, put together a two-article companion package under the headline "Who Was Sport's No. 1 Wrecker?" The legendary sportswriter Grantland Rice penned a piece endorsing baseball star Ty Cobb for the title. Conzelman wrote the story arguing Hutson was that character for football. Conzelman may have been in the service at the time, but Hutson was still active.

In part, Conzelman wrote:

> Professional coaches know the only way to keep a game with Green Bay from becoming a rout is to assign the safety man and the defensive right halfback to watch Don every time the Packers put the ball in motion. In spite of that, the statistics of any game he plays will show Hutson catching seven-to-10 passes and scoring at least one touchdown. That's only half of it. Here's the other half: Because the opponents must keep two men on him, a situation is created that yields gains for Curly Lambeau's team at other positions.
>
> Hutson's bewildering effectiveness in snaring passes is based on his speed, his shuffling gait, his feigned laziness that pays off when an opponent gets careless, the sureness of his grip, his unerring eye for a ball in flight, and his guile.[12]

That took care of the scouting report on Hutson.

As good as the Packers were that season, Pittsburgh was that weak. After a 54–7 wipeout, the Steelers were 1–8–1 and Green Bay was 9–1. For a short while, Pittsburgh had an upset on its mind, going ahead 7–0. Then the Packers ran up 26 points in the second period, and by the end of the game the biggest offensive producer was backup quarterback Hal Van Every. Hutson gathered in yet another touchdown pass, this one of eight yards from Isbell, and kicked two extra points. Clarke Hinkle got

Caught by Don Hutson!

his share on two short touchdown runs. Van Every tallied on two rushing touchdowns and an explosive 86-yard pass interception return.

That lined the Packers up against the Washington Redskins before 35,594 fans at Griffith Stadium in their final regular-season game on November 30. The Redskins were not as strong as they had been in recent years, but they were formidable this day. Perhaps the Packers were overconfident against a club that would be 5–5 by the end of the contest, but the Redskins piled up a 17–0 halftime lead.

Green Bay fans could thank the Isbell-Hutson partnership for this comeback. Not only did Hutson catch three touchdown passes off the arm of Isbell, but he kicked two extra points, too, for 20 points out of the Packers' total in a 22–17 victory. Hutson's touchdowns came on throws of 8, 3 and 40 yards as the Packers charged back before adding their last two points on a safety. Hutson's points gave him 95 for the season, setting a new NFL record. In 1934, the Bears' Jack Manders scored 76 points for the old mark. Hutson concluded the campaign with 395 points lifetime, also a new record. Manders was second at 385 points. Hutson's 12 touchdowns gave him one more than Washington's Andy Farkas scored in 1939. So his rousing finish helped him set three league scoring records at once.

That scoring burst made the Packers 10–1, the best record in the West and the best in the league. Except for the one blip early against the Bears, it had been a months-long, marvelous performance. The only problem was that the 10–1 record was equaled by Chicago, and the teams had split the season series. They were tied. The New York Giants took first place in the East with an 8–3 record. Without layers of playoffs, it was just winner of the East versus winner of the West for the crown. So the Bears and Packers had to meet a third time for the right to face New York.

A big crowd of 43,425 turned out at Wrigley Field to holler for the Bears on December 14. There was a scrappy first period with the Packers leading 7–6, but the Bears overran Green Bay with 24 points in the second period for the 33–14 win. Hutson wasn't much of a factor except for kicking two extra points. Hinkle, in his last game, and Van Every, of all people catching a toss from Isbell, scored the Packers' touchdowns.

The surprise was that so many people came out for the game, or perhaps that the game was played at all. In between the Packers' November 30 triumph over the Redskins and this meeting, the United States had been blindsided by the bombing of Pearl Harbor in Hawaii on

18. 1941

December 7, and the nation had entered the war. Football, even among the most fervent of fans, was no longer the top topic of conversation. The war had arrived on the country's doorstep, delivered with a vengeance of flame and explosions, and the immediate death count, military and civilian, was 2,403, plus 1,206 wounded. Overnight, football had lost importance, even at championship time.

President Roosevelt addressed the nation, and Congress swiftly declared war on Japan. The *Green Bay Press-Gazette* published a front-page editorial in the same edition as the war declaration and its report of Japan's morning sneak attack thousands of miles away. It read in part, "Japan has murderously attacked our country. Japan launched fire and death with all the treachery known to thugs and outlaws."[13] War was the only course of action.

The Packers were manhandled in Chicago a week after the shocking attack, and Curly Lambeau made no excuses and did not pretend that but for a few breaks, the game would have gone Green Bay's way. He had no reasons for why his team was listless, and he did not mention Pearl Harbor being a distraction. "Let's not alibi," Lambeau said. "Let's take it. The team wasn't fighting and they made a lot of mistakes."[14]

On December 21, back at Wrigley Field, the Bears batted around the Giants just as easily, winning the NFL title by a 37–9 spread. The crowd, perhaps with the reality of the world situation crossing American borders, was much smaller, with 13,341 in attendance. That is the smallest crowd ever to watch a league championship game.

The game concluded the professional football season, just in time, some might say. There was no way of knowing what the future might bring, soon or in the long run, and whether there would be a next football season. Two National Football League players who suited up for the Bears-Giants championship game were killed in action not so far in the future.

Ruey Bussey, known as "Young," was a Bears backup quarterback after playing collegiately for Louisiana State University and being chosen far down in the 1940 NFL draft of college players. He was the 187th player chosen and did not make the Bears' final roster that season. He played on a club in Newark, New Jersey, George Halas was subsidizing and then made the team in 1941. Bussey became a lieutenant in the Navy, but while home on leave predicted his own death to his Army brother in a coming military operation. On January 7, 1945, Young Bussey was killed in the Philippines at 27 years of age.

Caught by Don Hutson!

Jack Lummus was a member of the Giants team that lost to the Bears in the title game. Lummus had been a free agent signee for New York and was paid $100 a game. He enlisted in the Marine Corps Reserve about five weeks after the championship contest. Eventually, he landed at Iwo Jima on February 19, 1945. On March 8, Lummus' platoon was assigned an assault on a fortified position. While suffering some minor wounds, Lummus took out the enemy entrenchments. But he stepped on a land mine and was more grievously wounded. In conversation with a doctor, Lummus reportedly said, "Well, doc, the New York Giants lost a mighty good end today."[15] Lummus was given 18 pints of blood in transfusions but died on the operating table from internal injuries.

He was later awarded the Congressional Medal of Honor, and on November 28, 2020, Lummus, who had already been inducted into the New York Giants Ring of Honor, had a statue erected of him on the campus of Baylor University, where he played football and baseball.

The Packers scattered for the year after the loss to the Bears, those residents of Green Bay, such as Don Hutson, returning home to where they made their living. Over the coming years, as the same war they had read about from afar since 1939 dominated American consciousness, most of their lives would change in less dramatic ways than did Bussey's and Lummus'. Many would still get to play pro football while the war was fought in foreign lands.

19

War-Time Football

The fighting was fierce and the bombs were exploding for hundreds of thousands of American servicemen who marched to war with the U.S. Army, Navy, Marines, and what would soon be called the Air Force. But not in Green Bay, Wisconsin. That was where Don Hutson spent World War II.

Hutson did not enter any branch of the military. He was classified 1A, but as the sole support of his immediate family, his wife and three children, he was exempt from being drafted. And he did not volunteer. Situations were complicated for many professional athletes. Some were enthusiastic patriots who volunteered to defend the country almost immediately after the Japanese bombed Pearl Harbor. Some enlisted on their own timetable. And some were drafted.

These were terrible times, with American men dying by the thousands all over the globe, and with Americans on the home front performing essential services for the public and the military effort in manufacturing jobs and other professions. Washington Redskins star quarterback Sammy Baugh did not enter the military, but he raised beef on his Texas ranch for the government. Sid Luckman, the Chicago Bears' quarterback, eventually volunteered for the Merchant Marine and was a member of that outfit from 1943 to 1945. He was not able to practice with the Bears, but he traveled to the site of games and played his position on Sundays.

Baugh continued to suit up for the Redskins throughout the war—on game days only, spending the rest of his week in Texas raising cattle. During the 1943 season, Baugh regularly played the full 60 minutes of Washington's games. Like Hutson, Baugh was married with two children and was his family's sole support. His draft board cleared him to join the Redskins wherever they played as long as he worked five days a week providing meat for the Armed Forces. That was an essential civilian service.

Caught by Don Hutson!

Luckman played mostly a full schedule in two seasons in the 1940s while attached to the Merchant Marine, except for 1944, when he appeared in just seven games.

Luckman's boss, George Halas, who turned 47 in February of 1942, was an ensign in the Navy during World War I, but he demanded the chance to play an active role in World War II. Given the rank of lieutenant commander in the Navy, Halas spent 20 months overseas under Admiral Chester Nimitz. Halas earned a Bronze Star and left the service this time with the rank of captain. He was more than 50 years old at the time.

Such future Hall of Fame baseball players as Ted Williams, Bob Feller, and Warren Spahn distinguished themselves in battle and lost significant years of their careers. Williams, the star hitter for the Boston Red Sox, who had just batted .406 during the 1941 season, the last man to top that mark, was a Marine pilot flying many dangerous missions—and was called up again during the Korean War. At first, he was not called because he was the sole support of his mother, but then he was reclassified. Spahn was wounded at the Battle of the Bulge.

Feller was in his automobile, driving from his home in Van Meter, Iowa, to Chicago to rendezvous with Cleveland Indians team officials to negotiate a new contract, when he learned of the Pearl Harbor bombing on the radio. Instead of making a new deal, he joined the Navy, becoming a gun captain as part of a crew on a 40-mm anti-aircraft mount. He saw action in the North Atlantic and the Pacific Theatre. "Combat is an experience that you never forget," Feller wrote years later. "A war teaches you that baseball is only a game, after all, a minor thing compared to the sovereignty and security of the United States."[1]

When the war began, the czars of professional sports leagues were not even sure there would be sports played while the nation was at war. Baseball was the National Pastime and took the lead on the matter. FDR wrote the so-called "green light letter" to Commissioner Kenesaw Mountain Landis giving baseball the presidential stamp of approval to go forward. It was made abundantly clear, though, that athletes would not receive special treatment from draft boards in terms of being ruled exempt so they could play games. Roosevelt said he felt the public needed some diversionary entertainment, but with every other mother's son risking his life, and often losing it, he did not want to see talented baseball and football players gain special treatment.

Some famous athletes, heavyweight champion Joe Louis notable

19. War-Time Football

among them, made trips all over the world, and to the front in some instances, for troop morale building. Louis also lent his name to fund-raising for War Bonds.

Don Hutson did not go to war and tried to keep the war from his family, but things did not work out on that front. Hutson was not an only child. He had younger twin brothers, Robert and Ray, who later were the mainstays on a Pine Bluff High School football championship team. They followed Don's footsteps in another way, both heading to the University of Alabama for schooling in the fall of 1940.

Standing 5-foot-9 and weighing around 160 pounds, the twins were smaller than Don. They had excelled at football, basketball, and baseball in Pine Bluff and senior year their team was acknowledged as a national football champion. They could have played sports at any number of colleges, but Don's influence was paramount. "We had heard nothing but Alabama football since we were kids, so there was no question where we could go," Ray Hutson said.[2]

At that time, Bear Bryant, their older brother's close friend, was an assistant coach, and he was tasked with riding over to Pine Bluff to sign the younger Hutsons.

Being related to such an illustrious former player, it was impossible for the siblings to slip into Tuscaloosa under radar. They received considerable attention, but also demonstrated signs of deserving it. Ray Hutson's specialties were running, receiving, and punting. Robert was a thrower, a passer, who could also run. The Hutsons made an impact right away, combining for 19 points in their first game of the season, a 25–6 win over Howard.

They showed promise as freshmen, but with war clouds hovering and the Selective Service Act taking effect even before Pearl Harbor, the twins chose not to return to Alabama to start sophomore year. They were certain they would be drafted into the Army when they turned 21 later in 1941, but they preferred the idea of flying. So they joined the Army Air Corps, which soon became the United States Air Force.

After training, the brothers were split up. Ray remained in the United States, serving in Wilmington, Delaware. Robert was stationed in the South Pacific. It was in his capacity as a pilot, during a takeoff in the Himalayas in India, site of the tallest mountains on earth, including Mount Everest, that Robert Hutson crashed and perished. Initially, Robert was reported as missing on August 27, 1943.

At home in Arkansas, the Hutsons' mother heard of the rumor of

Caught by Don Hutson!

one son's death on September 5, 1943. The Packers' football season was soon to begin, but Don Hutson went home to mourn his brother. Ray said, "Several months later a solider came to our house to confirm that he had been killed."[3]

Hutson's parents wrote to the Air Force asking for information and received a letter from a major who had been flying directly behind Robert and watched his plane go down. He reported that a search party immediately combed the wreckage and found no indication of life, and all crew members were given "a Christian burial by a chaplain" in the group.[4]

Ray, the other brother, continued in the Air Corps until 1946. He flew 77 missions in the same territory where Robert died. Ray received the Distinguished Flying Cross with two oak clusters and the Air Medal with two oak clusters. Ray never returned to play football at Alabama. Saying he was lucky to survive so many missions under fire, Ray said he could have returned to the Crimson Tide with most of his eligibility intact, but so much time had passed. "I enjoyed both football and basketball at Alabama, but it just seemed too much to go back after nearly five years," he said.[5]

All across professional football, rosters thinned as men enlisted or were drafted into military service to defend the United States. The National Football League persevered with its schedule, and teams did the best they could with the players available. The Bears were leaderless in a manner they had never been before, with team founder and coach George Halas thousands of miles from Chicago. Halas appointed trusted aides Hunk Anderson and Luke Johnsos as co-coaches. That arrangement continued through 1945.

For those who were able, available, and willing to play, there was still uncertainty about how the National Football League season would play out. Gasoline rationing was imposed. Rubber was rationed. During World War I, citizens had been asked to conserve sliced bread under a program called "Wheatless Wednesdays." The idea was reborn during World War II with the belief it would save wax paper, but rather quickly the Secretary of Agriculture determined it wasn't saving as much as had been predicted. Butter, sugar, and canned milk were rationed. Nylon, used in women's stockings and ropes, was in limited supply. Old stockings donated for recycling were made into parachutes.

When FDR gave Major League Baseball the go-ahead to play in 1942, it became a guinea pig for the NFL to follow. Pro football only

19. War-Time Football

overlapped with baseball by a month or so in those days, so league officials could watch and learn from baseball's experiences. It became clear that playing games was popular with the public, that workers coming off their shifts enjoyed viewing games. By March, NFL Commissioner Elmer Layden, who as a college player gained fame as one of The Four Horsemen of Notre Dame, proclaimed that football would go forward.

Packers leader Curly Lambeau was a strong backer of playing the games and said baseball was a good barometer. "I feel confident that baseball will go through in 1942 and this means that football will, too," he said.[6]

Problems arose from gas rationing. Most of the NFL was contained in Eastern and Midwestern cities larger than Green Bay. The Packers were buttressed by regional support. They were truly Wisconsin's franchise. Gas rationing limited non-essential traveling by issuing stamps by household in the amount of three gallons of fuel weekly. Speed limits were reduced to 35 mph to save on tires' rubber wear and on gas. In those other cities, fans could take public transportation to stadiums. How would opponents reach Green Bay? Besides the Chicago Bears and Cardinals, the closest team to Green Bay was the Detroit Lions. "With the exception of Green Bay, where there are extenuating circumstances, National league teams are located in the nation's metropolitan centers." Layden said. "Parks are all easily accessible by street cars and busses, with handy connections to suburban traction lines and railroad terminals."[7]

Seven out of the eight cities in the league would be fine. It was Green Bay's future that provoked worry. For that matter, owners of teams in some of those big cities never wanted to make road trips to Green Bay, not only because it was out of the way, but because City Stadium at full capacity only held around 25,000 people. The Bears and Lions, the Packers' chief Western rivals, were willing to make the trek. Other teams pushed for Packers home games to be played in Milwaukee. None of this was fair to the Packers, the last small-market survivor of the NFL's early days, or their devoted fans. Other teams used the war to gang up on Green Bay. When hard-nosed bargaining was completed in hammering out the 1942 schedule, Green Bay received five home games, but the definition of "home" did include Milwaukee. Just three of the games would be played in Green Bay. That did beat going to Wrigley Field or Briggs Stadium twice each in a season, though.

Lambeau, who said other cities, Buffalo and Akron, Ohio, among

Caught by Don Hutson!

them, offered to step up and host Packers home games, said at one point in the debate that he only had a commitment from the Chicago Bears to travel to Green Bay. "But I wouldn't give in," Lambeau said.[8]

There was a fierce rivalry between the Bears and Packers, and George Halas and Curly Lambeau drove one another nuts annually, but whenever there was a crisis jeopardizing the Packers, Halas and his Bears always stood in Green Bay's corner.

Usually Packers problems revolved around finances for a club sustained by stockholders, who were not private millionaires. Almost always, the issues popped up because Green Bay was as small as it was. This time the United States government's gas rationing could crush the Packers unless team leadership could shrewdly maneuver around it while at the same time not alienating the team's own fans and supporting citizens around the state. The Packers managed their way through the challenges.

Always present, with the nation's freedom and future on the line, was the danger of being perceived as less than patriotic in devotion. It was a tricky position since there was a general sensitivity about so-called big-time athletes banging their apparently strong bodies around on the football field, yet not being well enough for military service. The optics were tough, though nationwide 30 percent of those reporting to Selective Service boards for physicals were rejected.

Initially, single men were selected for government service after those between 21 and 45 registered. There was a marriage exemption, as long as individuals had been married prior to the draft. It should be remembered that in the early 1940s, married women regularly gave up their careers after being wed and did not work outside the home.

A man walking down the street might look okay to the casual observer, but could be branded 4-F for bad vision, arthritis, asthma, flat feet, a punctured eardrum, mental illness, syphilis, or other frailties of health, yet still being well enough to compete in football. Also, he might be a player in time of war like Don Hutson, who was the sole financial support of his immediate family.

20

Making the Most of It

Just shy of 1,000 players, coaches and other National Football League personnel served in the United States military during World War II. While the game persevered and teams played out a schedule, that meant rosters were short-handed, coaching staffs had limited bodies, and so did front offices.

That created opportunities for some players to compete on professional teams who would never have made final rosters during peacetime, and some players who would otherwise have retired stayed around and played a little longer than they would have. Of course, others managed to play such as Don Hutson, who stayed out of the military, and Sammy Baugh and Sid Luckman, who were essentially once-a-week players. The phrase Monday morning quarterbacking about those who second-guess games did not come into parlance until later, but Baugh and Luckman were basically Sunday quarterbacks.

When news broke about Pearl Harbor on December 7, 1941, there were three NFL games under way. The Brooklyn Dodgers and New York Giants were playing at the Polo Grounds. The Chicago Bears were playing the Chicago Cardinals at Comiskey Park. And the Washington Redskins were hosting the Philadelphia Eagles at Griffith Stadium. The public address announcers in New York and in Chicago told servicemen in the stands to report to their outfits. In Washington, higher ranking government and military personnel present were paged. The games went on.

The Packers were not playing, but coach Curly Lambeau had journeyed to Chicago to scout the Bears and Cardinals. Player Tony Canadeo joined him there. Canadeo, who ended up serving in the Navy and the Army during World War II, said he didn't even know where Pearl Harbor was. That may have been true for many Americans. Hawaii was a possession, not yet a state, and it was only after the Japanese attack that

Caught by Don Hutson!

Pearl Harbor took on the semblance of being sacred ground. Canadeo was sitting in the stands when someone who carried a radio to the game announced to those in earshot that Pearl Harbor had been bombed. "Everyone was saying, 'Where the hell is Pearl Harbor?'"[1]

Soon, everyone in the stadium was aware of the breaking news. Bears star George McAfee said, "My wife was at the game. She said people just sat there stunned, with no one talking." After the game concluded, ending with listless play, he felt, "We went over to a Cardinal player's apartment and listened to all the news on the radio."[2]

From the Packers, Clarke Hinkle entered the Coast Guard. Another 16 members of the squad spent time in the service, including Canadeo, Hal Van Every, Carl Mulleneaux, George "Bud" Svendsen, Howard "Smiley" Johnson, and most of the draft picks the Packers had selected from colleges. Commissioner Layden and team owners hoped there would be enough players to have a season, and it turned out there were. All NFL teams faced the same conundrum. Young players they chose were drafted or enlisted, taking their fights to different trenches. Some 21 NFL-connected personnel, 19 of them current or former players, died in World War II. Three pro football individuals received the Congressional Medal of Honor, Jack Lummus of the Giants, Maurice Britt, who played for Detroit in 1941, and Joe Foss, who later served as commissioner of the new American Football League in the early 1960s.

In 1942, before things got even worse, the Packers still fielded a squad with many well-known names. They had Hutson, naturally, but they also retained quarterback Cecil Isbell and such other regulars as Joe Laws, Lou Brock, and Andy Uram, and they still had Canadeo, at least temporarily.

This year was really the "Don and Cecil Show." The 1942 campaign was the best of Hutson's career, and it was also the best of Isbell's career. Hutson set a new record for catches in a single season (breaking his own), and Isbell became the first quarterback to throw for more than 2,000 yards in a season. As long as they were going to play the games, even if they played with a war going on around them, the Packers made their time on the field count and went hard after the Western Division title and a sixth NFL championship.

The regular season opened September 27, a little later than usual, and lined up most of the usual suspects for the Packers. They opened versus the Bears in front of 20,007 fans at City Stadium. Although the Bears were minus many individuals who shifted to military service,

20. Making the Most of It

they remained a major power in the league and still retained many key weapons from a two-time defending titlist. In a pretty good scuffle, they acted as if nothing had changed, winning 44–28.

Green Bay fell behind at first, rallied with 21 points in the second quarter, and then watched the Bears pull away with a 31-point second half. Gary Famiglietti totaled three touchdowns for Chicago as the dominating offensive figure. While Hutson and Isbell could not produce the victory, they got off to a good start that reminded the rest of the league they were still around. Isbell hit Hutson on a 40-yard touchdown in the second period and with a 25-yard pass in the third period. Hutson also kicked two extra points.

The next week, October 4, the Packers lined up against the other Chicago team, the Cardinals, before 24,897 fans at Comiskey Park. In recent years, the Packers had the upper hand against this Chicago bunch in wins, but many of the contests were close. In this game, the Cardinals took a 13–3 lead into the fourth quarter. The Packers inched closer on a 5-yard TD throw from Isbell to Hutson, but the outcome appeared bleak until later. Green Bay survived on a stunning defensive play by Charley Brock for the decisive touchdown. Brock rambled 20 yards with a fumble, but it was no simple dropped pigskin that gave him the ball.

Long into retirement, Brock labeled this encounter "The Game I Will Never Forget." The reason? "I'll never forget the first time I stole a ball and scored a touchdown. We were losing 13–7 and Curly Lambeau was furious. This was the era of the two-way player and when we went on defense, Lambeau yelled, 'Go out and get that ball if you have to steal it!' On the very next play we stood up their fullback at the line of scrimmage and the ball was there for the asking. I just took it out of his arms and started running. But it seemed like three miles."[3]

Linemen, whose field of play is often confined to a 15-yard radius, routinely make such comments when they come into possession of the football and must run to daylight. Lambeau probably was furious because if the Packers lost this one, they would have been 0–2 for the season.

The Packers took a break from close calls in the following game, trouncing the Detroit Lions, 38–7. Isbell hurled three touchdown passes, two to Hutson, who kicked extra points after each of them, and one to Uram. The pass to Uram traveled six yards. The passes to Hutson traveled 20 and 69 yards. The Packers notched a fourth TD through the

Caught by Don Hutson!

air when Tony Canadeo hit Keith Ranspot on a 25-yarder to wrap up the scoring.

The Cleveland Rams had their way with the Packers' defense at selected moments on October 18 at City Stadium, notably in a 21-point second quarter. But Green Bay had sufficient firepower to deflect the threat and move to 3–1 on the season. Hutson scored on two touchdown passes, the longest of 26 yards, and contributed five extra points, Isbell scored on a run, and Joe Laws reined in a TD pass from Canadeo in the 45–28 decision.

The Packers were ahead, 31–21, when Isbell completed the shortest touchdown pass of his career to Hutson in the fourth quarter. The Packers were inside the Cleveland 1-yard line when Isbell caught both the defense and his own coach by surprise with his play call. Officially, the score was a 1-yard pass. Unofficially, the distance to the end zone was claimed to be four inches. Although Isbell and Hutson were devastatingly effective in the long game, sometimes the short game paid off well, too.

"I was also a good short passer, although no one probably knows that Don and I may [have] collaborated on the shortest touchdown pass of all time, four inches," Isbell said. It was first down and the ball was practically touching the goal line.

> Somebody asked me later why we'd throw from such a short distance. "That's why it wasn't as silly as it seemed," I explained. If it failed, we still had three shots for the touchdown. Besides, I always felt more confidence scoring with Hutson than with any other way. What made it remarkable was not the distance, but the catch. I was so excited that I threw the ball way over his head. It took a miraculous, one-handed catch to save the play. When I came off the field, our coach, Curly Lambeau, grabbed me and screamed, "Don't you ever do that again!" Maybe. "I won't," I said. But I'm not sure I wouldn't have tried it again.[4]

A rematch with the Lions followed in Detroit, but it was more of a replay, with the Packers in charge all the way with a TD in each quarter for a 28–7 victory. Andy Uram, who already had a 97-yard run from scrimmage on his resume from a previous year, ran back a kickoff 98 yards for a touchdown after Detroit collected its lone score. Detroit came out of this game with an 0–6 record.

Brock may have saved the Packers in the first meeting against the Cardinals, but the win gave Green Bay a major spark and they began a serious run. The second time the squads played, it was all-Green

20. Making the Most of It

Bay-all-the-time in a 55–24 triumph. Isbell threw five touchdown passes. Hutson scored on three of them, going 40, 73, and 65 yards in a rambunctious showing. Uram was not far behind, grabbing the other two touchdown tosses from Isbell on gains of 64 and 36 yards. But he caught another touchdown of 62 yards hurled by Joe Laws. In all, Green Bay gained 423 yards passing that day (333 by Isbell), and 539 yards total in the game.

Green Bay kept up its wicked offensive pace a week later by taking down the Rams for a second time, 30–12. The Packers were an unstoppable machine on offense, it seemed, particularly through the air. Hutson and Isbell (sometimes with an assist from a backup) beat up on defenses everywhere. This time Hutson grabbed three more touchdown passes, two from Isbell and one from Canadeo, the longest of 15 yards, and his foot added three more points. There was only a short time during the game when Cleveland got within reach. The Rams narrowed the margin to 16–12 before the Packers ran off two more touchdowns.

After six consecutive wins, Green Bay was after revenge in the November 18 game against the Bears at Wrigley Field. Wartime or not, attendance was logged at 42,787. FDR seemed correct that Americans were thirsty for entertainment. These were the types of games Green Bay fans and citizens loved, a chance to tweak the nose of the big-city representatives. But the Bears were riding a multi-year high, the 1940s, war interruptions or not, proving to be the most accomplished in the long history of the franchise.

This game went sour for the Packers from the start, and it was never close. Chicago won, 38–7, and Green Bay did not even get on the board until the fourth quarter. By the time Hutson grabbed a 7-yard touchdown pass from Isbell, the Packers were doomed. The contest started ignominiously for high-scoring Green Bay and got worse from there. Future Hall of Fame center-linebacker Clyde "Bulldog" Turner rambled 42 yards with a fumble for the Bears' first score. Then Sid Luckman, whose primary job was to hurl touchdown passes, intercepted a pass from the other side and ran it back 54 yards for another touchdown. It was 31–0 after three quarters, and it was apparent to observers that unless Chicago committed unanticipated missteps, no one was going to catch the Bears in the West.

As well as the Packers played all season against everyone except the Bears, if they had half a chance to come from behind in the standings, they had to win out. On November 22, up against the usually tough,

Caught by Don Hutson!

but this year faltering New York Giants, they produced a clunker. The 30,246 spectators squatting in the Polo Grounds were happy with a 21–21 tie, leaving their team 3–5–1. Green Bay even had to make a surge in the fourth quarter with a final TD to salvage that. Hutson scored two six-pointers launched on passes from Isbell and kicked three extra points, and the other Packers touchdown came from Canadeo.

Green Bay's record was 6–2–1. There was no indication the Bears were going to fall apart, and they had two wins in hand over the Packers with Green Bay having just two games left. Maybe the Packers were psyched out because they knew they were not going to win it all, but they did win two tight games to finish out. They beat the losing Philadelphia Eagles, 7–0, and the improved, now-named Pittsburgh Steelers, 24–21. The victories were not overly impressive, but they were wins.

Sure enough, the only touchdown scored in the game versus Philadelphia that left the Eagles 2–9–1, was recorded by Hutson on a 31-yard pass from Isbell. It was a microcosm of Green Bay's season, although in this one the defense was the true standout, holding Philadelphia to 130 yards of offense.

On a rare occasion for the time, Pittsburgh was better than average and better than it had been in a long while. The Steelers were hungrier, too, for an upset. Hutson booted a 20-yard field goal and three extra points. Isbell completed three touchdown passes, though none went to Hutson.

The Packers ended up 8–2–1, a solid season, but in second place in the West. No playoffs, no chance to capture another title. The Bears steamrolled the league, going 11–0, with 376 points scored and only 84 allowed. Green Bay was not the only one that had difficulty with Chicago that year. The Bears seemed certain to win a third straight world championship. The Redskins easily took the East with a 10–1 record. Memories were fresh of the Bears' 73–0 wipeout of the Redskins in the 1940 championship game. Maybe no devastation would occur, but the overall thinking was that the winner would be the Bears in a walk. Not so. The Redskins, playing for pride and revenge, won 14–6.

Green Bay had not won the prize it desired the most during the 1942 season. The Bears had proven to be the better team twice. But Don Hutson and Cecil Isbell showed they had no peers in the passing game. This was Hutson's finest season. His 74 catches set a new NFL record, improving on his own standard of 58 catches he established the year before. His 1,211 yards gained through the air led the league and also

20. Making the Most of It

set a new record. As did his 17 touchdown receptions. He attempted 34 points after touchdown, leading the NFL in that category, making all but one, or 97.1 percent. The 33 made was another league-leading statistic. The league was used to this sort of accomplishment from Hutson, and perhaps his numbers were up because the competition was down due to war departures, but he was still doing things no one else had done, or could do.

Isbell, who had more competition for quarterback recognition, had led the league in completions, yards gained, and touchdown passes in 1941. But in 1942 he did it all over again in louder, more emphatic fashion. He was tops in completions again with 146, and his tosses gained 2,021 yards. This was the first time in National Football League history a passer topped that barrier. He threw for 24 touchdowns, which was an average of more than two per game in an 11-game season. It was phenomenal production.

Although Isbell originally had to work his way past Arnie Herber, a future Hall of Fame, merely to become the main signal-caller for Green Bay, he never retained the amount of fame from his peak years that accrued to Sammy Baugh and Sid Luckman. For good reason. Those outstanding players, forever identified with a single franchise, remained in top form year after year. However, Isbell stunned Green Bay, Curly Lambeau, and the football world by retiring from the professional game after the 1942 season to go into coaching.

Isbell was making $10,000-a-year for Green Bay and accepted a two-thirds salary chop. The harsh world of pro football as a business got to him. He did not like the way the Packers parted with Herber, who had been a mainstay. "I saw Lambeau go around the locker room and tell players like Arnie Herber they were done," Isbell said. "I vowed it would never happen to me."[5]

Isbell competed for the Packers for just five seasons—his entire career included 54 regular-season games—and he was only 27 years old when his abrupt decision was made. He did not leave the Packers to enter military service, but to become an assistant coach for the football team at his alma mater, Purdue University, for one season before becoming the Boilermakers' head man for three years. Only the 1945 team, which finished 7–3, made a significant impact in the Big Ten. He resurfaced as head coach of the Baltimore Colts, then affiliated with the new All-America Football Conference, for parts of three seasons after World War II. His best year with that organization was 7–7.

Caught by Don Hutson!

Isbell and Hutson roomed together on the road for the five seasons they played together with the Packers and were very close. Somehow, it was misconstrued by some sportswriters that they did not get along and were not even speaking to one another. Isbell couldn't understand how such a rumor started. The first time Isbell saw such balderdash in print was the year he got married. Isbell used this example to illustrate how close he and Hutson were and to debunk commentary they were not on speaking terms. "Don and his wife went to Hawaii with us on our honeymoon," Isbell said.[6]

Hutson and Isbell were close enough that they discussed retiring from pro football at the same time, and initially Hutson planned to join Isbell on the sidelines after 1942. Lambeau lobbied the heck out of Hutson to return and also urged Isbell to sign a new contract. The effort worked on Hutson but failed with Isbell.

For a time in the 1930s and 1940s, the Joe Carr Memorial Trophy was the name attached to the NFL's Most Valuable Player Award. Carr was an early commissioner of the league. Hutson won the award for his play in 1941 and 1942 and was presented with the second piece of hardware at the start of the 1943 season. By then he was already wishing Isbell had stuck it out and stayed with the Packers. "I hope Cece changes his mind," Hutson said, "because I'm sure every fan and every writer would want to see him pitch again. Don't quote me [he was quoted anyway], but I even think the other coaches in the league would like it. He's that good tossing that pigskin."[7]

21

New Looks for 1943

While all NFL franchises conducted the business of play under great hardship during World War II, some franchises almost did not make it through in one piece. The Brooklyn Dodgers' roster was so depleted in 1943, many of the team's ex-players came out of retirement to help out. The Cleveland Rams chose not to play a schedule at all that year. The Pittsburgh Steelers and Philadelphia Eagles were hurting so badly for players they merged for the 1943 season, calling themselves the Steagles. In 1944, that arrangement dissolved, but the Steelers and the Cardinals worked together, using the unwieldy name Card-Pitt.

Those were major changes affecting league teams, as if all the personnel shifts were not. Rosters were in great flux, and even though Cecil Isbell's shocking retirement was a big change for the Green Bay Packers, not because of World War II. Coach Curly Lambeau knew there were going to be trying times for the Packers, but he had not anticipated being forced to round up another first-rate quarterback.

Herber joined the team in 1930, although he was not the passing leader until 1932, but for a decade, with few back-up moments of glory going to others, the Packers relied on Herber and Isbell as the on-field leaders. Now real NFL-caliber players were at a premium. There was a player shortage across the league, and being forced to find a top-notch starting quarterback with any level of experience was a challenge. The Packers, more than most teams, needed a Herber or Isbell since the team counted on the forward pass so much to feed Don Hutson. Hutson was a special talent who had fortunately meshed with the previous two star quarterbacks. Green Bay needed a high-caliber passer to get the ball into Hutson's hands downfield, or they would be limiting their own offensive power.

Lambeau was a hard-nosed man who fancied himself irresistible to women. He split up with his wife and seemingly dated anyone attractive

Caught by Don Hutson!

in a skirt. Some players even accused of him of making passes at their wives. During the war, however, especially when the Packers played home games elsewhere in Wisconsin, a soft and generous side of Lambeau shone through. When the Packers played in Wisconsin's biggest city, he provided tickets to youngsters living in orphanages and also made sure they got drinks and snacks.

Lambeau entreated Isbell to eschew retirement, but it was a futile appeal. Efforts to obtain a new veteran quarterback or pick one through the draft failed, since the only draft most college football players were paying attention to at the time was the Selective Service draft.

That meant the popular, multi-skilled Tony Canadeo, who had shown considerable aptitude for making clutch plays on offense during his young career, was now the full-time man behind center. Canadeo was born in Chicago and attended high school there. Then he drifted 2,000 miles westward to play college football at Gonzaga. In Spokane, Washington, he earned the nickname, "The Gray Ghost of Gonzaga." Unlike Red Grange, who had the more stirring "Galloping Ghost" moniker bestowed on him at the University of Illinois in the 1920s, Canadeo was not nicknamed that because his swift running made him as hard to tackle as a ghost. It was because his hair was prematurely graying at a young age.

Canadeo, who also boxed in college, was a star on the last Gonzaga Bulldogs team that played big-time football before the administration dropped the sport. Canadeo, selected by Green Bay in the 1941 college draft, has the distinction of being the last Gonzaga gridiron man to play professional football. He made the team despite being chosen in the ninth round. Canadeo had some sparkling moments for the Pack in 1941 and 1942, but in 1943 he had significant responsibility. He was 24 with some seasoning when he took over as quarterback.

Canadeo was 5-foot-11 and weighed 190 pounds. He was an all-around skilled football player, but he did not have the arm strength of Herber or Isbell, even if he was a well-respected leader. He might respect Hutson's value as a receiver, but that did not mean he could thread the needle or always find him open downfield. It took more work for the connection to be made. Canadeo was a better runner than Herber or Isbell, and that figured since that had been his primary occupation. Overall, Canadeo was as versatile as any player who ever suited up for the Packers, running the ball, catching the ball, throwing the ball, receiving punts and kickoffs and punting. Oh, and he played defense,

21. New Looks for 1943

too. He was a valuable man to have around and excelled sufficiently that he was elected to the Pro Football Hall of Fame.

Much later, in the 1970s, when the NFL was inhabited by specialists, someone asked Canadeo which position he would be playing. "I'd probably be an offensive back," Canadeo said. "There's no way I can see any player playing offense and defense now. With all the specialists teams have, there are 11 fresh men on the field at all times."[1]

There was no one else on the Packers to turn to as a new quarterback for the 1943 season. The United States was well into war footing by then with more and more players giving up their commitments to their sports to swear allegiance to the Armed Services. The safety and future of the country were paramount. Several NFL teams were hurting, but the league drew up a full schedule and the Packers prepared to play. Even with George Halas overseas, the juggernaut Bears were favored to win the West ahead of Green Bay and contend for another title.

Green Bay was the smallest home for a professional sports franchise, but the Packers had to play by the same rules as the big boys, compete against them not only on the field, but for players. The Green Bay residents were no less patriotic during World War II. Even with such a huge distraction and more significant events occurring elsewhere in the world, the passion for the Packers was undiluted. It may have been that Green Bay football fans always cared more about their guys than they did in other places.

By this point in Don Hutson's career, he was nationally known, but he was a local hero nonetheless. He lived in the community, and his family lived in the community. He may have been a transplant from Arkansas, but he was a Green Bay boy now. In shades of 2022, by the 1940s, Hutson even had some product endorsements. One supporter, so to speak, was Jockey Underwear, which through one of its nearby stores in Kenosha, Wisconsin, advertised in the Green Bay newspapers with such phrases as "There is Only One Don Hutson. There is Only One Jockey." Whether or not such discussions took place in a board room before the ad campaign was dreamed up, one thing Hutson excelled at was faking defensive backs out of their jocks.

He continued to do so during the 1943 season, even minus Cecil Isbell, overcoming his own reluctance to keep playing and gradually becoming attuned to Canadeo. Hutson set numerous pass receiving records in 1942 and although the Packers did not reach the

Caught by Don Hutson!

championship game, they put up pinball-like scoring numbers. The offense was not quite as efficient in 1943.

Opening day was September 26, and the first game of the new NFL season brought the Chicago Bears to town. Nice test right away. The tenacious rivals understood that getting the upper hand in the West Division meant winning the head-to-head encounters, and sometimes it took hand-to-hand confrontations. This game was well-hyped, but nothing much was settled, although it was a pretty good game. The outcome witnessed by 23,675 fans at City Stadium was a 21–21 tie.

The Bears scored first in the first quarter on a Sid Luckman touchdown pass, and the Packers knotted things at the half when one of the franchise's newer weapons, Ted Fritsch, Sr., the replacement for retired Clarke Hinkle, scored on a 4-yard run. This was Fritsch's first career TD. Hutson, by now pretty much the full-time designated booter, kicked the extra point, one of three he had in the game. Chicago led, 21–14, in the fourth period, but Canadeo, coping well with the pressure inherent in his new role, found an open Hutson for a 37-yard touchdown pass.

Green Bay followed with a 28–7 victory the next week in Chicago against the Cardinals. New weapon Joel Mason scored two touchdowns, Fritsch added one, and holdover Harry Jacunski contributed another. Jimmy Conzelman, who viewed Hutson as the ultimate game-breaker, didn't have to worry about the receiver this day, for two reasons. Hutson's only visit to the scoreboard came through four extra points, and Conzelman wasn't there. His first of two Cardinals coaching stints ended after the 1942 season.

Fritsch, a native of Spencer, Wisconsin, who attended Wisconsin-Stevens Point, was a fullback with a knack for bulling the ball into the end zone from close quarters. His importance to the team gradually grew, and he spent his entire NFL career, through 1950, with the Packers, in 1946 leading the league with nine touchdowns and scoring 100 points. Although he was born in Green Bay, where his family stayed, Ted Jr., at 242 pounds about 30 more pounds than his dad, also became a pro football player. Ted Jr. spent seven years in the league, but none with the Packers.

As they recently had, the Packers next had their way with the Detroit Lions in a home game, belting Detroit, 35–14, before 21,396 fans. Packers fans continued to turn out in good numbers for home gamers during the war. Except for five extra points, Hutson did not score, though Fritsch did once more and Andy Uram collected two

21. New Looks for 1943

touchdowns, both on passes from Canadeo. Lou Brock also caught a TD throw from Canadeo in one of the new QB's best passing games. On a day when Green Bay accumulated 445 yards of offense, the Packers gained 206 through the air.

Hutson and Canadeo connected just fine in an October 17 game, also at City Stadium, but the 23,058 in attendance did not leave with smiles on their faces. Hutson's touchdown covered 16 yards, but it came in the fourth quarter and was Green Bay's only TD of the day. Sammy Baugh riddled the Packers' secondary, firing four touchdown passes in a 33–7 victory. The Redskins had taken down the mighty Bears in the title game the preceding season and looked mighty good this day. In 1943, Baugh was on his way to a 23-touchdown-pass season while leading the league in completions, attempts, and yards gained through the air.

The licking-their-wounds defeat left the Packers with a 2–1–1 record and serious doubts. They then experienced a rematch against the Lions, and the easy 27–6 triumph made them feel better. Hutson caught a 16-yard touchdown pass, kicked a 21-yard field goal, and kicked three extra points. Lou Brock scored twice.

A year earlier, the Packers could not shake free of the New York Giants. This was a different chapter in the long-running string of games between the clubs. The Packers traveled to the Polo Grounds, where they were welcomed by 46,208 spectators, and outplayed the Giants, 35–21, with a strong finish after the game was tied 21–21 in the fourth quarter. Hutson nabbed touchdown throws of 17 and 12 yards from Canadeo, kicked five extra points, and even thew a touchdown pass to jump-start Green Bay's scoring in the first period. It came on a 38-yard pass play with Harry Jacunski.

The only blemish on the Chicago Bears' record at that point was the smudge of a tie with the Packers. In their second game, Chicago proved superior with a 21–7 victory at Wrigley Field. The fans continued to show up during the height of the war and at a time when the war news was not particularly encouraging. They bought 43,425 tickets for this one to see Sid Luckman direct traffic and score a TD himself. Canadeo ran for the only Green Bay six-pointer. The message was pretty much delivered that the Packers did not have the goods to go all the way this season—unless the Bears faltered.

As it so happened, the Packers acquitted themselves well after this loss, pretty much rampaging through the last three regular-season games. Green Bay clobbered the Chicago Cardinals, 35–14, who were

Caught by Don Hutson!

0–8 after their trip to Wisconsin. Hutson ruined the Cardinals by himself, catching touchdown passes of nine and four yards and scoring on an 84-yard interception return. And he contributed four extra points.

Hutson did the same kind of damage November 21 at Ebbets Field, where the Packers polished off the Brooklyn Dodgers, 31–7. It was too much Hutson all-around. He scored the game's opening points on a 51-yard TD throw from Canadeo, then kicked a 23-yard field goal in the second quarter. After halftime, Hutson burst away on a 79-yard touchdown pass play initiated by backup Irv Comp. All four Packers extra points were propelled by Hutson's foot.

On December 5, following a bye week, the Packers met the combined Philadelphia Eagles-Pittsburgh Steelers outfit, aka the Steagles, and closed the regular season with a 38–28 win. Hutson caught two more touchdown passes, both from Comp, and kicked a 23-yard field goal and five extra points. Green Bay concluded with a 7–2–1 record. The Bears won the West with an 8–1–1 mark. Washington and New York each posted 6–3–1 records in the East, but the Redskins became the title-game representative with a 28–0 playoff victory. Then the Bears topped Washington, 41–21, for the crown. In a bully-for-them moment, the Steagles recorded a 5–4–1 winning record.

In his first year directing the offense, Canadeo completed 56 passes in 129 attempts for 875 yards and nine touchdowns. Comp definitely had his shining moments, going 46 for 92 for 662 yards and seven touchdowns. Comp, who was a native of Milwaukee, was a rookie in 1943 and was not in danger of being drafted into the military because he only could see out of one eye. He had cataracts in his left eye that left him legally blind.

Comp was an all-around sports star in high school at Bay View High, and his arm strength was such he was sometimes called "The Bay View Bazooka." He enrolled at the University of Wisconsin but flunked out. Then he went on Benedictine College in Kansas, where he received no national attention. Still, Lambeau remembered him from high school and took a chance, drafting Comp in the third round of the NFL player selection sweepstakes.

"If I had to do it all over again," Comp said later about his competitive sports life, "I'd do the same thing. I played four sports and enjoyed them all. You get more attention at a place like [Benedictine]. At big schools you're just a number."[2]

As for Hutson that year, he did not approach his record-breaking

21. New Looks for 1943

stats achieved in 1942 in concert with Isbell. But playing with a new starter at the position in Canadeo and a backup with even less experience, he still led the NFL in all the basic receiving categories: Most catches, (47) yards (776), and touchdowns (11).

Pretty much Hutson's entire career would have been an ESPN highlight reel. He always said his biggest thrill with the Packers occurred when he scored his first touchdown on the long pass against the Bears. But later he gave some bonus points of excitement to two plays from the 1943 season. He touted a couple of his more off-beat scores rather than his more frequent long touchdown-catching scores. "My interception of a Cardinal pass in a 1943 game in which I made an 85-yard return for a touchdown was a big thrill, too," Hutson said, "and so was that touchdown pass I threw to Harry Jacunski."[3]

The interception return of his memory actually went into the books at 84 yards. The touchdown heave was in the tie versus the Giants. Maybe Hutson should have become his own quarterback.

Green Bay Packers 1944 team picture. The team won the NFL crown that year (courtesy Neville Public Museum of Brown County).

22

One More Crown

For all of those years, the Green Bay Packers found magic at quarterback, through Arnie Herber's prime and Cecil Isbell's too-short prime. Then coach Curly Lambeau pretty much manufactured a new quarterback out of thin air when Tony Canadeo stepped in for the 1943 season.

Canadeo was young and productive, looking as if he could fill the role for years, or at least until the end of World War II and the resumption of a more normal college draft. That would have been acceptable. Canadeo, who was in the Navy, like Sammy Baugh and Sid Luckman, finagled his weekends to play for the Packers in 1943. But after he received an early discharge, he managed just three games in 1944 because he went into the Army and didn't play again until 1946. In pro sports vernacular, it was almost as if Canadeo had been traded from the Navy to the Army. Along with Canadeo's departure in 1944 was Andy Uram's, another Packer on to the Armed Forces.

As if Lambeau didn't nurse a personnel headache for the entire length of the war, Don Hutson was again making noise about retiring. Once again, he changed his mind and committed to playing the 1944 season. Lambeau worked Hutson over verbally. He finally signed a contract on September 1. Lambeau gave Hutson a raise and made him an assistant coach, too. Lineman Buckets Goldenberg said he was retiring, missed the first game of the season, but was cajoled back into the line for a last go-around.

Still, it was getting kind of thin in the quarterback ranks. The only one left who seemed remotely capable of doing the job was second-year man Irv Comp, who was not fit for military service because of his lack of vision in the left eye. Yet he emerged as the QB for Green Bay, doing a remarkable job with his overall athletic gifts despite the handicap. Every team was hurting for players and top-quality players, as the war was of

22. One More Crown

primary attention in towns and cities, at the work place, and at sporting venues. Things were improving on that front, in fact, on several fronts, better by all accounts in all ways than they were at the nadir on the morning after the assault on Pearl Harbor.

As did many others in the civilian population, citizens of Green Bay not in the military were employed in critical stateside jobs for the war effort. Curly Lambeau was in touch with Commissioner Elmer Layden, who said he favored players taking factory jobs or the like that would help the country, and it was okay for them to play for the Packers on Sundays.

At one point, there was a short story in the *Green Bay Press-Gazette* which read, "If you want to be a fullback on the Green Bay Packer football team this fall you may have to learn how to back up a rivet as well as you can back up a line."[1]

Lambeau said such workers could do their country a service by working at other jobs at the same time they were employed by the Packers.

> If the War Manpower Commission believes pro football players should work on war jobs, we see no reason why they can't do so and play football, too. They could start work on an early shift and be through in time to get in daily drills. If they need be, they could practice at night under the lights. In the old days of pro football, most of the players worked at other jobs and played football on Sunday. There's no reason why they can't do the same thing to keep the game alive.[2]

In some ways, pro football was hanging by a thread, with more and more players going to war. The Chicago Bears, a mini-dynasty of the first few years of the 1940s, sent more and more players into the service, so lost some stature as a powerhouse. The Bears won the NFL title in 1940, 1941, and 1943 and lost in the championship game in 1942. Then they lost more men to the Armed Forces. The Packers, without any kind of experience to speak of at quarterback, were in no position to make rash predictions about their own fortunes, except expressing a willingness and preparedness to keep playing.

During January of 1944, Royal Air Force planes unleashed a bombardment on Berlin, the heart of Germany, giving the Nazis back some of the same medicine poured on England. Late in the month, the siege of Leningrad ended after 872 days, the Soviet Union finally hurling back the German advance.

At various atolls and other locations in the South Pacific, American

Caught by Don Hutson!

troops drove out Japanese invaders in bloody battles. Allied forces in Europe kept making gains, and on June 6, 1944, the D-Day invasion was launched at Normandy in France by 155,000 Allied troops to take back the continent. In the weeks and months leading up to the fall football season, there was much more good news from the war fronts, including victories by the Free French, the Soviets, and Americans. Japanese forces were starting to demonstrate increased desperation when 4,300 men unleashed a Banzai charge on Saipan and were slaughtered.

German generals plotted to overthrow and assassinate dictator Adolf Hitler, but the plan failed. Parts of France, Italy, Luxembourg, and Belgium were being liberated from German occupation by advancing Allied forces, and the first of that wave crossed into Germany proper.

Packers regular-season play began for 1944 on September 17 at Wisconsin State Fair Park before 12,994 fans. It was the first of five straight home games awarded the team to start the year. Then they went on the road for the rest of the season. The visiting team was the Brooklyn Tigers, who had changed their nickname from Dodgers. The result was the usual, though, favoring Green Bay, 14–7.

The Packers took the lead in the first quarter, Brooklyn tied it in the third quarter, and the Packers finished the scoring in that same period. Appropriately, Hutson scored Green Bay's first touchdown of the season on a 24-yard completion from Irv Comp. Lou Brock scored the other TD on a 17-yard run, and Hutson kicked two extra points.

The Packers did not have to wait long for the first test barometer of the season, with the Bears arriving at Wisconsin State Fair Park on September 24. Attendance was double at 24,362, and the Bears were not as doubly good as they had been. It was a grand, 42–28 victory for Green Bay and a pretty good game for spectators. Green Bay led 14–0 after the first quarter and 28–7 at halftime, but still had to fight off the Bears late when they clawed back to 28–28.

The Pack needed its two fourth-quarter touchdowns. Lou Brock gave the lead back to Green Bay on a 42-yard TD run, and Ted Fritsch scored the clinching touchdown on a 50-yard pass interception. Hutson and Comp connected on a 26-yard TD throw, Comp ran for a score himself, and Hutson kicked six useful extra points. Green Bay's offense totaled 364 yards.

On October 1, the Packers moved to 3–0, handling the Detroit Lions as they had consistently in recent years by posting a 27–6 win. Hutson caught a 3-yard touchdown pass from Comp, but in perhaps

22. One More Crown

the niftiest play of the game, the young quarterback caught a touchdown pass himself, thrown for 11 yards by Lou Brock. As had gradually become a regular thing, Hutson kicked three extra points. Hutson was the man with the leg these days, unlike a few seasons earlier when as many as three different Packers booted the point after on any given Sunday.

The next visitor, this time at City Stadium, was the hanging-in-there Card-Pitt (Chicago Cardinals and Pittsburgh Steelers) combined team. This was a no-mercy game with the Packers raising their record to 4–0 with a 34–7 romp. Hutson welcomed the amalgamated team to Wisconsin with a first-period 55-yard touchdown reception from Comp and caught a second, 7-yard touchdown pass from him in the second quarter. The Packers scored heavily, early and late.

Green Bay gained 388 yards to the other guys' 187, and that included 241 yards through the air. The defense held the visitors to 61 yards rushing.

Over and over, no matter who tried to cover him, Hutson kept proving he could wiggle into the open and catch long passes resulting in touchdowns, whether thrown by Arnie Herber or Cecil Isbell, or flung by Tony Canadeo or Irv Comp. Some arms were better than others, some quarterbacks were better than others, but it did not seem to make much difference. If the ball went into the air anywhere near Hutson's grasp, he could get a hand on it, pull it in, and run to the end zone.

Legendary Clark Shaughnessy, the College Football Hall of Fame coach who developed the T-formation and installed it for the Bears and Sid Luckman, was looking ahead when he analyzed Hutson's impact on football. "In the years to come, whenever forward-pass catching is mentioned, one name will always be mentioned first, Don Hutson, without a doubt the greatest pass catcher the game of football has ever known and probably the greatest it will ever know," Shaughnessy said. "No one but Superman could perform the feats Don Hutson has performed in catching passes."[3]

Although Shaughnessy's vantage point was contemporary, while the man was still playing, the coach's analysis was pretty much spot on. Bud Lea, a long-time Milwaukee newspaper sports columnist, who was born and grew up in Green Bay, saw Hutson play live as a youth. One thing he noted, nearly 55 years after Shaughnessy made his comment, was, "He was always referred to as 'The Great Don Hutson.' Once you saw him play, you knew the reasons why."[4]

Caught by Don Hutson!

Lambeau saw Hutson play over and over again, year after year, and never tired of watching his man out-smart and out-play the opposition. "He would glide downfield, leaning forward as if to steady himself close to the ground," Lambeau said. "Then, as suddenly as you gulp, or blink an eye, he would feint one way and go the other, reach up like a dancer, gracefully squeeze the ball and leave the scene of the accident. The accident being the defensive backs who tangled their feet up and fell trying to cover him."[5]

In the final game in this lengthy home skein, the Packers took on the Cleveland Rams, winning 30–21, but needed a strong second-half defensive effort to hold back the visitors. The Rams got as close as 28–21 in the fourth quarter before a Packers safety clinched matters. Hutson kicked four extra points but was kept out of the end zone. Then the Packers waved goodbye to Green Bay.

The first game on the road took place in Detroit against the Lions, who were weak enough to be 1–3–1 after the Packers beat them, 14–0, at Briggs Stadium. The attendance was reasonably robust given the Lions' status and the continuing war, with 30,844 paying ticket-holders. The Packers were the bosses in this one although the point differential was not huge. Ted Fritsch scored on a 1-yard run, and Joe Laws scored on a 29-yard touchdown pass from Comp. Hutson kicked two extra points. Detroit was held to 196 total yards.

In early November, the 6–0 Packers brought their act to Chicago for Round 2 versus the Bears, and while the Bears were just 3–2–1 after the game, they bullied the Packers with a 21–0 shutout. QB Sid Luckman was involved in all three Bears touchdowns, getting one himself on a 1-yard run and throwing two TD passes. There were 45,553 fans in the house at Wrigley Field, an impressive turnout, who got what they were after. Green Bay gained only 49 yards rushing in 28 attempts and just 97 through the air. It was a forget-it day for the Packers.

Granted, the Cleveland Rams were not in the same class as the Bears, but they were a near-.500 team when the Packers invaded League Park on November 17. This was a start-to-finish, 42–7 Green Bay romp, raising the Packers' first-place record to 7–1. Hutson caught touchdown passes of 33 and 15 yards from Comp and kicked six extra points. Cleveland did not score until the second half and already trailed 21-zip.

Maybe the performance lulled the Packers, but the next week, November 19, a massive crowd of 56,481 spectators at the Polo Grounds rooted the Giants on every step of the way in a thorough 24–0 wipeout

22. One More Crown

that was more complete than what the Bears had only recently accomplished. The Giants, 5–1–1 afterwards, had the answer for everything Green Bay tried on offense or defense.

New York banked the shutout in bend-do-not-break fashion, permitting 283 yards of offense, but with strict patrolling of the end zone. The Packers could never make the big play when they needed it, even after moving the ball. The margin was a bit of a shock to the Packers.

Only one regular-season game remained on November 26, and fortunately for Green Bay, the schedule provided an opportunity against one of the least challenging NFL teams. That Sunday offered up the winless Cardinals-Steelers group. When the Packers won, 35–20, it completed their regular season at 8–2. The mixed team, which also seemed like a mixed-up team under its extenuating circumstances, ended 0–10. Hutson grabbed touchdown passes of 36 yards and 6 yards and kicked five extra points.

Green Bay won the West, with the Bears and late-rallying Lions finishing in a second-place tie with 6–3–1 records. The Giants captured the East with an 8–1–1 mark that barely outdid the surprising 7–1–2 Philadelphia Eagles. Given the mauling the Packers took against the Giants, the match-up for the league crown on December 17, back in New York, did not look favorable.

Even with a new quarterback in 1944, Hutson excelled, making 58 catches for 866 yards and nine touchdown receptions. Comp did all right, completing 80 of 177 passes for 1,159 yards and 12 touchdowns. Hutson made 31 out of 33 extra point tries and led the National Football League in scoring with 85 points, 19 more than the second-highest total. This was the seventh time Hutson led the league in catches, the seventh time he led in yards gained through passing, and the ninth time he led in touchdown catches.

The showdown with New York did not figure to be any picnic, but there was an intriguing sidebar to the meeting. The Giants' quarterback was Arnie Herber. Herber had come out of his early retirement from the Packers. Sure enough, he led his new team into the title game to face his old team. Herber had not played since 1940, yet he returned for two successful seasons with New York in 1944 and 1945 before retiring for good.

The irony would have been supreme if Herber had prevented the Packers, Lambeau, and Hutson from winning a third title together. That's not how the game played out. There were 46,015 fans present who

Caught by Don Hutson!

guessed the Giants would dispose of the Packers the way they had earlier that season.

It was a scoreless first period, and that was already a moral victory for Green Bay compared to the first outing. The Packers ended up gathering all the points they needed in the second quarter when fullback Ted Fritsch scored twice, on a 1-yard run and a 28-yard pass from Comp. Hutson, who had just two catches in the game, kicked both extra points. The Giants did not score until the fourth quarter and could never come back. Neither team ripped off huge amounts of yardage.

The man who ended up with possession of the game ball for Green Bay was defensive lineman Baby Ray, who played 11 seasons with the Packers. Earlier in the same season, Curly Lambeau cheered up Ray after a weak game against the Eagles by saying the Packers would win the crown and he would get that prize of a game ball. Ray said afterwards that team captain Charley Brock tried to scoop up the ball, but Lambeau told him he couldn't keep it, it was going to Ray.

At least Herber didn't burn them. Herber was just 8-for-22 on throws and was saddled with four interceptions, not one of the finer outings of his career. Although it was not in a championship game, a year later, in December of 1945 near the end of the regular season, Herber atoned with the game he said was his greatest achievement in football. On December 2 at the Polo Grounds, he lifted New York to a 28–21 victory over the Philadelphia Eagles by throwing four touchdown passes in the second half. For a 35-year-old on the verge of true retirement, it was a glorious last hurrah. Herber called the performance "a thrill that can hardly be matched for me. When you get old and past your prime, to have a good day—any kind of good day—is a memorable thing in a player's life."[6]

The old Packer and pal of Hutson's went out in style, albeit with another team. Hutson believed he was going to beat Herber to the sidelines permanently after his third championship with the Packers in 1944. He again told Lambeau he was definitely retiring. He made the announcement at a Green Bay luncheon after the title was won, saying he would stick around long enough to play in the summer All-Star charity game, though he still hedged. "I've tried to retire for the past three years," Hutson said. "I intend to retire after the All-Star game. But if the Packers need me to defend their title next year, I'll probably be in there playing again. I intend to sign a new contract as the backfield coach of the Packers, but any reports of my definite retirement before the season

22. One More Crown

starts are premature. I want to quit playing. Ten years in this league is enough."[7]

Lambeau once again put on the full-court verbal press to talk Hutson out of the drastic retirement step. He dangled a raise, but Hutson replied, "Not enough. If I come back next year, I want $15,000." Lambeau acted as if he had taken a stake through the heart, or at least his wallet. "Never," he answered. "Nobody makes $15,000." Hutson was prepared. "Sammy Baugh does," Hutson said. "That will be two of us."[8]

And it was. Lambeau ultimately did not quibble over a thousand dollars here or there, not with Hutson. Years later, Hutson recounted the story and said, "That's the kind of business deal I always liked to make—one that was good for both parties."[9]

23

The Last Go-Around

Don Hutson's pro football career and World War II both ended in 1945, one of them too soon and one of them too late. Hutson was only 32, so he probably could have kept on playing. The end of the war, which began with Germany's invasion of Poland six years earlier, had dragged on and on with extreme devastation.

In January, Franklin D. Roosevelt was sworn in for an unprecedented fourth term as president of the United States. In February, FDR, Winston Churchill, and Josef Stalin met at Yalta to discuss a post-war world as they became convinced Germany and Japan would be defeated and the United States, England, and the Soviet Union would be the superpowers standing. Later that month, American Marines invaded Iwo Jima.

By spring, in early May, Germany surrendered to the Allies unconditionally. In August, after the United States unleashed the atomic bomb on Hiroshima and Nagasaki in Japan, wreaking destruction and horror, the war in the South Pacific ended.

What that meant was that by the time pro football teams were gathering for training camps and beginning a new season, the war had at last concluded. Football players wearing those other uniforms were anxious to return home. Some would never play ball again, due to death, wounds, or rusted skills. Some were not released from their service commitments by the time the season began.

The Packers still had Hutson, sweet-talked into one more year by Curly Lambeau. Thirty-four-year-old veteran Joe Laws was still around. Ted Fritsch and Lou Brock were still in the lineup, and Carl Mulleneaux was back.

One Packer never returned. Howard "Smiley" Johnson, 28, a guard, who entered the service in 1942, played for Green Bay in 1940 and 1941 after attending the University of Georgia. Johnson, who joined the

23. The Last Go-Around

Marines and earned two Purple Hearts and two Silver Stars, was killed in action at Iwo Jima in 1945. The second Silver Star was awarded posthumously. He had attained the rank of lieutenant.

Another Packers lineman, Pete Tinsley, who also played with Johnson in college, said, "He was a tough one."[1] Tinsley had predicted stardom for Johnson if he returned to the Packers after World War II. The VFW Post in Clarksville, Tennessee, Johnson's hometown, was named for him.

While Hutson was in Chicago for the All-Star game, the spot the Packers earned by winning the 1944 championship, he overlapped with old friend Paul "Bear" Bryant. He played a small role in recommending Bryant for his first head coaching job. Hutson was a decade into his pro playing career, but after graduating from Alabama, Bryant had promptly embarked on a college football coaching career.

Between 1936 and 1944, Bryant had been an assistant coach at Union College, Alabama, and Vanderbilt, and for two service teams, Georgia Pre-Flight and North Carolina Pre-Flight, while in the military. With the war over, Bryant wanted to hasten his discharge from the military and obtain a head coaching job.

Hutson and Bryant approached the same climax of a story from two different directions.

Bryant's version of what transpired is this: He and Hutson found themselves at the same cocktail party at the All-Star game hosted by the *Chicago Tribune*, the game's sponsor, and caught up on their lives. More importantly for Bryant, apparently, was the presence of George Preston Marshall, the Washington Redskins owner. Bryant had done some scouting of collegians for Marshall, who wanted to hire him to become an assistant for Washington. But Bryant wanted to be a head man. Hutson said nice things about his pal to anyone who would listen, but when Bryant turned Marshall down and said he wanted to run his own program, Marshall essentially said, "Why didn't you say so?" He immediately pulled strings and got Bryant an offer to become head coach at the University of Maryland.

Hutson's version of what transpired is this: Hutson was in his hotel room when the phone rang, and Marshall was on the other end of the line. Marshall said he was trying to get in touch with Bryant and did Hutson know where he was. "I can get Bryant the coaching job at Maryland if I can find him tonight," Marshall said. Hutson responded, "I just got him a ticket to the game. He's sitting right here on my bed." Marshall

Caught by Don Hutson!

said, "Put him on the line." Hutson said the conversation "launched Bear on the greatest coaching career in football history."[2]

That fall Bryant, 32, did begin his first year as a head college football coach with the Terrapins. Over the coming seasons, Bryant developed his style and leadership as head of programs at Kentucky and Texas A&M before taking over at Alabama, where between 1958 and 1982 he became a bigger legend in Tuscaloosa than Hutson.

The 1945 pro season began on the late side for Green Bay, September 30, with the good old Chicago Bears journeying to City Stadium and 24,525 fans responding. This day, the Packers did more damage on the ground than through the air. Fritsch scored two touchdowns and kicked a field goal, but Hutson collected the extra points, four of them. The Packers led the whole way, but it was as close as 17–14 in the second half.

"The boys came through when the chips were down," Curly Lambeau said of his men. "I was pleased with the way the boys fought." Quarterback Comp was injured, and the Packers had to count on backup Roy McKay, perhaps one reason the ball did not find Hutson deep downfield.[3]

Still, Hutson drew heavy attention on defense and caught what passes he could, three for 83 yards. Bears owner-coach George Halas was still not back on the sideline, and Luke Johnsos, one of his co-coach fill-ins, still felt Hutson made a big impact. "It was old man Hutson," Johnsos said. "Without him they would be equal to us. I hope the fifth time he retires, he means it."[4]

It is difficult to imagine what praise Johnsos would have issued if he had run across Hutson the next week. The Packers invited the Detroit Lions to Wisconsin State Park October 7 and smoked them, 57–21, in front of 20,463. That was the listed attendance for the greatest performance of Hutson's career.

Irv Comp bounced back part-time from his injury of the week before, but Hutson seemed to bond with McKay. They connected on four touchdown passes, covering 56, 46, 17, and 6 yards, all in the second quarter. Hutson kicked extra points after all his own touchdowns, plus another extra point following another Green Bay TD for 29 points himself in a single quarter (and 31 for the game). The Packers scored 41 points in the period, but no individual had so distinguished himself in an NFL game with that kind of scoring in such a short time. More than 75 years later, no one has bested Hutson's one-quarter scoring mark.

This time Hutson left observers agog and sportswriters searching

23. The Last Go-Around

for apt descriptions. One press box inhabitant wrote: "Hutson has had other great days—many of them—in 10 full seasons of play, but he's never had one like Sunday. He made the Detroit defense—composed of veterans, mind you—look silly."[5]

Hutson's 31 points in a game lasted for 16 years as a league record, and it was broken by Green Bay great Paul Hornung when he scored 33 points in one contest. As it so happened, Hutson was in the stands that day to see his record busted.

More than three decades after the occasion, Hutson said he remembered the windy weather more vividly than the 29-point quarter. "It must have been coming out of the north at better than 30 mph," he said. "The stadium was located at the state fairgrounds in the Milwaukee suburb of West Allis and the wind just whipped right down the field. Finally, we got the wind at our backs and there was no stopping us."[6] Hutson said Lambeau guessed correctly that the Packers would steamroll the Lions in this manner once the wind was behind them. After that 41-point second quarter outburst, Hutson said the only other time he played the rest of the day was to kick extra points.

Hutson said he had felt ready to retire from pro football for a couple of years, but being a star on the team in a town that loved its football about as much as its children, he couldn't bring himself to do it each time football season rolled around and each time Lambeau appealed to him.

Yes, he wanted to go on to something new, "But it's hard to retire in Green Bay. Everybody is crazy about football up there and playing the way I had, it was hard to quit," he said. Hutson, a two-way player in accordance with the era, played offense and defense, as well as kicking, so was easily on the gridiron more than 40 minutes out of the 60 played. He had been remarkably healthy but felt it could not last. "The odds were against my going on and not getting hurt."[7]

After such a powerful showing and the buzz created by Hutson's points record, Green Bay sold out City Stadium for a second week in a row for the first time in club history. While fans may not have been expecting a struggle from the Cleveland Rams, Curly Lambeau recognized that the Rams, who had shut out the Chicago Bears, brought a new threat level to town. He had to sell the notion to his players, too.

"The boys are beginning to appreciate that they'll have a battle on their hands against the Rams," Lambeau said during practice. "They're beginning to come up for the game."[8]

Caught by Don Hutson!

The Packers promptly went out and lost, 27–14, before the sellout crowd of 24,000-plus. At 3-0 after this one, the Rams looked stronger than they had in years. Cleveland led 6–0 at halftime and salted the victory away with a 21-point fourth quarter. This was the start of a new-look Rams that carried over to Los Angeles and introduced ex-UCLA star Bob Waterfield to the NFL. Waterfield, a future acting star and member of the Pro Football Hall of Fame, threw for two touchdown passes and ran for another himself. He was also the Rams' new kicker and booted four extra points that day.

Green Bay's next foe was a team that combined forces between the former Brooklyn bunch, the Tigers, and the Yanks, based in Boston. The Packers started the weird team's tailspin with a 38–14 triumph. The Packers' explosiveness included Hutson grabbing two touchdown passes, one from Irv Comp of 75 yards and the other from Roy McKay of 7 yards. Hutson also provided five extra points.

Once again, Green Bay's regular-season schedule was top-heavy with home games, the first five in a row, including the October 28 game against the Chicago Cardinals. This meant the contest versus the Cardinals, which became a 33–14 win, was the last time Packers fans saw Hutson play in person. Hutson was by then determined not to play another season after 1945. He really did expect to retire this time.

The 19,221 fans at City Stadium got vintage Hutson as the Packers raised their record to 4–1 to move into a tie for first place in the West at the expense of the 1–5 Cardinals. Comp found Hutson alone for a 19-yard TD pass in the first quarter and an early Green Bay lead. The Pack produced a 20-point second-quarter eruption that decided the game and was mightily helped by Hutson. He scored the next touchdown on a 12-yard run and followed up with his third touchdown on a 39-yard pass from Comp. He also kicked three extra points that day.

This was not one of the Bears' better seasons, so the Packers arrived in Chicago optimistic for the November 4 meeting at Wrigley Field. Fans did not seem to care if the Bears were out of sorts, they still turned out 45,527 strong. Then they were rewarded with a 28–24 upset. The Packers got out to a 14–0 lead, but the Bears fought back, overtook them, and held on. Hutson's main contributions were three extra points. This would be a huge blow to the Packers' ability to capture another Western Division crown. They basically lost their chance to defend the 1944 championship by dropping to 4–2 in this game.

The defeat came at a terrible time as well. A week later, Green Bay

23. The Last Go-Around

journeyed to Cleveland to face the Rams for the second time. If ever they needed a win in this season, the November 11 game was the one. But the Packers were even flatter against the good Rams than they had been against the off-year Bears, losing 20–7. The Rams ambushed the Packers with 20 points in the first period, and the only touchdown Green Bay scored came on a 75-yard pass from Comp to Clyde Goodnight. Hutson's extra point put him on the board, but neither team scored after the first quarter.

From there, the Packers were chasing a wisp. They thumped the Tigers-Yanks combination, 28–0, and Hutson found the end zone on a 10-yard pass while adding four extra-point boots. For baseball aficionados, it may be noted that the game was played in front of 31,923 fans in the Boston Red Sox's Fenway Park. Nobody realized it, especially since Green Bay had two more games, but that pass reception was the final touchdown of Hutson's career.

Early Thanksgiving week, before the Packers' November 25 game against the usually formidable Giants at the Polo Grounds, Lambeau attended a New York sportswriters' luncheon and took the opportunity to discuss advances made in the passing game. He joked about how every team suddenly claimed to be unearthing slick pass receivers like Don Hutson. "It tickles me to read about all these 'new' Hutsons," Lambeau said. "It seems as if every team has one."[9] The reality was that no other team had one.

This was not New York's year, although loyal fans still supported the Giants to the tune of 52,681 in the house that day. New York did take an early 7–0 lead, but the Packers gradually eroded the margin and inched ahead to win, 23–14. The loss dropped the Giants to 2–5–1. The Packers, although not contending for a title, improved to 6–3. Hutson kicked a 15-yard field goal and two extra points.

The Packers did not even return to Green Bay to practice for the last regular-season game at Detroit, December 2. They worked out in Rye, New York, in Westchester County, before embarking for a second-place showdown versus the Lions. It was not so long ago that the Packers rang up 57 points on Detroit, so they didn't worry too much before this one. They should have worried more. Humiliated by the last result, the Lions handled the Packers, 14–3, in this one. Hutson kicked a 15-yard field goal in his last pro football game. Green Bay finished 6–4, but Detroit's win gave the Lions a 7–3 record.

One might have expected Green Bay sportswriters to make a big

Caught by Don Hutson!

deal out of Hutson's finale, but they did not, perhaps not trusting that he would truly retire. They had been teased before. The biggest aspect of the loss to Detroit was that it ended a 10-game Packers winning streak over the Lions dating to 1940.

Hutson had a first-quarter fumble but caught four passes during the game. He concluded his last season with 47 catches to lead the NFL again. He totaled 834 yards and scored nine TDs through the air, too, though those numbers did not top the league. Hutson also scored 97 points, but that did not lead the league, either.

Green Bay Packers receiving star Don Hutson on the occasion of his induction into the Pro Football Hall of Fame in Canton, Ohio in 1963 (courtesy Pro Football Hall of Fame).

23. *The Last Go-Around*

Right after the final game, United Press International announced its annual professional football all-league team. Fullback Ted Fritsch and center Charley Brock were chosen from Green Bay, joined by Don Hutson. It was the seventh straight year Hutson was selected for that all-star recognition.

Although at least one newspaper made a little bit of fun of Hutson's annual retirement announcements, this time he meant it. The 1945 season was his last.

24

Legacy

When Don Hutson finally did retire from the Green Bay Packers and the National Football League after the 1945 season, he owned 19 league records for receiving and scoring, including all of the big ones. When a pro football annual was published, his achievements took up a full page in the record book.

Key records included catching 488 passes during his 11-year career when passes were not thrown nearly as often as they are in the present-day NFL, catching 99 touchdown passes, and scoring 105 touchdowns in all. His yardage total was 7,991. His career points total was 825, with a high of 138 in a season. Between points scored, catches made, passing yards gained, and touchdowns caught, Hutson led the NFL in those major categories 29 times.

Hutson set the record for most receiving yards in one game with 209 at a time when often whole teams did not reach that total. He totaled 1,211 yards in a season for another record. He also held the mark for most catches in one game with 14.

In 1942, when Hutson set the record for single-season receptions with 74 catches, second place was 27. At the time of his retirement, those 99 touchdown grabs were first on the career list by a margin of 62 touchdowns. That 488 total catches? Second place was 190 catches. His stature as leader in categories ranked first by hundreds ahead of anyone else on the all-time lists, and in some instances it took 40 or 50 years for his records to be broken.

It should not be forgotten that when Hutson played, a season consisted of 10, 11, or 12 games. In 1960, the NFL expanded to 14 regular-season games a year and in 1978 moved to a 16-game season. For 2021, the league shifted to a 17-game season. Not only did the emphasis on the forward pass increase dramatically in those decades after Hutson's playing days ended, receivers had many more opportunities to catch passes by playing many more games.

24. Legacy

The almost-always placid Hutson never expressed regret about the change in the nature of the sport resulting in his numbers being surpassed. In 1989, he generously said, "I love to see my records broken, I really do. You get a chance to relive a part of your life, the whole experience."[1]

There was a bit of confusion over one record, however. It was said that Hutson caught a pass in 95 straight games. But upon further review in 1991, it was discovered he had a 44-game catch streak that ended in 1941 and then started a new one of 50 straight games. The shutout game had been overlooked by statisticians.

During his playing days, Hutson was mostly listed as being 6-foot-1-inch tall and weighing 183 pounds. However, when he first broke into the league from Alabama, he was labeled almost too light to play at something around 168 pounds. Even Curly Lambeau, the coach and front office guru who always believed in Hutson, had doubts that his spindly end could hold up to the beating he might receive playing both ways on NFL Sundays.

In a rare outlook on diet and nutrition, when Lambeau urged Hutson to beef up his weight a little bit, the coach sprang for a lunch-time beer and a dinner-time beer, which he felt wasn't enough alcohol to do Hutson any harm, but would add some calories. At the least, Lambeau felt a beer here and there would not hurt Hutson. It was akin to the period of time much later when doctors reviewing the effects of alcohol on the body announced that a glass of wine every day was good for a person.

When Hutson bowed out, opposing team leaders who had watched him roam the gridiron like the "Alabama Antelope" he was called, uttered lengthy tributes of praise. Repeatedly asked about his biggest thrill on the field, Hutson settled on his first touchdown, the 83-yarder against the Chicago Bears as a rookie, and stuck with that story. He scored many more against Chicago and other teams.

Bears owner-coach George Halas returned from World War II service just as Hutson was departing the Packers, had briefly chased the Crimson Tide alum for his own team, but dropped out of the signing competition when faced with the Packers' and Brooklyn's willingness to bid much higher. That meant Halas had to face Hutson on the field twice a season for years. Sometimes the Bears were good enough to win titles anyway, and sometimes the Packers got the best of the Bears.

"For the next 10 years, Hutson was doing that sort of thing to every

Caught by Don Hutson!

club in the National Football League," Halas said of the player pointing to his inaugural score versus Chicago as a special one. "I just concede him two touchdowns a game and I hope we can score more."[2]

Clyde "Bulldog" Turner, the lineman-linebacker who was also enshrined in the Pro Football Hall of Fame in Canton, Ohio, was a member of those Bears teams grappling with the Packers each season. Turner said he hated to compare players from different eras in 1997, but he made an exception for his viewpoint on Hutson. "He was the best I've ever seen," Turner said. "I don't like to compare players then with players now, but he was head and shoulders above the ones in that era."[3]

The Bears, who saw as much of Hutson as any other team, lined up with praiseworthy comments about Hutson's greatness. In their long memories, he was the one who stood out, even among the best Chicago players such as lineman Dan Fortmann, another Hall of Fame lineman who became a doctor.

"He was so much better than the rest of the players of his day," Fortmann said, "that he could dominate a game. He was also a great defensive back when he wasn't catching passes."[4] That is something often overlooked.

Ken Kavanaugh, an outstanding end for the Bears after an All-American college career, said his pro football education began as a member of the charity All-Star team that faced the Packers in late August of 1940. It should be remembered that Kavanaugh became one of the best receivers in the league during his World War II-interrupted career. He was a three-time All-Pro and twice led the NFL in receiving touchdowns—after Hutson retired. His first impressions of Hutson at the All-Star game left him dizzy. "Our trouble was that we couldn't contain Don Hutson," Kavanaugh said of the 42–28 loss. "He showed me tricks I didn't believe possible, caught three touchdown passes and murdered us."[5]

Those who saw Hutson perform understood he was unique for the time, but many great NFL receivers came much later and couldn't be blamed for not knowing much about his ability. One who knew his history, and at one point held the career receptions record, was Raymond Berry. The Colts receiver was a precise pass-route runner and made the big play during his career spanning 1955 to 1967, when he gathered in 631 balls. The sharpest observers recognized how well Berry ran his routes, but Berry said he never did do anything to get open Don Hutson hadn't already done.

24. Legacy

Maybe so. In a 1942 road game against the Cleveland Rams, Hutson made a one-of-a-kind catch he was happy to reminisce about 47 years later, and so was passer Cecil Isbell. The Rams were sick of Hutson literally running rings around the defensive backfield. This time, Cleveland coach Dutch Clark improvised a double-team of Hutson, but in basketball parlance came close to devising a box-and-one defense to stop him.

Given the statistics from the game reports and memories constructing the event three times, this telling may only be 90 percent accurate. In 1970, Isbell remembered the touchdown pass (one of three Hutson caught that day despite the full-court coverage of him) this way:

> [Clark] told Dante Magnani, the fastest man on their squad, "You go anywhere Hutson goes. I don't care what he does, you stay with him." [Hutson] ran diagonally toward the goal post with Magnani right with him. Suddenly, Don just shifted gears and took off, but Magnani stayed with him. At about the 10-yard-line, Hutson gave it the jet propulsion, but Magnani still stayed with him. So what happens? Don ran straight at the goal post and hooked one of the uprights with his left arm. His feet left the ground and his momentum spun him around the goal post. Just about that time the ball was getting there (I had floated a long pass) and he reached up and caught it with one hand. Magnani liked to have blown a fuse.[6]

In 1989, in a lengthy interview in his home with the *Los Angeles Times*, Hutson recounted the play, in part with more detail, in part with different detail. In Hutson's telling, the Packers had the ball on the 15-yard line, on the outskirts of the end zone, and he was triple-covered. But Hutson said he improvised ahead of time in the huddle, and the quarterback he spoke to was Arnie Herber. "I'm going to run straight at the right goal post," Hutson said, "and when I get there, I'm going to stick out my right arm and whirl around it. Throw the ball just as I hit the post. And be sure to throw it to the other side, where I'll be when I'm turned around."[7]

The play clicked for the score. "If it was illegal, they didn't call it," Hutson said. "I never tried it again, but I take a lot of pride in one thing. That was the first post pattern."[8] Hah, hah.

When a sportswriter from *Sports Illustrated* visited and asked about the play, looking for confirmation that the goal-post catch occurred in real life, Hutson said, "That actually happened."[9] He added that Magnani was his shadow and said it was Isbell who threw the ball. The Packers *did* score on a 15-yard pass from Isbell to Hutson in what seems to be the Cleveland game involved, but Magnani was playing and

Caught by Don Hutson!

Herber was not. His last season with the Packers was 1940, so perhaps Hutson just misspoke in his *Los Angeles Times* interview.

The faux 95-game consecutive games catch record didn't matter as much as it once might have because by the time it was discovered, it had not only already been broken, but Hutson was on the premises to see it done. Brilliant San Diego Chargers receiver Lance Alworth, who was nicknamed "Bambi," caught a pass in his 96th straight game near the end of the 1969 season when the Chargers belted the Buffalo Bills, 45–6.

Hutson, who was 56 years old at the time, met with Alworth on the field to offer salutations. "I just told him congratulations," Hutson said. "But it has been a pleasure for me to have Alworth break the record. He has to be among the top all-time receivers. He has all the moves and he can run with it after he catches it."[10]

The record-breaker was a 9-yard toss from Chargers quarterback John Hadl. Alworth, who at 6 feet tall and 184 pounds was built much like Hutson, caught 542 passes in his NFL career that ran from 1962 to 1972. He played his last year at 32, and his single-season high for catches was 73, one less than Hutson's top season.

Hutson made receiving sound simple across time. "It's still the same old thing with receivers," he said. "First you try to catch it. Second, if you can't catch it, you try to keep the other people from catching it. Then you run with it."[11]

While Hutson was self-effacing and was quick with compliments for more modern-day receivers and quarterbacks, once in a while in his old age he slipped in a deadpan joke about his own prowess. An *Akron-Beacon Journal* sports columnist once wrote about an exchange with Hutson in the late 1980s, when he was asked how many passes he might catch. "I could catch 50 passes a season," Hutson said. This surprised the listener, since Hutson caught that high of 74 in 1942. Prodded to elaborate, Hutson said, "Well, I'd be catching those passes during the year of my 75th birthday. The important things today were the important things 40 years ago. I had 9.7 speed. I had the ability to get open. I had the ability to catch the ball."[12] That will basically do it.

As he approached three-quarters of a century in age on the calendar, Hutson still held 11 NFL records. He said his most appreciated record was his 99 touchdown receptions. "That means I contributed for a long time," he said.[13]

That record did last decades. Seattle Seahawk Steve Largent, a native of Oklahoma who was an All-American at the University of

24. Legacy

Tulsa, superseded many of Hutson's records (although they have in turn been broken). Largent scored 100 touchdowns through the air, caught 819 passes, and gained 13,039 yards on passes before retiring in 1989 after playing in 200 games. Largent later served four terms in Congress as a Republican representative from Oklahoma.

Hutson could have been present for Largent's 100th TD, but he didn't want to travel from California to Washington for no reason and it was not clear when Largent would break the record. Hutson's California neighbor was Seattle coach Chuck Knox, and when Knox asked him to come, Hutson retorted, "I will be glad to come up, if you'll just let me know when he's going to get it."[14]

Hutson was a young man with a wife, Julia, and three daughters, Julia, Martha, and Jane, when he retired from pro football. From the time he was a teenager, Hutson aspired to be a businessman, and he majored in business at the University of Alabama. Before he left the playing field, Hutson was already making moves to set up the rest of his life. For one, he was an assistant coach for the Packers. He did the job in 1944 and 1945 while he was still playing and stayed on through 1948.

From then on, Hutson was pretty much Citizen Don. He had a bowling alley called the Packer Playdium. He opened a car dealership in Green Bay and became a Chevrolet and Cadillac dealer while moving to Racine, on the outskirts of Milwaukee. He spent years growing the firm into one that had 150 employees.

"I can't remember when I didn't want to be a businessman," Hutson said. "At the university, I was the only athlete in the business school. The only reason I wanted to play pro sports was to get a stake. I never aimed for automobiles. That just happened to be the thing I got into. I just wanted to run a business, any business."[15]

Hutson was involved in many civic ventures as an out-of-the-game civilian, including working with the Boy Scouts of America, in many capacities locally and nationally, as an active member of the First Presbyterian Church of Racine, and in the Racine Chamber of Commerce. He was a participant in the Racine Goodfellows Organization and was a key individual fund-raising for the Masonic Brotherhood. He donated use of cars for the driver-education program at Racine schools and adult driver-training courses for adults.

Among other memberships, Hutson was linked to the Elks, the Racine Country Club, the Milwaukee Athletic Club, the Harbor Island

Caught by Don Hutson!

Yacht Club, the Racine Yacht Club, and the Fishing Club of Ontario, Canada, and he was an Honorary Kentucky Colonel.

As time passed, many honors accrued stemming from his Packers playing days. Some came fairly quickly. In 1951, Hutson was chosen as a charter member of the College Football Hall of Fame. That same year, Hutson was selected in the first class of the Wisconsin Athletic Hall of

Green Bay Packers great Don Hutson gives golf pointers to Green Bay Packers legendary coach Vince Lombardi (courtesy of Neville Public Museum of Brown County).

24. Legacy

Fame, and again in 1951 the Packers retired his No. 14 uniform jersey, the first one set aside by the Green Bay franchise. As the NFL aged, historians selected a 1930s All-Decade team, a 50th anniversary all-league team in 1970, and a 75th anniversary all-league team in 1994. He was chosen for all of them.

Unlike Major League Baseball, which has been around since 1876, the National Football League did not establish itself until 1920. Baseball opened its Hall of Fame doors in 1939 in Cooperstown, New York (though they had been picking enshrinees since 1936), and football opened its Hall of Fame doors in 1963 in Canton, Ohio. The first football Hall class included 17 men: Jim Thorpe, Red Grange, Bronko Nagurski, Sammy Baugh, Johnny "Blood" McNally, Mel Hein, Dutch Clark, Pete Henry, Cal Hubbard, Ernie Nevers, George Halas, Curly Lambeau, Bert Bell, Joe Carr, Tim Mara, George Marshall—and Don Hutson.

Johnny Blood and Hubbard were Packers teammates of Hutson's. Lambeau, of course, was the coach and founder of the team. Hubbard, who became an umpire, has the distinction of being the only football figure inducted into the National Baseball Hall of Fame, too.

In 1994, when he was 81 years old, the Packers invited Don Hutson back to Green Bay for the unveiling of the team's new Don Hutson Center indoor training facility (author photo).

Caught by Don Hutson!

The inaugural pro football Hall class was announced on January 29, 1963, and the enshrinement ceremony was conducted on September 7. Hutson's presenter was Dante Lavelli, the retired star receiver of the Cleveland Browns, who caught 386 passes himself. "Don Hutson set records for pass catching which only legislation can wipe out," Lavelli said. "He is a football yardstick. Hutson created pass patterns and developed faking to an almost federal offense. His impossible catches were not luck."[16]

Quite typically of his entire life, Hutson's acceptance speech was very brief, and he simply praised the other men he was entering the Hall with in that first class of players.

"Ladies and gentlemen, for me to fully appreciate the honor of being inducted here today, all I have to do is look at the names of the persons on the list that are also going in," Hutson said. "I know all of them, and while I played I got to know some of them, too well, you might say. That's why I appreciate it. It is a great honor and I thank you very much."[17]

In business, in sports, in life, Hutson always acknowledged one thing about his journey after Pine Bluff.

"I've always been lucky," he said.[18]

Epilogue

After the Green Bay Packers won their sixth world championship in 1944, the team did not win another title for 17 years, until the legendary Vince Lombardi took command of the club and ignited the dormant passion in a struggling franchise. It was on Lombardi's watch that the Packers lived out their most glorious years, winning five more National Football League crowns between 1961 and 1967, including the first two Super Bowls.

There had been some hard times after Don Hutson retired and some shocking ones. Team founder Curly Lambeau, who coached the club for 31 years, had a bitter split with the operation and even ended up coaching the Chicago Cardinals in 1950 and 1951 and the Washington Redskins in 1952 and 1953, unthinkable developments.

Lambeau, born in 1898, was only 67 when he died in 1965 in Sturgeon Bay, Wisconsin, collapsing from a heart attack on a neighbor's lawn. Hutson, worked as an assistant coach for a few years, said he never wanted to be a head coach and definitely did not want to make a switch back to the sport from the business world.

Lombardi, along with such fresh legends and future Hall of Famers as Paul Hornung, Jim Taylor, Bart Starr, Willie Davis, Ray Nitschke, Herb Adderley, Jerry Kramer, Forrest Gregg, and Jim Ringo, and other players became the new heroes in the smallest town in professional sports. Gradually, the old heroes like Cal Hubbard, Johnny Blood, Arnie Herber, Cecil Isbell, and Tony Canadeo began dying off.

Green Bay Packers faithful were treated to or developed new traditions, such as the Ice Bowl playoff victory of December 31, 1967, over the Dallas Cowboy (when it was -13 degrees with a -46 wind-chill), the phrase, "The Frozen Tundra," and fanatic fans wearing "cheesehead" head gear. The Styrofoam lids are immediately recognizable around the country as identifying Packers supporters.

Epilogue

Don Hutson's children grew up, married, and had their own children. When he surrendered his Wisconsin business interests, he moved to Rancho Mirage, in the Coachella Valley of Southern California, a desert climate instead of a snowy one. Hutson became somewhat of a California homebody, at least in the sense that he had to have a good reason to budge from his daily routines, which often included playing gin rummy at the Thunderbird Country Club.

Other pursuits included watching football on television and playing golf. Once, when he made a charity golf appearance back in Wisconsin, Hutson played a round with Vince Lombardi. He was photographed giving the coach some pointers on this other game.

Hutson represented an early NFL version of the pro game, when there were fewer teams, there was no television, even the best players often went both ways on offense and defense, and those phenomenally accurate place-kicking specialists were unknown. Many times, two or three different Packers booted extra points until a little bit later, after Clarke Hinkle retired, and Hutson was the last one standing, he become the regular Green Bay kicker.

"In my day, we didn't have a designated kicker," Hutson said. "We just got in the huddle, looked around, and asked, 'Who wants to kick this one?' I only volunteered once in a while." That was an overly casual summation, since Hutson did eventually take over for good. "I'd never kicked a football anywhere until I got to Green Bay."[1]

Over the years in retirement, Hutson had the occasional health issue. Once, the Green Bay newspaper reported he had "a seizure" but was okay. The seizure, at 56, was a heart attack. Although he had gone gray with a somewhat, if not dramatically receding hairline, Hutson maintained his playing weight of about 185 pounds (no update was provided in interviews about him still chugging a beer with lunch and dinner, or not, though clearly Lambeau had not been buying for years).

In 1988, with Super Bowl XXII being held virtually right down the street from him in San Diego, Hutson was invited to flip the coin during the ceremony to start the game between the Washington Redskins and Denver Broncos at Jack Murphy Stadium. The date, January 31, was Hutson's 75th birthday. "I'm very honored to be here and toss the coin," Hutson said. "The people that have been ahead of me like George Halas, Art Rooney and Bronko Nagurski, I remember very well. I'm in pretty fast company."[2]

For years, Hutson served on the Packers' board of directors.

Epilogue

Anyway, he always was glad for visits back to Green Bay for good reasons, whether from not-so-distant Racine, or California. The Packers and the city always warmly welcomed him.

In 1994, Hutson was given a big reason to return. City Stadium had long since been renamed Lambeau Field for the founder of the team, and the team kept developing a plot of land in the same vicinity, adding structures to include a Packers Hall of Fame, club executive offices, a gargantuan, 22,000-square-foot team gift shop (where replica No. 14 Don Hutson jerseys were sold for $150), and practice fields named after Clarke Hinkle and Ray Nitschke, made it all somewhat resemble a college campus.

In a frequently cold and snowy environment, that year the Packers added a new feature to the grounds, the 112,000-square-foot Don Hutson Center, an indoor practice facility built for $4.7 million. The name of the facility is emblazoned on the side in eight-foot-tall letters, large enough that a zoning variance was needed to approve it. When the building was dedicated on July 18, 1994, Hutson, then 81, was present to bless it. The team made sure of that by flying him from California on a private jet. At the time, Green Bay general manager Ron Wolf said meeting Hutson was like being in the presence of royalty, or at least sporting royalty such as Babe Ruth or heavyweight champ Jack Dempsey.

Hutson still followed pro football closely as he aged. He couldn't get over the continuing emphasis on specialists, where some defenders only played two downs to rush the passer and a different man came in to stop the run, where different fellows ran back punts than ran back kickoffs, and kickers didn't play at all except to use their foot. Since he played both offensive and defensive end, though switching to safety on defense eventually, Hutson used to say he played the equivalent of 22 NFL seasons, not 11.

There was so much more emphasis on the passing game than when he played between 1935 and 1945, it was only a matter of time before many long-time receivers surpassed his record of 488 catches. Hutson greatly admired those who excelled at doing what he used to do, however. Lance Alworth, the Chargers' star, and Steve Largent, who broke Hutson's record of 99 touchdown catches, were both players he respected and whose skills he respected.

It was Hall of Famer Jerry Rice, though, who caught his eye, and Hutson came to believe Rice was the greatest wide receiver of all time. The San Francisco 49ers great left ample supporting evidence in the

Epilogue

record book to generate such enthusiasm. The 6-foot-2, 200-pound Rice broke into the league in 1985 and played through 2004, catching a record 1,549 passes for a record 22,895 yards and a record 197 touchdowns. A 13-time All-Pro selection, Rice did play 20 seasons. To Hutson, Rice was the best.

"Including everybody," Hutson said, including himself. "I've watched a lot of football on TV. A lot of these people are still missing passes trying to catch it with the arms. Rice catches with the hands and that's that. He's No. 1 as far as I'm concerned."[3]

Green Bay, two decades into the 21st century, is practically a Packers company town. Inside a convenience store a few blocks from the stadium on Lombardi Avenue, there was a drawing of Lombardi on a wall, and there were Lombardi quotes on the men's room wall. "Titletown" indeed.

A film shown inside the Packers Hall of Fame includes narration saying, "There is no place quite like Green Bay. There is no team quite like Green Bay. Without the Packers, Green Bay would be an ordinary town."[4] The rest of the displays demonstrate why the Packers, with their 13 team championships, are far from ordinary.

There are plenty of artifacts commemorating Don Hutson's career inside the Hall of Fame, whether they are newspaper articles displayed about his playing days, a Hutson-worn game jersey, a 1944 Wheaties cartoon, or a sign reading, "Don Hutson, Football Royalty." A tape plays of long-time *Sports Illustrated* football writer Peter King saying, "I think Don Hutson was the best player in NFL history."

Anyone who saw Don Hutson play live in the NFL is beyond the minimum age for collecting Social Security payments. He died a quarter of a century ago, so there are not many people connected to the team today who got to know him at all. However, a couple of football old-timers who were also wide receivers did so.

Carroll Dale, born in 1938, broke into the NFL in 1960 with the Los Angeles Rams after his college career at Virginia Tech. A three-time Pro Bowl selection, Dale played for the Packers between 1965 and 1972. He came along long after Hutson's pioneering days, but when the passing game was truly beginning to expand and jump-start higher scoring performances.

"When I went to Green Bay you really became aware of him," Dale said. "It is really amazing what he did in his day. He is someone credited with this wide open offense. Even in the 1960s, the running game was a bigger part of your offense. In the '60s, people who threw a lot of

Epilogue

A view of Lambeau Field, where the Green Bay Packers play their home games today (author photo).

passes were trying to catch up. They were people who didn't win championships. I was really fortunate to get traded to Green Bay in the '60s."[5]

Dale, who caught 438 passes, including 52 for touchdowns, was part of three Green Bay teams that won championships. Dale is enough of a student of the game to recognize that Hutson was unique for his time. "They [the Packers] had Hutson and they had a quarterback and a coach who believed in him," Dale said. "They opened up the offense. He was absolutely so far ahead of his time. Just to look at those numbers that would match today's offenses. I've seen a few clips [of Hutson playing]. It is just amazing for that era."[6]

Boyd Dowler, another prominent Packers wide receiver from the 1960s who was slotted into a role called flanker with five Packers title teams, is slightly older than Dale. He caught 474 passes between 1959, when he was Rookie of the Year, and 1971.

Dowler said he met Hutson but did not know him well and spent some time with him when he attended a Packers game in Green Bay. Subsequently, Dowler, defensive back Jesse Whittenton, and their wives visited a bar with Hutson.

"Of course, I'd heard a lot about him," Dowler said.

Epilogue

He seemed like a nice fella. Of course, I'd admired his career. They had some film on him and I looked at some of it just out of curiosity. Quite frankly, it looked like he just out-ran everybody. He sure could run. He flew down the field. It looked to me like he could have played for us in the '60s.

They didn't have that many people in pro football who could run that fast. He did things so naturally. His numbers proved it. The athletic ability is the first thing you notice. Speed is speed. If you have the speed at the start, you have a leg up.[7]

Dale and Dowler were of a later generation of football players, but Hutson's stature never really diminished from the time he first took the field for Green Bay. He did face declining health during the few years following his appearance at the opening of the Don Hutson Center, and after undergoing heart surgery and losing some of his hearing, he became increasingly frail.

When the end came for Hutson, he had been in a hospital in Rancho Mirage with an undisclosed illness, then was transferred to a nursing home on June 17, 1997. He died 11 days later at the nursing home at age 84, and his body was taken to Wiefels & Son Funeral Home in Palm Springs.

Secrecy shrouded the developments, from the illness, to cause of death, to burial arrangements. A memorial service was conducted for family members only, and family members instructed the funeral home not to release any additional information. No death notice was placed in newspapers. Hutson was survived by Julia, his wife of 60 years.

Whether it was through the Associated Press, press statements made by the Packers, or sportswriters, newspapers took care of themselves with glowing tributes to the man they

This is a replica Don Hutson uniform jersey of the kind sold in the Packers' team gift stop for $150 (author photo).

Epilogue

credited with being one of the greatest football players of all time, someone who set records by the bushel and who was hailed as an innovator on the gridiron roughly equal to Babe Ruth on the diamond.

Don Hutson was not a flamboyant man, nor a colorful, outgoing one. He was level-headed but behaved with directness and simplicity, on and off the field. He was a football player ahead of his time and understood what he accomplished, but while enjoying those accomplishments did not brag about them. He was one of those star players whose economy of motion belied his greatness, but his pass-catching confidence was expressed in a personal philosophy once summarized.

"I know I'm going to run like the devil and try to get free," Hutson said, "and then look over my shoulder and say, 'Hello, football, I've been expecting you' and then catch the ball."[8]

The "Alabama Antelope" and "The Ghost of Green Bay" ran like the wind until that ball landed in his hands.

Chapter Notes

Preface

1. David Zimmerman, *Curly Lambeau: The Man Behind the Mystique* (Hales Corner, WI: Eagle Books, 2003), 111.
2. Creg Stephenson, "Don Hutson, the Babe Ruth of Wide Receivers and Alabama's Greatest Football Player," www.al.com, July 1, 2016/updated January 13, 2019.

Introduction

1. Frank P. Maggio, *Notre Dame and the Game That Changed Football* (New York: Carroll & Graf, 2007), 84.

Chapter 1

1. Bob Oates, "Don Hutson: After Helping Invent the Forward Pass, the Former Packer Star Grabbed the Brass Ring of Life, as Well," *Los Angeles Times*, April 30, 1989.
2. Dave Anderson, "Sports of the Times: The Bear Who Really Was One," *New York Times*, November 2, 1983.
3. Danique Lewis, "NFL in the 1920s," Prezi (slide show), https://prezi.com/cipkmvr-usey/nfl-in-the-1920s.
4. Jeremy Cluff, "Highest Paid Players in NFL: Ranking Players by Salary for 2020 Season," *Arizona Republic*, March 30, 2021.
5. Paul W. Bryant and John Underwood, *Bear: The Hard Life and Good Times of Alabama's Coach Bryant* (New York: Bantam Books, 1975), 7.
6. *Ibid.*, 19.
7. "The Alabama Antelope: One of Football's Greatest Pioneers," Paul W. Bryant Museum Archive, http://bryantmuseum.com/stories.asp?ID=34.
8. Bryant and Underwood, *Hard Life*, 26–27.
9. *Ibid.*, 27–28.
10. *Ibid.*, 40.
11. *Ibid.*, 43.

Chapter 2

1. *The Zebra* (Pine Bluff, AR, High School Yearbook), 1931.
2. *Ibid.*, 1931.
3. Advertisement, *Pine Bluff (AR) Commercial*, September 12, 1930.
4. Delbert Cutrell, "Squad Is Put Through Another Stiff Workout," *Pine Bluff (AR) Commercial*, September 5, 1930.
5. Delbert Cutrell, "Old Sol Puts the Kayo to 4 Football Men," *Pine Bluff (AR) Commercial*, September 9, 1930.
6. Leroy Morwood, "Pine Bluff Football Camp Has Appearance of Big Family Earnestly Engaged in Building Good Team," *Daily Graphic* (Pine Bluff, AR), September 4, 1930.
7. *Ibid.*
8. "Zebras Open 1930 Grid Season," *Daily Graphic* (Pine Bluff, AR), September 13, 1930.
9. Advertisement, *Daily Graphic* (Pine Bluff, AR), September 13, 1930.
10. George Heister, "Zebras Defeat Benton," *Pine Bluff (AR) Commercial*, September 15, 1930.
11. *Ibid.*

Chapter Notes

12. Ed L. Campbell, "Zebras Take to Air to Trounce North Little Rock," *Daily Graphic* (Pine Bluff, AR), October 5, 1930.
13. Ed L. Campbell, "Hutson Out of Fordyce Game with Injury," *Daily Graphic* (Pine Bluff, AR), October 14, 1930.
14. Ed L. Campbell, "Camden Achieves Life Long Ambition in Beating Locals," *Daily Graphic* (Pine Bluff, AR), October 26, 1930.

Chapter 3

1. George Halas, "Halas Calls Friedman Pioneer Passer—Rest Came by Design," *Chicago Daily News*, February 4, 1967.
2. Barry Gottehrer, *The Giants of New York: The History of Professional Football's Most Fabulous Dynasty* (New York: G.P. Putnam's, 1963), 65.
3. Eric Kennedy, "Benny Friedman: The QB Who May Have Saved the New York Giants," February 13, 2006. www.bigblueinteractive.com, https://www.bigblueinteractive.com/2006/02/13/the-quarterback-who-may-have-saved-the-giants-benny-friedman/.
4. *Ibid.*
5. David Zimmerman, *Curly Lambeau, the Man Behind the Mystique* (Hales Corners, WI: Eagle Books, 2003), 79.
6. *Ibid.*, 79.
7. *Ibid.*, 57.
8. Denis J. Gullickson, *Vagabond Halfback: The Life and Times of Johnny 'Blood' McNally* (Madison, WI: Trails Books, 2006), 77.
9. *Ibid.*

Chapter 4

1. University of Alabama Center for Public Radio & Television, press release, "The Football Game That Changed the South," http://www.cptr.ua.edu/news, February 20, 2007.
2. Paul W. Bryant and John Underwood, *Bear: The Hard Life and Good Times of Alabama's Coach Bryant* (New York: Bantam Books, 1975), 43.
3. (No byline), "Crimson Legend, Don Hutson: Football's Most Decorated Hero," Paul W. Bryant Museum Archives, 1994.
4. Bryant and Underwood, *Hard Life*, 45.
5. *Ibid.*

Chapter 5

1. (No byline), "Hutson Hit Bottom at 'Bama Before Soaring," Associated Press/*Montgomery Advertiser*, July 1, 1997.
2. *Ibid.*
3. *Ibid.*
4. (No byline), "Bama Regards Bulldogs as Tough Opening Foe," *Tuscaloosa News*, September 20, 1934.
5. Jay Thornton, "Clemson Eleven to Meet Tide on Homecoming Day," *Tuscaloosa News*, November 5, 1934.
6. Damon Runyon, Syndicated Column, "Alabama Is the Team," *Tuscaloosa News*, November 8, 1934.
7. Jay Thornton, "Big Homecoming Crowd of 8,000 Sees Raging Tide," *Tuscaloosa News*, November 11, 1934.
8. (No byline), "Howell Scores Twice as 'Bama Wins with Ease," *Tuscaloosa News*, November 18, 1934.
9. (No byline), "Alabama Accepts Rose Bowl Bid: Crimson Invited for Fourth Time in Grid Classic," Associated Press/*Tuscaloosa News*, November 30, 1934.

Chapter 6

1. John Horne and Mortimer Jordan, *A Year at Alabama*, University of Alabama, Student Body Press, 1935, 206.
2. Ralph McGill, "Tide to Face Butterfly Defense in Bowl Battle," *Atlanta Constitution*, December 26, 1934.
3. *Ibid.*
4. Ralph McGill, "The Party Meets Stars on Movie Studio Trip," *Atlanta Constitution*, December 27, 1934.

Chapter Notes

5. *Ibid.*
6. *Ibid.*
7. Paul W. Bryant and John Underwood, *Bear: The Hard Life and Good Times of Alabama's Coach Bryant* (New York: Bantam Books, 1975), 53.
8. *Ibid.*
9. *Ibid.*, 54.
10. *Ibid.*
11. *Ibid.*, 54–55.
12. *Ibid.*, 55.
13. Bryant and Underwood, *Hard Life*, 56–57.
14. *Ibid.*, 58.
15. *Ibid.*, 58–59.
16. *Ibid.*, 59.
17. *Ibid.*, 55.

Chapter 7

1. Mark Kelley, "Howell-Hutson Combine Hailed as Game's Best," *Los Angeles Examiner*, January 2, 1935.
2. *Ibid.*
3. (No byline), "Alabama Hailed as Finest Eleven in Bowl History," *Tuscaloosa News*, January 2, 1935.
4. Maxwell Stiles, "Alabama Called Best Team Ever to Play in Bowl," *Los Angeles Examiner*, January 3, 1935.
5. Frank Thomas, "Great Victory, Says Thomas," Associated Press, January 2, 1935.
6. *Ibid.*
7. (No byline), "Telegrams and Paper Clippings Hail Champions," *Tuscaloosa News*, January 3, 1935.
8. Paul W. Bryant and John Underwood, *Bear: The Hard Life and Good Times of Alabama's Coach Bryant* (New York: Bantam Books, 1975), 61.
9. *Ibid.*, 62.

Chapter 8

1. Christopher Smith, "25 Interesting Facts About Former Alabama Legend Don Hutson," https://www.saturdaydownsouth.com/alabama-football/ April 11, 2015.
2. Lew Freedman, *Baugh to Brady: The Evolution of the Forward Pass* (Lubbock: Texas Tech University Press, 2018), 56.
3. David Zimmerman, *Curly Lambeau: The Man Behind the Mystique*, (Hales Corner, WI: Eagle Books, 2003), 112.
4. *Ibid.*, 112.
5. Freedman, *Baugh to Brady*, 58.

Chapter 9

1. Lee Remmel, "Feathers 'Assisted' on Hutson's First Pro TD; 17 Seasons Enough: Joe Perry," *Green Bay Press-Gazette*, June 11, 1964.
2. *Ibid.*

Chapter 10

1. Lee Remmel, "Greatest Packer Games: No. 8," NFL game program, August 30, 1975.
2. *Ibid.*
3. *Ibid.*
4. *Ibid.*
5. *Ibid.*
6. *Ibid.*
7. *Ibid.*
8. John Walter, "Green Bay Crushes Detroit, 31–7," *Green Bay Press-Gazette*, November 11, 1935.
9. Stoney McGlynn, "Packer Passes Smother Detroit, 31–7," *Milwaukee Sentinel*, November 11, 1935.
10. Denis J., Gullickson, *Vagabond Halfback: The Life and Times of Johnny 'Blood' McNally* (Madison, WI: Trails Books, 2006), 116.
11. (No byline), News Release, Pro Football Hall of Fame, March 12, 1968.
12. Oliver E. Kuechle, "Johnny Blood: Pro Football's Happiest Wanderer," *Milwaukee Journal*, September 28, 1965.
13. (No byline), "Hutson Goes to Hospital," *Green Bay Press-Gazette*, November 19, 1935.
14. John Steadman, "Hall of Famer Herber Made $75 a Game," *Baltimore News American*, December 21, 1966.
15. David Whitley, "Hutson Was First Modern Receiver," www.espn.com/sportscentury/features. No date.

Chapter Notes

Chapter 11

1. (No byline), "Don Hutson to Play in Judges Outfield," *Pine Bluff Commercial*, March 16, 1936.
2. *Ibid.*
3. Jimmy Cannon, "Hutson 'Taught' Mays to Catch Ball," *Los Angeles Herald-Examiner*, April 24, 1964.
4. *Ibid.*
5. Chris Willis, "Don Hutson," *Coffin Corner* 27, No. 4 (2005).
6. David Whitley, "Hutson Was First Modern Receiver," www.espn.com/sportscentury/features.
7. Pat Livingston, "Hutson Brings Down the House!" *Coffin Corner*, Volume 2, No. 12, 1980.
8. (No byline) "The Greatest, the Legend," Nostalgia, Club 66 Newsletter, Historical Perspective of the Green Bay Packers and the NFL, 1999.

Chapter 12

1. John Steadman, "Hall of Famer Herber Made $75 a Game," *Baltimore News-American*, 21, 1966.
2. *Ibid.*
3. Jack Yuenger, "Arnie Herber: He Came to Play," *Green Bay Press-Gazette*, no date. Article reproduced in the Green Bay Packers Yearbook, 1962, 32–33.
4. "Arnie Herber: The Greatest Long Passer," Green Bay Packers Yearbook, 1965.
5. *Ibid.*
6. (No byline) (Advertisement), "COMING TO GREEN BAY," *Green Bay Press-Gazette*, November 5, 1936.
7. Stanley Woodward, "Rout of Redskins Emphasizes Inferiority of Eastern Pros," *New York Herald-Tribune*, December 14, 1936.
8. *Ibid.*

Chapter 13

1. David Zimmerman, *Curly Lambeau: The Man Behind the Mystique*, (Hales Corner, WI: Eagle Books, 2003), 125.
2. (No byline), "Former Packer Stars Laud Lambeau as 'Great Leader, *Milwaukee Sentinel*, June 2, 1965.
3. Zimmerman, *Curly Lambeau*, 130.
4. Oliver E. Kuechle, "Packers Bow to Bears, 14 to 2," *Milwaukee Journal*, September 20, 1937.
5. Kuechle, "Packers Bow."
6. Gary D'Amato and Cliff Christl, *Mudbaths & Bloodbaths: The Inside Story of the Bears-Packers Rivalry* (Madison, WI: Prairie Oak Press, 1997), 30.

Chapter 14

1. Chuck Johnson, "Cecil Isbell's Passing Left a Lasting Impression," *Milwaukee Journal*, November 23, 1965.
2. *Ibid.*
3. Cecil Isbell, "I Remember Don Hutson," NFL game program, December 14, 1970.
4. *Ibid.*

Chapter 15

1. Larry Williams, "The Ghost of Green Bay," *Sport Magazine*, December 1960.
2. John Walter, "Late Touchdown Pass Gives Packers Cleveland Win," *Green Bay Press-Gazette*, November 29, 1937.
3. Stan Grosshandler, "'39 Packers—One of Green Bay's Greatest Teams," *Football Digest*, November 1971.
4. *Ibid.*
5. (No byline), "It's in the Old Sock," (Advertisement), *Green Bay Press-Gazette*, December 9, 1939.
6. (No byline), "ONE MORE GAME," (Advertisement), *Green Bay Press-Gazette*, December 9, 1939.
7. (No byline), "The Packers Are a Sweet Ball Club," (Advertisement), *Green Bay Press-Gazette*, December 9, 1939.
8. (No byline), "WORLD CHAMPIONS," (Advertisement) *Green Bay Press-Gazette*, December 9, 1939.
9. John Walter, "Play Magnificent Football in Final Contest Before, 32,279," *Green Bay Press-Gazette*, December 11, 1939.

Chapter Notes

10. John Walter, "Looking Up in the Realm of Sports," *Green Bay Press-Gazette*, December 11, 1939.

Chapter 16

1. Russ Davis, "Little Town That Leads 'Em," *Saturday Evening Post*, November 30, 1940.
2. *Ibid.*
3. *Ibid.*
4. *Ibid.*
5. Lew Freedman, *Baugh to Brady: The Evolution of the Forward Pass* (Lubbock: Texas Tech University Press, 2018), 127.

Chapter 17

1. Winston Churchill, speech to cabinet, May 13, 1940. https://WinstonChurchill.org. International Winston Churchill Society.
2. Winston Churchill, speech to House of Commons, June 4, 1940. https://www.presentationmagazine.com/winston-churchill-speech-we-shall-fight-them-on-the-beaches.
3. Franklin D. Roosevelt, speech, Fireside Chat radio, May 26, 1940, https://millercenter.org/the-presidency/presidential-speeches/May-26-1940-fireside-chat-15-national-defense.
4. (No byline), "Arnie Herber," Pro Football Hall of Fame press release, 1966.
5. Oliver E. Kuechle, "Time Out for Talk," *Milwaukee Journal*, June 30, 1969.
6. Oliver, E Kuechle. "Packers Win Exhibition Game, 28 to 20," *Milwaukee Journal*, September 3, 1940.

Chapter 18

1. Don Hutson, AZ Quotes, https://www.azquotes.com/quote.
2. Creg Stephenson, "Don Hutson, the Babe Ruth of Wide Receivers, and Alabama's Greatest Football Player," https://www.al.com/sports. July 1, 2016.
3. *Ibid.*
4. *Ibid.*

5. *Ibid.*
6. Packer Icons: "Don Hutson, Poetry In Motion," NFL Films, July 3, 2014.
7. *Ibid.*
8. *Ibid.*
9. (No byline), Pro Football Hall of Fame, press release, September 6, 1964.
10. *Ibid.*
11. Cliff Christl, "Lou Brock," Green Bay Packers Hall of Fame, December 24, 2018.
12. Jimmy Conzelman, "Who Was Sport's No. 1 Wrecker? *Look*, November 1939.
13. (No byline), "We Have Only One Course," *Green Bay Press-Gazette*, December 8, 1941.
14. (No byline), "No Substitute for Victory, and Coach Lambeau Isn't Offering Any Alibi for Inadequate Showing Sunday," *Green Bay Press-Gazette*, December 15, 1941.
15. Fred Haynes and James Warren, *The Lions of Iwo Jima—The Story of Combat Team 28 and the Bloodiest Battle in Marine Corps History* (New York: Henry Holt, 2008), 114–115.

Chapter 19

1. Bob Feller, "Gun-Captain to Legendary Pitcher," Answering the Call, U.S. Naval Institute, June, 2008. https://www.usni.org/magazines/proceedings/2008/June/answering-call-im-still-navy-man-heart.
2. Delbert Reed, "When Winning Was Everything: Alabama Football Players in World War II," (Tuscaloosa, AL: Paul W. Bryant Museum, January 20, 2013), 111.
3. *Ibid.*, 111.
4. *Ibid.*, 112.
5. *Ibid.*, 113.
6. Cliff Christl, "When Green Bay Almost Lost the Packers," https://www.packers.com/news/when-green-bay-almost-lost-thepackers, December 17, 2020.
7. *Ibid.*
8. David Zimmerman, *Curly Lambeau: The Man Behind the Mystique* (Hales Corner, WI: Eagle Books, 2003).

Chapter Notes

Chapter 20

1. David Zimmerman, *Curly Lambeau: The Man Behind the Mystique*, (Hales Corner, WI: Eagle Books, 2003), 151.
2. *Ibid.*, 152.
3. Charley Brock, "The Game I Will Never Forget," *Milwaukee Sentinel*, September 20, 1969.
4. Cecil Isbell, "I Remember Don Hutson," NFL Game Program., December 14, 1970.
5. (No byline), "Cecil Isbell: A Short Time in the Spotlight," *Coffin Corner* XIX, No. 19 (1997).
6. Isbell, "I Remember Don Hutson."
7. Harry Sheer, "Isbell May Play Again for Packers," *Chicago Daily News*, September 27, 1943.

Chapter 21

1. (No byline) "Tony Canadeo," Pro Hall of Fame Edition, Remembrances of the Four New Enshrinees for 1974. (1974)
2. (No byline), "Packers Saw Great Things from Irv Comp," *Milwaukee Journal-Sentinel*, December 20, 2007.
3. Larry Williams, "The Ghost of Green Bay," *Sport Magazine*, December 1960.

Chapter 22

1. (No byline), "Packers Plan to Use Work as Conditioner," Associated Press/*Green Bay Press-Gazette*, May 7, 1943.
2. *Ibid.*
3. Cliff Christl, "Don Hutson: Green Bay Packers History," https://www.packers.com/news/history-hof-don-hutson, June 6, 2018.
4. Bud Lea, "Last of the Legends: Don Hutson One of a Kind," *Packer Plus*, July 16, 1997.
5. *Ibid.*
6. Len Wagner, "Arnie's Greatest Day Came with Giants," *Green Bay Press-Gazette*, October 16, 1969.
7. Jimmy Jordan, "Don Hutson Hopes to Retire After All-Star Game in 1945," Associated Press, December 20, 1944.
8. Bob Oates, "Don Hutson: After Helping Invent the Forward Pass, the Former Packer Star Grabbed the Brass Ring of Life as Well," *Los Angeles Times*, April 30, 1989.
9. *Ibid.*

Chapter 23

1. Cliff Christl, "Packers' Smiley Johnson Gave His Life for His Country," https://www.packers.com/news/packers-smiley-johnson-gave-his-life-for-his-country.
2. Bob Oates, "Don Hutson: After Helping Invent the Forward Pass, the Former Packer Star Grabbed the Brass Ring of Life, as Well," *Los Angeles Times*, April 30, 1989.
3. Lee Remmel, "Packers Smash Bears, 31–21 to Open," *Green Bay Press-Gazette*, October 1, 1945.
4. *Ibid.*
5. Dave Yuenger, "Hutson Leads Packers to 57–21 Win Over Lions," *Green Bay Press-Gazette*, October 8, 1945.
6. Don Hutson, and A. Smith, "I Remember: A 29-Point Quarter in 1945," NFL Game Program, October 17, 1976.
7. *Ibid.*
8. (No byline), "Second Sellout Crowd of Year to See Packer-Ram Tilt Sunday," *Green Bay Press-Gazette*, October 12, 1945.
9. Oscar Fraley, "Lambeau Laughing About All These New Hutsons in League," United Press International/*Green Bay Press-Gazette*, November 30, 1945.

Chapter 24

1. David Whitley, "Hutson Was First Modern Receiver," no date (accessed August 18, 2021), www.espn.com/sportscentury/features.
2. Frank LItsky, "Don Hutson: A Star Receiver for the Packers, Is Dead at 84," *New York Times*, June 28, 1997.
3. Cliff Christl, "Superstar: Hutson's

Chapter Notes

Legendary Status Continues to Live On," *Milwaukee Journal-Sentinel*, June 29, 1997.

4. Dan Fortmann, "A Conversation with Dan Fortmann," *Pro! Magazine*, no date.

5. Arthur Daley, "Sports of the Times: Among Those Honored," *New York Times*, December 11, 1963.

6. Cecil Isbell, "I Remember Don Hutson," NFL Game Program, December 14, 1970.

7. Bob Oates, "Don Hutson: After Helping Invent the Forward Pass, the Former Packer Star Grabbed the Brass Ring of Life, as Well," *Los Angeles Times*, April 30, 1989.

8. *Ibid.*

9. John Garrity, "The Game's Greatest Receiver Don Hutson Remains the Standard by Which All Wideouts Are Measured," *Sports Illustrated*, October 6, 1995.

10. Howard Hagen, "Hutson Praises Alworth's Catch to Crack Record," *San Diego Union*, December 15, 1969.

11. *Ibid.*

12. Tom Melody, "Sports Memories," *Akron Beacon-Journal* magazine, March 1988.

13. *Ibid.*

14. Oates, "Don Hutson."

15. *Ibid.*

16. Pro Football Hall of Fame, Canton, Ohio, website, Don Hutson, http://www.profootballhof.com/players/don-hutson.

17. *Ibid.*

18. Oates, "Don Hutson."

Epilogue

1. Bob Oates, "Don Hutson: After Helping Invent the Forward Pass, the Former Packer Star Grabbed the Brass Ring of Life, as Well," *Los Angeles Times*, April 30, 1989.

2. Al Pohl, "Birthday: Hutson Flips a Coin to Celebrate 75th," *Packer Report*, February 15, 1988.

3. (No byline) Associated Press, "Don Hutson Envies Rice: Hall of Famer Says 49er Great Best Ever," *Wilmington (DE) News-Journal*, September 14, 1994.

4. Green Bay Packers Hall of Fame tourist film, Green Bay Packers team Hall of Fame.

5. Carroll Dale, interview with author, May 13, 2019.

6. *Ibid.*

7. Boyd Dowler, interview with author, May 14, 2019.

8. Jack Miles, "The Living End," *Milestones in Sports/Catholic Boy*, December 1966.

Bibliography

Books

Bryant, Paul W., and John Underwood. *Bear: The Hard Life and Good Times of Alabama's Coach Bryant.* New York: Bantam Books, 1975.

D'Amato, Gary, and Cliff Christl. *Mudbaths & Bloodbaths: The Inside Story of the Bears-Packers Rivalry.* Madison, WI: Prairie Oak, 1997.

Freedman, Lew. *Baugh to Brady: The Evolution of the Forward Pass.* Lubbock: Texas Tech University Press, 2018.

Gottehrer, Barry. *The Giants of New York: The History of Professional Football's Most Fabulous Dynasty.* New York: G.P. Putnam's Sons, 1963.

Gullickson, Denis J. *Vagabond Halfback: The Life and Times of Johnny "Blood" McNally.* Madison, WI: Trails Books, 2006.

Haynes, Fred, and James Warren. The *Lions of Iwo Jima: The Story of Combat Team 28 and the Bloodiest Battle in Marine Corps History.* New York: Henry Holt, 2008.

Maggio, Frank P. *Notre Dame and the Game That Changed Football.* New York: Carroll & Graf, 2007.

Reed, Delbert. *When Winning Was Everything: Alabama Football Players In World War II.* Tuscaloosa, AL: Paul W. Bryant Museum, 2013.

Zimmerman, David. *Curly Lambeau: The Man Behind the Mystique.* Hales Corner, WI: Eagle Books, 2003.

Magazines

Coffin Corner (Newsletter of the Professional Football Researchers Association)
Football Digest
Green Bay Packers Yearbook
National Football League Game Programs
Saturday Evening Post
Sport
Sports Illustrated

Newspapers

Akron Beacon-Journal
Arizona Republic
Atlanta Constitution
Baltimore News-American
Chicago Daily News
Daily Graphic (Pine Bluff, AR)
Green Bay (WI) Press-Gazette
Los Angeles Examiner
Los Angeles Times
Milwaukee Journal
Milwaukee Sentinel
New York Herald-Tribune
New York Times
Pine Bluff (AR) Commercial
San Diego Union
Tuscaloosa (AL) News

Bibliography

Online Sources

ESPN, www.espn.com/sportscentury/features.d.
Franklin D. Roosevelt speeches, Miller Center, University of Virginia, https://millercenter.org/the-presidency/presidential-speeches/May-26-1940-fireside-chat-15-national-defense.
Green Bay Packers team website, https://www.packers.com.
New York Giants, www.bigblueinteractive.com.
Packers Report, https://247sports.com/nfl/green-bay-packers/.
Pro Football Hall of Fame website, http://www.profootballhof.com.
United States Naval Institute, https://www.usni.com.
University of Alabama sports, www.al.com.
Winston Churchill speeches, https://WinstonChurchill.org.

Wire Services

Associated Press
United Press International

Other Sources

Catholic Boy
Green Bay Packers Hall of Fame
NFL Films
Paul W. Bryant Museum Archives
Packer Plus
Pro Football Hall of Fame Press Release
The Zebra, 1931 (Pine Bluff, Arkansas, High School Yearbook)
University of Alabama Center for Public Radio and Television, press release

Interviews

Carroll Dale
Boyd Dowler

Index

Adderley, Herb 201
Africa 146
Akron, Ohio 159
Akron Beacon-Journal 196
Akron Pros 7
Alabama 30, 31, 37, 40, 45, 87
Alabama Club of Southern California 46
All-America Football Conference 167
Allegheny Athletic Association 5
Allied war forces 178
Alworth, Lance (Bambi) 196, 203
American Football League 75, 76, 162
Anderson, Broncho Billy 10
Anderson, Hunk 158
Andover Academy 31
Arizona Cardinals 12
Arkansas 3, 9, 18, 20, 24, 31, 35, 37, 47, 157, 171
Arkansas River 9
Army (West Point) 6, 32
Asia 135
Associated Press 55, 206
Atlanta, Georgia 41
Atlanta Constitution 46
Auburn University 39
Australia 146

Badgro, Red 73
Baker Bowl 83
Balasz, Frank 124, 148
Ballard's Drug Store 18
Baltic States 135
Baltimore 99
Baltimore Colts 76, 167, 194
Barnum, Len 141
Baseball Hall of Fame 90, 199
Baton Rouge, Louisiana 74
Battle of Bristol 52
Battle of Britain 134
Battle of Pine Bluff 10

Battle of the Bulge 156
Baugh, Sammy 109, 113, 121, 131, 132, 134, 155, 161, 167, 173, 176, 183, 199
Baum, Cecil 97, 98, 99, 101
Baum's Dry Goods 97, 98
Bay View Bazooka 174
Bay View High (Wisconsin) 174
Baylor University 75
Belgium 135, 178
Belichick, Bill 150
Belichick, Steve 150
Bell, Bert 138, 199
Benedictine College 174
Benton, Jim 123
Berlin 177
Berry, Raymond 143, 194
Berwanger, Jay 60, 61, 63
Bible, Dana X. 75
Biemeret, Alex 129
Big Ten Conference 15, 32, 60
Birmingham, Alabama 31, 42, 46, 87
Birmingham Black Barons 87
Blood and Sand (movie) 81
Bogart, Humphrey 115
Boozer, Young 38
Boston 98, 128, 189
Boston Patriots (New England Patriots) 76, 93, 150
Boston Red Sox 156
Boston Yanks 188, 189
Boy Scouts 9, 197
Brandt, Gil 143, 144, 145
Brenda Starr (comic strip) 63
Briggs Stadium 117, 124, 141, 159, 180
Bristol Motor Speedway 52
British Commonwealth 99
Britt, Maurice 162
Brock, Charley 149, 163, 182, 191
Brock, Lou (baseball) 149
Brock, Lou (football) 149, 150, 162, 164, 173, 178, 179, 184

219

Index

Brooklyn 98
Brooklyn Dodgers (football, Tigers) 2, 25, 62, 65, 98, 116, 122, 145, 149, 161, 169, 174, 178, 188, 189, 193
Brown, Joe E., 47
Brown, Johnny Mack (Dothan Antelope) 32
Broyles, Frank 31
Bruder, Hank 73, 107, 121
Brumbaugh, Carl 93
Bryant, Ida 12
Bryant, Mary Harmon 48
Bryant, Paul "Bear" 1, 3, 11, 12, 13, 14, 15, 21, 31, 33, 34, 35, 36, 37, 38, 39, 42, 47, 48, 49, 50, 51, 56, 57, 58, 157, 185, 186
Bryant, Wilson 12
Buckingham Palace 146
Bucknell University 148
Buffalo (New York) 114, 159
Buffalo All-Americans 7
Buffalo Bills 196
Buss, Art 60
Bussey, Ruey (Young) 153

Caddell, Ernie 77, 94
Calhoun, George 7, 29
California 32, 42, 45, 46, 50, 61, 86, 197, 203
Camden, Arkansas 22
Camp, Walter 5
Canada 128
Canadeo, Tony 90, 91, 145, 148, 150, 161, 162, 164, 165, 166, 170, 171, 172, 173, 174, 175, 176, 179, 201
Candlestick Park 88
Cannon, Jimmy 87
Canton, Ohio 4, 7, 81, 128, 199
Canton AC (Bulldogs) 7, 144
Captain Kidd's Cleaners 35
Card-Pitt 169, 181
Carr, Henry 89
Carr, Joe 65, 199
Carroll College 6
Casablanca (movie) 115
Chattanooga Choo-Choos 87
Chicago 128, 135, 144, 156, 158, 170, 185
Chicago Bears 2, 11, 12, 25, 27, 29, 60, 67, 67, 69, 70, 72, 77, 78, 79, 80, 83, 96, 97, 99, 101, 103, 104, 105, 107, 108, 109, 113, 114, 115, 116, 117, 119, 121, 129, 131, 133, 134, 136, 139, 140, 142, 143, 145, 147, 148, 149, 150, 152, 152, 153, 154, 155, 159, 160, 161, 162, 163, 165, 166, 171, 172, 173, 174, 175, 177, 180, 181, 186, 187, 188, 189, 193, 194
Chicago Cardinals 68, 69, 76, 83, 92, 93, 99, 104, 105, 106, 114, 119, 120, 139, 140, 149, 150, 151, 159, 161, 162, 163, 164, 169, 172, 173, 174, 179, 181, 188, 201
Chicago Charities College All Star Game 68, 69, 78, 105, 126, 137, 185, 194
Chicago Tigers 7
Chicago Tribune 69, 126, 185
Chicago White Sox 140
China 135, 146
Chippewa Falls Marines 69
Churchill, Winston 134, 140, 184
Cincinnati Reds 144
City Stadium 27, 29, 67, 69, 73, 80, 92, 93, 95, 104, 106, 113, 138, 139, 149, 159, 162, 164, 172, 173, 179, 186, 187, 188, 203
Civil War 9, 32
Clark, Earl (Dutch) 77, 94, 99, 107, 195, 199
Clark, Potsy 77
Clarksville, Tennessee 185
Clemson University 40, 41
Cleveland (Ohio) 14, 35
Cleveland Browns 200
Cleveland Bulldogs 25
Cleveland County, Arkansas 12
Cleveland Indians 87, 156
Cleveland Municipal Stadium 123, 141
Cleveland Rams 107, 108, 113, 116, 120, 123, 131, 139, 141, 148, 150, 164, 165, 169, 180, 187, 188, 189, 195
Cleveland Tigers 7
Coachella Valley, California 202
Cobb, Ty 151
Cochems, Eddie 6
College Football Hall of Fame 4, 25, 77, 179, 198
Columbia University 121, 132, 147
Columbus Club (Green Bay) 126
Columbus Panhandles 7
Comiskey Park 140, 161, 163
Comp, Irv 174, 176, 179, 180, 181, 182, 186, 188, 189
Confederate Army 10
Congress 146, 153, 197
Congressional Medal of Honor 154
Conzelman, Jimmy 151, 172
Cooperstown, New York 199
Cotton Belt Railroad 10, 18
Cotton States League 85, 86
Cramton Bowl 39

220

Index

Crisp, Hank 47, 49, 50, 56
Cutrell, J.W. 22

D-Day invasion 178
Dale, Carroll 204, 205, 206
Daley, Art 145
Daley, Arthur 145
Dallas, Texas 34
Dallas Cowboys, 88, 143, 201
Danowski, Ed 118
Davis, Harold 20
Davis, Red 20
Davis, Willie 201
Dayton Triangles 7
Decatur Staleys 7, 151
de Champlain, Samuel 67
de Gaulle, Charles 135
Del Rio, Texas 45, 46
Democratic Party 135
Dempsey, Jack 203
Denmark 135
Denver Broncos 202
Dermott, Arkansas 20
Detroit 98, 128, 189
Detroit Heralds 7
Detroit Lions 76, 80, 82, 84, 94, 96, 98, 99, 101, 106, 112, 115, 116, 117, 120, 121, 124, 129, 139, 140, 141, 148, 150, 159, 162, 163, 172, 173, 178, 180, 181, 186, 187, 190
Detroit Tigers 77, 147
Detroit Wolverines 25
Dildy, Jim 37, 48
Dilwig, Lavvie 27, 67
DiMaggio, Joe 70
Distinguished Flying Cross 158
Ditka, Mike 12
Dixie Amateur League 85
Don Hutson Center (Green Bay, Wisconsin) 203, 206
Don Hutson Park (Pine Bluff, Arkansas) 17
Donnelly, Ben (Sport) 5
Dorais, Charley (Gus) 6, 54
Dowler, Boyd 205, 206
Doyle, Andrew 33
Drake, Johnny 131
Duchess of Windsor 100
Duke of Windsor 100
Duke of York 100
Duke University 33
Duluth Eskimos 81
Dunaway, Allen 20
Dunkirk 134

Eagle Scouts 9
Eastwood, Clint 44
Ebbets Field, 98, 122, 174
El Dorado, Arkansas 22
El Paso, Texas 43
Elks (Racine, Wisconsin) 197
Emmy Awards 145
Engebretsen, Paul (Tiny) 67, 94, 106, 111, 114, 115, 118, 121, 123, 124, 136, 138, 148
England 74, 99, 146, 177, 184
ESPN 175
Ethiopia 74
Europe 9, 122, 135, 147, 178

Fairfield High, Alabama 87
Famiglietti, Gary 163
Farkas, Andy 152
FBI 63
Feathers, Beattie 68, 70, 73, 136
Feller, Bob 156
Fenway Park 189
Finland 135
First Presbyterian Church of Racine (Wisconsin) 197
Fishing Club of Ontario, Canada 198
Fitzgerald, Larry 143
Flaherty, Ray 27, 73
Florida 63
Forbes Field 75, 82
Ford, Gerald (president) 60
Fordyce High (Arkansas) 13, 14, 15, 21, 22, 34, 35
Fortmann, Dan 194
Foss, Joe 162
The Four Horsemen of Notre Dame 159
France 122, 135, 146, 178
Francis, Kavanaugh 47
Frankford Yellow Jackets 27
Frazier, Brenda 63
Friedman, Benny 25, 26, 27, 29, 54, 73, 96
Friedman, Sam 49
Fritsch, Ted, Jr. 172
Fritsch, Ted, Sr. 172, 178, 180, 182, 184, 186, 191

Galloping Ghost 170
Gantenbein, Milt 69, 82, 94, 100, 106, 111, 121, 126, 131, 136
Garner, James Nance 97
Georgia Pre-Flight football 185
Georgia Tech University 32, 40, 41

Index

Germany 74, 122, 134, 135, 146, 147, 177, 178, 184
The Ghost of Green Bay 207
Gipp, George 56
"God Bless America" 130
Goldenberg, Charles (Buckets) 67, 103, 104, 109, 111, 136, 148, 176
Goodnight, Clyde 189
Gonzaga University 170
Gordon Bent Co. 126
Grange, Red 25, 26, 68, 170, 199
The Gray Ghost of Gonzaga 170
Grayson, Bobby 46, 53, 55
Great Britain 122, 146
Great Depression 12, 35, 68, 74, 75, 97
Green Bay 25, 29, 66, 67, 98, 101, 115, 122, 125, 126, 128, 129, 130, 133, 137, 142, 145, 155, 159, 160, 171, 172, 177, 187, 189, 203, 204
Green Bay Packers 1, 4, 7, 8, 27, 28, 59, 62, 65, 66, 67, 68, 69, 70, 72, 73, 74, 75, 76, 77, 78, 79, 81, 82, 83, 84, 89, 92, 93, 94, 95, 97, 98, 100, 101, 102, 103, 104, 105, 106, 107, 108, 109, 110, 111, 112, 113, 114, 115, 116, 117, 118, 120, 121, 122, 123, 124, 125, 126, 129, 130, 131, 133, 135, 135, 137, 138, 139, 140, 141, 142, 143, 144, 145, 147, 149, 150, 151, 152, 153, 154, 160, 162, 163, 164, 165, 166, 167, 168, 169, 170, 171, 172, 172, 173, 176, 179, 180, 181, 182, 184, 185, 186, 187, 188, 189, 190, 192, 196, 197, 201, 202, 203, 204, 205, 206; Hall of Fame 4, 89, 203, 204
Green Bay Press-Gazette 76, 78, 80, 97, 101, 125, 126, 153, 177
Green Bay West High 29
green light letter 156
Greenberg, Hank 147
Greene, Charlie 10
USS *Greer* 146
Gregg, Forrest 201
Griffith Stadium 109, 133, 152, 161
Guys and Dolls 40

Hadl, John 196
Halas, George 2, 11, 12, 25, 26, 29, 60, 63, 68, 97, 103, 107, 108, 121, 132, 134, 147, 151, 153, 156, 158, 160, 171, 186, 193, 194, 199, 202
Hammond Pros 7
Harbor Island Yacht Club 197
Harrison, Marvin 143
Hawaii 152, 161, 168

Hayes, Bob 88
Heffelfinger, William (Pudge) 5
Hein, Mel 73, 117, 130, 131, 199
Heisman Trophy 60
Henry, Pete 199
Herber, Arnie 28, 29, 30, 59, 67, 68, 70, 76, 78, 79, 80, 81, 83, 89, 92, 94, 95, 96, 97, 98, 99, 100, 104, 106, 107, 108, 109, 111, 112, 113, 114, 116, 118, 119, 120, 121, 122, 124, 126, 131, 132, 133, 136, 137, 138, 139, 140, 147, 167, 169, 176, 179, 181, 182, 195, 196, 201
Hess, Rudolf 146
Hewitt, Bill 93, 97
Himalayan Mountain Range 157
Himes, Chester 10
Hines, Jim 89
Hinkle, Clarke 67, 80, 82, 83, 93, 97, 99, 102, 104, 105, 106, 107, 108, 111, 114, 116, 119, 120, 121, 122, 124, 127, 136, 140, 141, 148, 149, 150, 151, 152, 162, 172, 202, 203
Hiroshima 184
Hitler, Adolf 122, 135, 146, 178
Hollywood 132
Holocaust 135
Hopkins, DeAndre 12
Hornung, Paul 187, 201
Hotel Pines 10
House of Commons 134
Howard College (Samford) 38, 157
Howard University 38
Howell, Millard (Dixie) 36, 39, 40, 41, 42, 45, 46, 52, 53, 54, 55, 56, 57, 61
Hubbard, Cal 67, 74, 90, 92, 111, 199, 201
Huckabee, Mike 10
Hudson River 141
Hughes, Buck 37
Hunter, Torii 10
Hutson, Don (Alabama Antelope) 1, 2, 3, 4, 8, 9, 10, 11, 12, 13, 14, 15, 16, 17, 18, 19, 21, 23, 24, 29, 30, 31, 33, 34, 35, 36, 37, 38, 39, 40, 41, 42, 44, 45, 47, 48, 49, 50, 51, 52, 53, 54, 55, 56, 57, 58, 59, 61, 62, 63, 65, 66, 67, 68, 69, 70, 72, 73, 75, 76, 77, 78, 79, 81, 82, 83, 84, 85, 86, 87, 88, 89, 90, 91, 92, 94, 95, 97, 98, 100, 104, 105, 106, 107, 108, 109, 111, 112, 113, 114, 115, 116, 118, 119, 120, 121, 122, 123, 124, 126, 127, 130, 131, 132, 133, 136, 137, 138, 140, 141, 142, 143, 144, 145, 148, 149, 150, 151, 152, 154, 155, 157, 158, 160, 161, 162, 163, 164, 165, 166, 168, 169, 171, 174, 175, 176, 178,

Index

179, 180, 181, 182, 183, 184, 185, 186, 187, 189, 190, 191, 192, 193, 194, 195, 196, 197, 198, 199, 200, 201, 202, 204, 205, 206, 207
Hutson, Jane (daughter) 197
Hutson, Julia (daughter) 197
Hutson, Julia (wife) 197, 206
Hutson, Mabel (mother) 10, 120, 157
Hutson, Martha (daughter) 197
Hutson, Ray (brother) 157, 158
Hutson, Robert (brother) 157, 158
Hutson, Roy B. (father) 10

Ice Bowl 129, 201
Ice Service Company (Sam Cook, A.H. Miller) 19
India 146, 157
Indian Packing Company 7
Iowa 60
Isbell, Cecil 112, 113, 114, 115, 116, 119, 120, 121, 122, 123, 124, 129, 131, 133, 138, 139, 147, 148, 149, 151, 152, 162, 163, 164, 165, 166, 167, 168, 169, 171, 176, 179, 195, 201
Israel 147
Italy 74, 122, 134, 178
Ivy League 32, 132
Iwo Jima 184, 185

Jack Murphy Stadium 202
Jackson Senators 86
Jacunski, Harry 123, 172, 173, 175
Jankowski, Ed 107, 108, 121, 123, 136, 141, 148
Japan 122, 134, 135, 146, 152, 155, 161, 178, 184
The Jazz Singer 46
J.C. Penney Co. 19
Joannes, Leland 125
Joe Carr Memorial Trophy (MVP award) 168
Johnson, Howard (Smiley) 162, 184
Johnsos, Luke 158, 186
Johnston, Swede 93
Jolson, Al 46, 47
Jones, L.L. (Cowboy) 85
Jonesboro, Arkansas 22
Jordan, Michael 87

Kansas 97
Kansas City Chiefs 12
Kansas University 75
Karl, Eric 130
Kavanaugh, Ken 139, 149, 194

Keeler, Ruby 47
Kelly, John (Shipwreck) 2, 62, 63, 65, 145
Kelly, Dr. W.W. 83
Kenosha, Wisconsin 171
Kentucky 62
King, Peter 204
King Edward VIII 99, 100, 101
Knox, Chuck 197
Knoxville, Tennessee 86
Korean War 156
Kramer, Jerry 201
Krystal's (hamburgers) 13

La Crosse Lagers 69
Lake Michigan 66
Lambeau, Earle (Curly) 1, 7, 8, 27, 28, 29, 59, 61, 62, 63, 65, 67, 68, 69, 70, 76, 78, 81, 92, 95, 96, 100, 103, 104, 105, 107, 109, 110, 111, 112, 113, 115, 118, 124, 125, 128, 129, 130, 131, 134, 136, 137, 140, 142, 145, 147, 149, 150, 151, 153, 159, 160, 161, 163, 164, 167, 168, 169, 170, 174, 176, 177, 180, 181, 182, 183, 184, 186, 187, 189, 193, 199, 201
Lambeau Field 67, 203
Landis, Kenesaw Mountain 86, 156
Landon, Alf 97
Largent, Steve 196, 197, 203
Las Vegas 9
Lavelli, Dante 200
Laws, Joe 76, 93, 96, 107, 116, 121, 123, 126, 136, 148, 162, 164, 180, 184
Layden, Elmer 159, 162, 177
Lea, Bud 179
League of Nations 74
Ledbetter, Dr. H.P., 46
Lee, Bill 42
Leemans, Tuffy 117
Legion Field 42
Lend-Lease Act 146
Leningrad 146, 177
Lepke, Louis 147
Lever, Lafayette 10
Lewellen, Verne 27
Liberty Ships 146
Lions Club (Green Bay) 126
Lithuania 147
Little, William 31
Little Rock, Arkansas 9, 22, 47
Livingston, Pat 91
Lombardi, Vince 67, 201, 202
Lombardi Avenue 204
London 134
Long, Dallas 10

223

Index

Long, Huey 74
Look Magazine 151
Los Angeles 43, 188
Los Angeles Examiner 54
Los Angeles Rams 204
Los Angeles Times 195, 196
Louis, Joe 156, 157
Louisiana 21
Louisiana State University 39, 50, 74
Luckman, Ethel 147
Luckman, Meyer 147
Luckman, Sid 113, 121, 131, 132, 133, 134, 139, 147, 155, 156, 161, 165, 167, 172, 173, 176, 179, 180
Luftwaffe 146
Lummus, Jack 154, 162
Luxembourg 135, 147, 178

Maccabiah Games 147
Madison, Wisconsin 66, 103
Magnani, Dante 195
Mahomes, Patrick 12
Major League Baseball 7, 11, 16, 66, 69, 118, 128, 158, 199
Malvern, Arkansas 22
Manders, Jack 78, 93, 97, 140, 152
Maniaci, Joe 140
Mara, Tim 199
Marr, Charlie 15, 42, 49
Marshall, George Preston 94, 100, 132, 133, 185, 199
Marshall, Texas 21
Mason, Joel 172
Masonic Brotherhood (Wisconsin) 197
Massachusetts 31
Massillon Tigers 7
Masters, Alfred 42
Masterson, Bernie 78, 79
Mays, Carl 87
Mays, Willie 87, 88
McAfee, George 139, 149, 162
McBride, Charlie 92
McDonald's (hamburgers) 13
McGill, Ralph 46
McKay, Roy 186, 188
McNally, Johnny (Blood) 27, 28, 29, 30, 67, 80, 81, 82, 83, 94, 96, 111, 131, 199, 201
Menominee Sugar Co. 125
Merrill Foxes 69
Miami Dolphins 89
Michalske, Mike 29, 30, 67, 95, 111
Michigan 7
Miller, Paul 94, 96, 106

Milwaukee 66, 103, 130, 159, 174, 179, 187, 197
Milwaukee Athletic Club 197
Milwaukee Badgers 81, 151
Milwaukee Journal 105
The Milwaukee Road Menu 101, 102
Milwaukee Sentinel 80
Mississippi State 39
Molesworth, Keith 79
Monnett, Bob 69, 70, 74, 82, 101, 104, 106, 107, 108, 109, 112, 116, 119
Montgomery, Alabama 39, 50
Monticello, Arkansas 21
Montreal 128
Moran, Hap 27
Moro Bottom, Arkansas 12
Moscow 146
Moscrip, Monk 55
Moss, Randy 143
Mount Everest 157
Mulleneaux, Carl 115, 118, 119, 121, 127, 136, 139, 150, 162, 184
Muncie Flyers 7
Mussolini, Benito 74

Nagasaki 184
Nagurski, Bronko 68, 148, 149, 199, 202
Namath, Joe 76, 144
National Basketball Association 66, 128
National Football League (American Professional Football Association) 1, 4, 7, 11, 12, 24, 25, 29, 44, 59, 60, 61, 62, 65, 66, 68, 71, 74, 77, 81, 84, 87, 89, 92, 93, 101, 104, 105, 106, 107, 109, 112, 115, 119, 122, 123, 124, 125, 128, 129, 131, 132, 133, 135, 137, 142, 143, 144, 145, 146, 147, 148, 150, 152, 153, 158, 159, 161, 162, 166, 167, 169, 172, 174, 175, 177, 181, 192, 193, 194, 196, 199, 201, 202, 204
National Hockey League 11, 66, 128
National League 86
National Pastime 156
National Register of Historic Places 10
Nazis 63, 122, 146, 177
NASCAR 52
NCAA 34, 38
Neale, Greasy 91, 144
Netherlands 135
Nevers, Ernie 199
New Jersey 145
New Orleans 56
New York City 62, 98, 100, 101, 128, 144
New York Giants (baseball) 87

Index

New York Giants (football) 25, 26, 27, 62, 68, 73, 75, 84, 88, 98, 109, 117, 118, 123, 124, 125, 126, 130, 131, 141, 152, 153, 154, 161, 166, 173, 174, 175, 180, 181, 182, 189; Ring of Honor 154
New York Herald-Tribune 101
New York Mets 87
New York-Penn League 86
New York Times 145
New York Titans (New York Jets) 75, 76
Newark, New Jersey 153
Newman, Harry 73
Newspaper Enterprise Association 41
Neyland, Robert 39
NFL Films 145
NFL Network 145
Nicolet, Jean 67
Nimitz, Adm. Chester 156
Nitschke, Ray 201, 203
Nolting, Ray 139
Normandy 178
North Carolina Pre-Flight football 185
North Little Rock, Arkansas 21
Norway 135
Notre Dame 6, 24, 32, 54, 56, 81
Nuremburg 146

O'Brien, Davey 138
O'Brien, Pat 47
Occidental College 46
Odessa, Russia 103
Ohio 7, 76
Ohio State University 52
Oklahoma 196, 197
Old Bailey 146
Oosterbaan, Bennie 54
Osmanski, Bill 121
Owen, Steve 125
Owens, Jesse 34
Owens, Terrell 143

Pac-10 Conference (Pac-12, Pacific Coast Conference) 15
Packer Playdium 197;
Packers Corporation 125
Palm Springs, California 206
Pardonner, Paul 76
Paris 135
Parker, Buddy 114
Pasadena, California 2, 15, 42, 45, 54
Pearl Harbor 152, 153, 155, 156, 157, 161, 162, 177
Pennsylvania 7
Philadelphia 83, 128, 144

Philadelphia Athletics 7
Philadelphia Eagles 12, 27, 60, 83, 91, 108, 121, 138, 139, 161, 166, 169, 174, 181, 182
Philadelphia Municipal Stadium 121
Philadelphia Phillies 7, 144
Philippines 153
Pine Bluff, Arkansas 2, 3, 9, 10, 12, 13, 17, 85, 200
Pine Bluff Commercial 18, 19, 20, 22, 85
Pine Bluff Daily Graphic 18, 19, 21, 22
Pine Bluff High School (Zebras) 10, 11, 15, 17, 18, 19, 20, 21, 22, 23, 34, 85, 157
Pine Bluff Judges 85
Pine Bluff School District 10
Pittsburgh Athletic Club 5
Pittsburgh Pirates (football, Steelers) 75, 76, 77, 81, 82, 83, 96, 99, 112, 116, 140, 151, 166, 169, 174, 179, 181
Poland 122, 184
Polo Grounds 87, 98, 100, 109, 117, 141, 161, 166, 173, 180, 182, 189
Portsmouth, Ohio 128
Portsmouth Spartans 67, 76, 77
Pottsville Maroons 81
Powell, Dick 47
Princeton University 5
Professional Football Hall of Fame 4, 12, 26, 27, 28, 34, 37, 38, 67, 75, 77, 90, 106, 112, 121, 132, 139, 144, 145, 149, 165, 167, 171, 188, 194, 199, 200
Profootballreference.com 27
Providence Steam Roller 151
Purdue University Boilermakers 112, 116, 167
Pyle, C.C. 25

Racine (Wisconsin) 197, 203
Racine Cardinals 7
Racine Chamber of Commerce 197
Racine Country Club 197
Racine Goodfellows Organization 197
Racine Yacht Club 198
Rancho Mirage, California 202, 206
Ranspot, Keith 164
Ray, Buford (Baby) 182
Reconstruction 32
Reeves, Guy 20
Regis College 29
Remmel, Lee 78
Renter, Pug 100
Rice, Grantland 151
Rice, Jerry 143, 203, 204
Richards, George 77

225

Index

Rickey, Branch 86
Riley, Joe 40
Ringo, Jim 201
Ritz-Carlton Hotel (Philadelphia) 59
Roaf, Willie 10
Robinson, Bradbury 6
Rochester Jeffersons 7
Rock Island Independents 7, 151
Rockne, Knute 6, 26, 54, 56
Rodgers, Aaron 144
Rommel, Gen. Erwin 146
Ronzani, Gene 78, 79, 93
Rooney, Art 75, 202
Roosevelt, Franklin D. (president) 74, 97, 122, 135, 146, 153, 156, 158, 165, 184
Roosevelt, Theodore (president) 6
Rose, Al 69
Rose Bowl 2, 15, 32, 33, 34, 36, 40, 42, 44, 46, 47, 50, 51, 52, 53, 55, 56, 57, 61, 62, 63
Rosh Hashanah 147
Royal Air Force 177
Runyan, Damon 40
Russia 135, 147
Rutgers University 5
Ruth, Babe 4, 68, 203, 207
Rye, New York 189

Saban, Nick 31
Sabol, Ed 145
Sabol, Steve 145
St. John's University (Minnesota) 80, 81
St. Louis Cardinals 85
St. Louis University 6, 24
St. Norbert College 129
St. Vincent's Hospital 82
Saipan 178
San Antonio, Texas 45
San Diego 202
San Diego Chargers 196, 203
San Francisco 49ers 203
San Francisco Giants 87
Sarboe, Phil 92
Satterwhite, Annie 87
Saturday Evening Post 129
Sauer, George, Jr. 76
Sauer, George, Sr. 75, 76, 80, 82, 83, 92, 97, 98
Scherber, Bernie 107
Schneider, Jack 6
Schneidman, Herb 107
Schwammel, Ade 75, 77, 78, 83, 93, 107
Scotland 146
Scott, Xen 31

Sears Roebuck and Co. 19
Seattle Seahawks 196
Secretary of Agriculture 158
Selective Service 157, 160, 170
Selma Cloverleafs 86
Sewanee, the University of the South 38, 40, 50
Shaffer, Lee 141
Shaughnessy, Clark 179
Shepherd, Bill 82
Simpson, Wallis 99
Sing Sing 147
Sisk, Johnny 78
Sloan, Dwight (Paddlefoot) 124
Smith, Ernie 77, 80, 82, 83, 93, 94, 97, 100, 107, 108, 124
Smith, Riley 48, 53, 54
Snyder, Bob 108, 139, 149
Soar, Hank 118
South Pacific 122, 157, 177, 184
Southeastern Conference 15, 39, 40, 42
Southeastern League 86
Southern Conference 32
Southern Pacific Lines 42
Soviet Union 122, 146, 177, 184
Spahn, Warren 156
Spencer, Wisconsin 172
Sports Illustrated 195, 204
Stalin, Josef 184
Stanford University 2, 33, 42, 44, 46, 47, 51, 52, 53, 54, 55, 56, 57, 61
Starr, Bart 201
Steagles 169, 174
Steel City 75
Stevens Point (football) 69
Stork Club 63
Strong, Ken 73
Sturgeon Bay, Wisconsin 201
Super Bowl 76, 100, 201, 202
Svenson, George (Bud) 123, 162

Taylor, Jim 201
Tennessee 32, 38
Texarkana 20
Texas 21, 35, 131, 155
Texas A&M University 40, 186
Texas Christian University 109, 131, 138
Thomas, Frank 33, 34, 35, 36, 38, 39, 41, 46, 47, 49, 50, 53, 55, 61
Thompson, Oliver 6
Thomsen, Fred 33, 34
Thornhill, Claude (Tiny) 53, 56
Thorpe, Jim 7, 199

Index

Thunderbird Country Club (California) 202
Time (magazine) 25
Tinsley, Pete 185
Titletown (Green Bay, Wisconsin) 204
Toronto 128
Tournament of Roses Parade 53
Troy, Alabama 85
Tucson, Arizona 46
Tulane University 40
Turner, Clyde (Bulldog) 165, 194
Turner, Lana 57
Tuscaloosa, Alabama 2, 16, 32, 33, 35, 36, 42, 46, 56, 63, 64, 157, 186
Tuscaloosa News 41, 55
Tuskegee Airmen 146
21 Club 63

Union Army 9
Union College 185
United Press International 41, 191
United Kingdom 134
United Nations 74
United States 122, 128, 134, 135, 146, 147, 156, 157, 158, 160, 171, 184
U.S. Air Army Corps (Air Force) 155, 157, 158
U.S. Army 155, 161, 176
U.S. Coast Guard 162
U.S. Marine Corps 154, 155, 156, 184, 185
U.S. Merchant Marine 155, 156
U.S. Navy 139, 155, 156, 161, 176
United States Naval Academy 75, 150
University of Alabama (Crimson Tide) 1, 2, 4, 11, 14, 15, 16, 23, 31, 32, 33, 34, 35, 36, 37, 38, 39, 40, 41, 42, 43, 44, 45, 46, 47, 51, 52, 53, 54, 55, 56, 61, 62, 63, 69, 85, 87, 157, 158, 185, 193, 197
University of Arkansas 15, 31, 33, 40
University of Chattanooga 33
University of Chicago 60
University of Detroit 82; stadium 107
University of Florida 32, 39
University of Georgia 32, 39, 184
University of Illinois 25, 170
University of Kentucky 32, 40, 62, 186
University of Maryland 185, 186
University of Michigan 25, 54, 60, 73
University of Mississippi 39
University of Missouri 40
University of Nebraska 75
University of New Hampshire 75
University of South Carolina 40
University of Southern California 46, 52
University of Southern California–Los Angeles 188
University of Tennessee 39, 40, 52
University of Texas 76
University of Tulsa 196
University of Washington 32
University of Wisconsin 29, 103, 137, 143, 174
University of Wisconsin–Stevens Point 172
Uram, Andy 116, 117, 120, 121, 136, 139, 141, 150, 162, 163, 164, 165, 172, 176
Ussery, Sterling Virginia 23

Van Avery, Hal 136, 140, 141, 147, 151, 152, 162
Van Dellen, Buck 54
Van de Graaff, Bully 31
Van Meter, Iowa 156
Vanderbilt University 32, 39, 41, 42, 185
Vermont 67
Vichy French 146
Virginia Tech 52, 204

Wade, Wallace 15, 31, 33, 34
Walker, Hillman 49
Walter, John 80
War Bonds 157
Ward, Arch 69, 126
War Manpower Commission 177
Warner Brothers 46
Washington, D.C. 100, 133, 144, 161
Washington State 197
Washington Redskins (Boston Redskins, Commanders) 93, 94, 98, 99, 100, 101, 109, 113, 117, 121, 123, 124, 131, 132, 133, 138, 142, 149, 152, 155, 161, 166, 173, 174, 185, 201, 202
Washington State University 33, 34
Waterfield, Bob 188
Wertz, Vic 87, 88
West Allis, Wisconsin 76, 187
Westfield, Alabama 87
West Lafayette, Indiana 113
Wheaties 204
Wheatless Wednesdays 158
White, Byron 112
White Christmas 130
Whittenton, Jesse 205
Wiefels & Son Funeral Home 206
Williams, Ted 156
Wilmington, Delaware 157
Wisconsin 2, 6, 7, 61, 98, 103, 112, 129,

Index

130, 138, 143, 147, 149, 159, 170, 174, 179, 202
Wisconsin Athletic Hall of Fame 198
Wisconsin State Fair Park 76, 93, 108, 114, 121, 125, 140, 148, 178, 186
Winthrop University 33
Wojciechowicz, Alex 112
Wolf, Ron 203
Woodward, Stanley 101
World Series 87
World War I 122, 156, 158
World War II 11, 63, 139, 147, 151, 155, 156, 158, 161, 167, 169, 171, 176, 184, 185, 193, 194
Wrigley Field 77, 79, 83, 96, 107, 121, 150, 152, 153, 159, 165, 173, 180, 188
Wyckoff, Frank 34

Yale University 5
Yalta 184
Yom Kippur 147
Yost, Fielding 25
Young, Bill 45, 46

www.ingramcontent.com/pod-product-compliance
Ingram Content Group UK Ltd.
Pitfield, Milton Keynes, MK11 3LW, UK
UKHW041948140426
5217IPUK00014B/695